DESIGNING BUILDINGS FOR PEOPLE

Sustainable liveable architecture

Derek Clements-Croome

THE CROWOOD PRESS

First published in 2020 by
The Crowood Press Ltd
Ramsbury, Marlborough
Wiltshire SN8 2HR

enquiries@crowood.com

www.crowood.com

© Derek Clements-Croome 2020

All rights reserved. No part of this publication may be reproduced or transmitted in any form or by any means, electronic or mechanical, including photocopy, recording, or any information storage and retrieval system, without permission in writing from the publishers.

British Library Cataloguing-in-Publication Data
A catalogue record for this book is available from the British Library.

ISBN 978 1 78500 709 5

Typeset by Jean Cussons Typesetting, Diss, Norfolk
Printed and bound in India by Parksons Graphics

Contents

Acknowledgements   4

Preface   5

Chapter One   Sustainable intelligent buildings for people   6

Chapter Two   Vernacular architecture   21

Chapter Three   Lessons from nature – biomimetic and biophilic architecture   4

Chapter Four   Buildings for health and wellbeing   57

Chapter Five   Technology as an enabler   88

Chapter Six   Sustainable architecture   103

Chapter Seven   Decision-making   126

Chapter Eight   Gallery of case studies   137

Appendix   180

References   183

Index   206

Acknowledgements

I HAVE SO MANY PEOPLE among my friends and colleagues to thank for their help, advice and input. Firstly my gratitude to my photo manager Tong Yang for her deft processing of all the photos and arranging drawings with Desislava Veleva; and to Gulay Ozkan and Norma Diaz for checking and formatting the references.

I am indebted to Mina Hasman at Skidmore Owings and Merrill (SOM); Clare Bowman at RCZM Architects; Professor Alberto Estevez at University International Catalunya; Petra Gruber at University of Akron in Ohio; Barbara Imhof at Liquifer Systems Group; Michael Beaven and his colleagues at Arup; Patrick Bellew at Atelier Ten; Stefan Jakobek at HOK; Joyce Chan Schoof at Parliament and Loughborough University; Ann Marie Aguilar at Well Certified; Sandra Gritti at Edge; Renzo Piano Building Workshop (RPBW); Amanda Levete at AL_A; Alexander Bond at Biophilic Designs; Alexandra Morris at Mitie; David Benjamin at The Living Architects New York; James Law Architects, Hong Kong; Neveen Hamza at Newcastle University, UK; Howard Morgan at Real Service; Debra Corey, Global Head of Engagement at Reward Gateway; Marylis Ramos at PRP; Midori Ainoura and her colleagues at PLP; Vyt Garnys and Paul Abijoye at CETEC; Nicola Gillen at Cushman Wakefield; Charlotte Hermans at AECOM; Briony Turner at Institute for Environmental Analytics; Neil Pennell at Land Securities; Toby Benzecry at Workplace Futures Group and Modus; Britni Stone at NBBJ; Farrah Hassan – Hardwick (HOK); among many others for discussions that opened my mind to new ideas. Photos are credited, as are companies where appropriate, on the pages where their work appears. Case studies have been generously offered by those above and many others.

A special thank you to my colleagues at the British Council for Offices for their help and encouragement, and also to members of the CIBSE Intelligent Buildings Group. Last but not least, I would like to pay tribute to all the students past and present with whom I have exchanged ideas over many years in the UK, China and other countries. It has been a rich knowledge exchange.

Derek Clements-Croome
Professor Emeritus at Reading University
Visiting Professor at Queen Mary University
London
August 2019

Preface

EVERY GENERATION seeks change and this is reflected by the shifting outlooks in society and advancements in technology. There is a growing sense that we are moving towards an open society in which personalization is strongly evident. Today many people want to work in adaptable environments denoted by such terms as flexi-time and flexi-space.

Many people are involved in the processes that underlie architecture – and hence the buildings being newly created or older ones being refurbished. It is important that connectivity between everyone is seamless so that the communication between them all is effective; all too often it is not. There has to be an openness to consider fresh ideas besides an awareness of long-term implications. It is the value of our endeavours that is important, expressed by, for example, the benefits to costs ratio or the social return on investment that should be a vital part of decision-making. Too often perceptions based on costs alone are misplaced.

We spend much of our time throughout our life in buildings. How do they affect us and how does our behaviour affect their performance? Today sustainable development and climate change, together with health and well-being, are two issues that permeate our thinking worldwide. Is it any longer enough to carry on thinking in the same way about how we design, plan and manage buildings? Buildings are viewed here more as organisms rather that static lifeless blocks of materials.

Chapters 1 to 7 of this book discuss and illustrate some principal areas of development that influence our thinking. We see here how lessons from Nature and history provide powerful insights into how we approach planning, designing and managing sustainability, whilst at the same time achieving flourishing environments in which people live and work. A gallery of examples which demonstrate these objectives is illustrated in Chapter 8.

I welcome readers to write to me care of the publishers with their ideas and experiences, which I can then reference in any possible future edition.

Derek Clements-Croome
September 2019

Chapter One

Sustainable intelligent buildings for people

> We never just look at one thing: we are always looking at the relation between things and ourselves. Our vision is continually active, continually moving....
>
> John Berger, *Ways of Seeing* (1972)

BERGER IS REFERRING to viewing art but what he says is true of how we sense the environment around us and the places we inhabit too. What do we mean by an 'intelligent building'? It is one that serves the needs of people in functional ways but is also beautiful – not just visually but in its simplicity and in the sensory ways it meets these human needs. Intelligent buildings have existed for thousands of years but different centuries and cultures express them in different ways; examples might be an igloo, a Japanese tea house, the traditional Malaysian house or a courtyard design. There are many other vernacular types throughout history, each offering ingredients that make up the recipe for what is the essence of an intelligent building.

Sir Henry Wotton's work, *The Elements of Architecture* (published in 1624), a loose translation of *de Architectura* by the Roman author and architect Vitruvius, includes the quotation, 'Well building hath three conditions: firmness, commodity, and delight,' which might today be paraphrased, 'durability, resilience, function and beauty.'

Of course these are basic, primary needs but they can be interpreted in various ways. Each building will be nuanced according to the way the client and design team interact. A building is a composition, but unlike a music score composed by one mind, buildings are a composite of thoughts and ideas from many minds that make up the design, construction and operation team. The variety of personnel constituting the team are educated in different ways too, and therein lies the source of many problems: the basic language of building and architecture is interpreted with different priorities by the various players. Attaining seamless connectivity of thoughts to achieve a vision is not easy but when successful it is very powerful.

Architecture can stir our emotions; how and why this happens is a complex but beautiful story and has been a topic of philosophical debate for many centuries. A cathedral evokes a special feeling within us as soon as we step over its threshold. Perhaps the sight of it has prepared us, but stepping inside, our sensory perception reaches deeper into our minds. The atmosphere is tangible, and even more so if music plays within the cathedral walls because it evokes another emotion in our sensory response beyond the visual impact. For those who have experienced music in King's College Chapel in Cambridge, St Paul's Cathedral in London, or Coventry Cathedral, for example, know how the visual and aural senses in those places evoke our emotions and wellbeing in a heightened way.

Terminology

In the twenty-first century, 'intelligent' buildings tend to be those that are technologically driven, but already we can see the impact of a shift in society's values: there is an increasing desire for buildings to be designed for the health and wellbeing of their occupants, a more caring and humane approach that offsets the hard face of construction and technology. Too often an intelligent building is reduced down to the choice of a building management system but there is much more to it than that; this is why I prefer the term 'intelligent' to 'smart'.

The words 'intelligent' and 'smart' are often used interchangeably but there is a distinction. Intelligence is the faculty of reasoning with a capacity to quickly comprehend. It is characterized by sound thought and good judgement. When a person is inherently intelligent they can also be smart but a smart person may not be very intelligent by nature. Smartness comes from responding to the situation or circumstances being experienced.

There are three types of intelligence, which recognize cognitive, emotional and practical reasoning and abilities. Smartness concentrates mainly on cognitive intelligence whereas most decisions in life depend on a mixture of all three types of intelligence. We can conclude that an intelligent building has a higher level of demands than a smart one. It has to

PHILOSOPHY OF OVE ARUP

Arup wrote about the theory and practice of design throughout his life. Central to his thinking was the notion of total design which advocated closer collaboration not only between architects and engineers but across the whole building supply chain. His firm, founded in 1938, became a test bed for this design philosophy. He believed that a design should be developed by individuals with diverse skills coming together from the beginning of the project. Traditionally engineers were not involved in the early stages of design. He believed that the architect should be part an engineer and the engineer should be part an architect in order to achieve a fruitful collaboration. We see this creed being continued not only in practice but in the growing trend towards university degree courses in architectural engineering today.

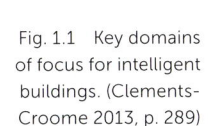

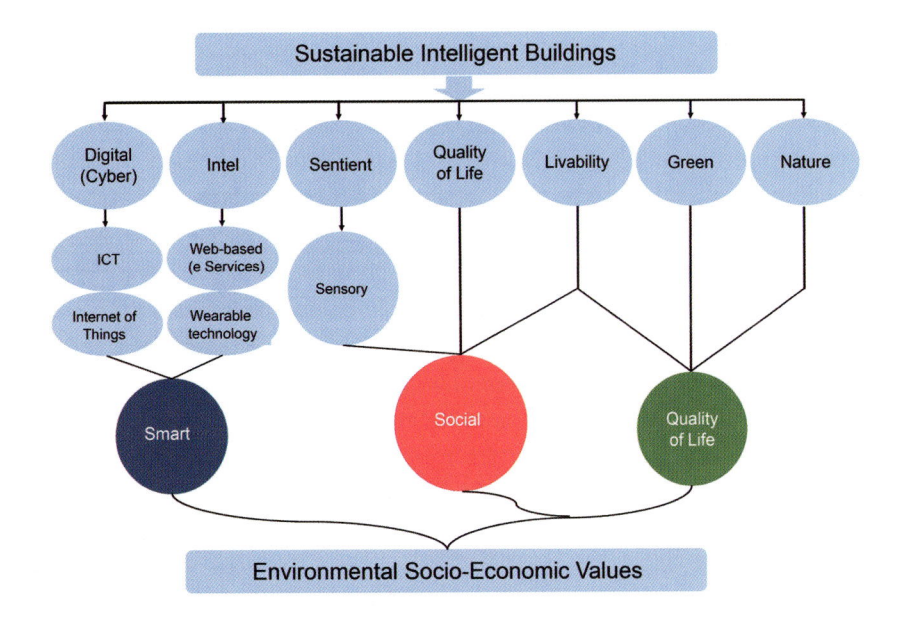

Fig. 1.1 Key domains of focus for intelligent buildings. (Clements-Croome 2013, p. 289)

enhance health and wellbeing by providing a wholesome sensory experience; it has to be sustainable in its use of resources but it also needs to be 'smart' in order to deal with quick changes of demand in temperature, ventilation or lighting, for example.

Digital technology can enable a building to be smart. The EDGE Olympic building in Amsterdam with its 15,000 sensors might be an example of a smart building but it also embraces other features that show it to be an intelligent one too as it aims to reduce energy costs and environmental impact whilst providing an optimal indoor environment for the occupants.

On the other hand, a low-tech building can be effective using passive control: measures like building form, orientation, mass and materials respond to changes in a more natural way. An igloo is an example of an intelligent building in the Arctic context. We can see that intelligence is a more embracing term than smartness; hence the use of these terms needs to be differentiated.

Can intelligent buildings provide alternative and more sustainable approaches to heating, ventilating and air-conditioning of buildings? Lessons from history as well as the natural world show us that they can. Some of these approaches feature in Chapters 2 and 3. Throughout history clean air, sunlight, sound and water have been fundamental to the needs of people. Today, sensitive control of these needs may use either traditional or new solutions, or a blend of both, but we have to remember that the built environment is fundamental to mankind's sense of wellbeing and it is the totality of this idea that we need to understand and value, even in a zero-carbon economy.

Intelligent buildings respect the needs of the individual, the business organization and the wider society, and we can learn a lot about intelligent buildings by looking at the history of world architecture and seeing how people have adapted buildings to deal with the rigours of climate and the changing face of civilization. There are also lessons to be learned from nature: animals and plants have evolved to use materials and expend energy optimally in the various changing and dynamic environments across the world, whether in deserts, arctic regions, hot-humid, hot-dry or temperate climates. Similarly, buildings are now having to absorb the impact of the technological age; the implications of climate change and the need for healthy working conditions are now dominating our thinking as people become more knowledgeable about the impact of the environment on individuals and within the context of local and global communities.

Intelligent buildings should be sustainable, healthy, and technologically aware, meet the needs of occupants and business, and should be flexible and adaptable to deal with change. The processes of planning, design, construction, commissioning and facilities management – including evaluating the building, referred to as post-occupancy evaluation (POE) – are all vitally important when defining an intelligent building. Buildings comprise many systems devised by many people, yet the relationship between buildings and people can only work satisfactorily if there is an integrated design, construction and operational team possessing a common holistic vision by working together right from the commencement of a project. This means that planners, consultants, contractors, facilities managers, manufacturers and clients must share a common vision with a set of intrinsic values, and must also develop a mutual understanding of how the culture of an organization with its patterns of work are best suited to a particular building form and layout and served by the most appropriate environmental systems. A host of technologies are emerging that help these processes, but in the end, it is how we think about achieving responsive buildings that matters. Intelligent buildings can cope with social and technological change and should be adaptable to short-term and long-term human needs. The design brief must reflect this vision and understanding.

We need to consider how buildings affect people in various ways. They need to be aesthetically expressive in sensory terms as well as satisfying our primeval needs of warmth, safety and security. The environments they create can help us work more effectively because they can present a wide range of stimuli for our senses to react to. Intelligent buildings enable their occupants to experience delight, freshness, a feeling of space; they should invite daylight into their interiors, and should provide a social ambience which contributes to a general sense of pleasure and improvement in mood. In Chapter 4, I introduce the idea of 'flourishing' environments in which people can thrive. Of course, the culture, the management and job satisfaction are key but this does not diminish the importance of the built environment.

Buildings consume a great amount of energy and water in their construction and during their total life-cycle. They use large quantities of materials and aggregates and they generate waste and pollution at every stage of their production. It is no longer acceptable to consider a building and its systems in isolation from its wider social impact. This has become critical with the growth of megacities, which is part of a rising trend towards urban living. Modern liveable cities comprise intelligent and sustainable buildings and infrastructures; however, they should also be designed to show respect for the natural environment and the health of the inhabitants. In other words, sustainable and intelligent cities are composed of buildings supported by intelligent infrastructures created for the wellbeing of residential, commercial and industrial communities.

The key criteria for good quality intelligent buildings are that they should:

- satisfy client and users in a sustainable manner (the main objective for supply stakeholders);
- meet social and community needs;
- respect the health and wellbeing of occupants; and
- recognize available resources.

An intelligent building starts with a comprehensive brief, which should include:

- a clearly articulated project with a holistic vision and mission;
- a recognition of the planning, design and procurement realities;
- a whole-life value approach;
- an embedded monitoring system; and
- a comprehensive operating system for the building.

The creation of shared visions, effective teams, clear structures and robust processes ensures that the intelligent building being constructed will demonstrate the purpose for which it was conceived. As we move towards sustainable futures there needs to be a long-term outlook by the project team; it is no longer valid to think short-term. This book is about change brought about by societal pressures as well as the technology we create.

We need intelligent buildings for humanity as well as for functionality and efficiency. They are our twenty-first-century signature to a better, kinder world in which health, wellbeing and happiness can be integral in our planning, design and management thinking. Many of the ideas discussed apply to the refurbishment of older buildings as well as new ones.

Too often there are barriers which make these ideals difficult to achieve. Short-termism; a lack of design thinking time; silo thinking where there is a lack of communication between all the stakeholders involved in the design, construction and management processes; besides an over-conservative outlook are some of the issues. Chapter 7 advocates a more open, transdisciplinary approach to our decision-making.

Deconstructing intelligent buildings

We can often deepen our understanding of architecture by deconstructing ideas first and then reconstructing them. Francis Duffy (formerly of DEGW and President of the UK Royal Institute of British

Architects 1993–95) described the nature of buildings as being composed of four layers of components: Shell, Services, Scenery and Set. The Shell is the structure, which has a lifetime of about fifty years or more; the Services are all the systems covering power, digital, air, water and transportation, having a lifetime ranging from three to twenty years; Scenery is the layout of partitions, including false ceilings, which can change about every five to seven years; Set is the furniture and contents, which can be changed every few weeks or months. Stewart Brand in his book *How Buildings Learn: What Happens After They're Built* interprets these factors and recasts them in terms of six 'S's; to these I have added Senses, Spirit and Soul:

The nine S's
Site: the geographical setting
Structure: the foundation and load-bearing elements
Skin: exterior surfaces
Services: operational systems of a building, including information technology and communications systems
Space plan: the interior layout
Stuff: the contents, including furniture
Senses: the human being
Spirit: the joy and mood induced by a place
Soul: the atmosphere or aura of a place

Brand considers one design imperative to be that 'an adapted building has to allow slippage between the differently paced systems of Site, Structure, Skin, Services, Space Plan, and Stuff.'

The concept of layering also defines how a building relates to people: the building interacts with the occupants at the levels of the Senses, Spirit, Soul and Stuff; with the tenant organization at the Space plan level; with the landlord via the Services that have to be maintained; with the public via the Skin and entry to the building; and with the whole community concerning the plan and size of the Structure and the Site. Occupants use the building and its systems in different ways depending on their use patterns of behaviour, lifestyle and expectations. Occupancy behaviour gives rise to the largest differences between patterns of consumption of energy or water, for example.

Buildings and their interiors should evoke a sensory experience and the quality of that experience will depend on the interaction between the individual and the building together with the environment that the building creates. Juhani Pallasmaa, in *The Eyes of the Skin: Architecture and the Senses* (1996), gives an elegant exposition about how architecture touches our perception of the world around us:

> Architecture is essentially an extension of nature into the man-made realm, providing the ground for perception and the horizon of experiencing and understanding the world. It is not an isolated and self-sufficient artifact; it directs our attention and existential experience to wider horizons. Architecture also gives a conceptual and material structure to societal institutions, as well as to the conditions of daily life. It concretises the cycle of the year, the course of the sun and the passing of the hours of the day.
>
> Juhani Pallasmaa

Buildings are subject to technological and sociological change. Christopher Alexander has posed the question, 'What does it take to build something so that it is really easy to make comfortable little modifications in a way that once you have made them, they feel integral with the nature and structure of what is already there?' (Refer to his books *The Timeless Way of Building* (1979) and *A Pattern Language* (1977).) Age plus adaptability make a building come to be loved. The building learns from its occupants and they learn from it. People like to have some control over their environment and also over the way that the building can be rearranged to deal with changing needs.

Old, cheap buildings offer high adaptability and opportunities for high-risk, creative ventures to be housed with little capital (Thorburn, 2002). Brand describes how the electronics firm Hewlett-Packard was founded in a garage in 1939 in California, with a $538 loan from their electronics teacher. Low rent space leaves tenants free to improve the space to suit their needs. Constant revision is the fate of the institutional and expensive buildings, but even they can be designed in an adaptable, loose-fit way to suit whole life expectancies.

Kincaid (2002) offers a note of caution about intelligent buildings and their tendency to be judged by the levels of system integration that they demonstrate. He argues that this approach can limit the adaptability potential of sustainable intelligent buildings. He goes on to suggest that the capability for re-differentiation or flexibility allows systems to be reconfigured and this will enhance the adaptability of the building and ease the problems of managing the information and communication technology systems.

Over fifty years there can be three generations of services and ten or more generations of space plan changes, and together with continual updating of information and communication systems the resulting costs are much higher than that of the original building.

Cathedrals appear to be monumental and impervious to change. The exterior of Salisbury Cathedral looks much as it did in 1266 yet, as Brand describes, the tower and spire were added in the fourteenth century; in 1754 the original choir screen was removed; in 1865 the screen and old organ were replaced with a new screen and a new organ; in 1929 the organ was removed and the screen demolished, to be replaced by an open metalwork one; in 1965 the screen was removed entirely to give an uninterrupted vista from end to end. What will be the next change?

Sir Richard Rogers, in an essay entitled 'The artist and the scientist', wrote:

> One of the things that we are searching for is a form of architecture which, unlike classical architecture, is not perfect and finite upon completion … we are looking for an architecture rather like some music and poetry which can actually be changed by the users, a kind of architecture of improvisation.
>
> Richard Rogers (quoted in Gans (ed.), 1991)

Architecture, like music, needs a technical resource to function in a myriad of ways, but at a higher level it requires interpretation which will ignite the spirit of the users.

The nature of aesthetics is broader than generally supposed. There is the direct visual aesthetic but there is also a sensory aesthetic which relates to the invisible. So the sounds, the feel, and the smell of the atmosphere in the building are part of the aesthetic. Freshness is one attribute of aesthetic, for example, and is a word which can apply to colour (visual sense), air quality (including air movement), one's sense of space, or the degree of tidiness (it is widely recognized that people often feel better when they declutter a space).

The title of Sybil Kapoor's book – *Sight, Smell, Touch, Taste, Sound: A New Way to Cook* – again reflects the power of our senses in all we do. Professor Charles Spence in the Experimental Psychology Department at the University of Oxford is an expert in 'gastrophysics', which he refers to as multisensory dining. This cross-sensory modal approach is evident when we experience the environment the building creates and is the root of the 'flourish' approach to assessing our state of health and wellbeing (*see* Chapter 4).

Aesthetics are also about how a building adapts and matures over time. How were the aesthetics of a Georgian building viewed in the eighteenth century in contrast to how they are seen today? There is an aesthetic linked to words such as mature, durable and mellow, and this aesthetic develops with time; buildings cannot learn if they do not last. Old buildings embody history and give a glimpse of it. There is also a social and environmental aesthetic, reflecting how well the building communicates with people inside and outside.

People often ask me to name my favourite intel-

Fig. 1.2 The Fallingwater Home by Frank Lloyd Wright. (Photo: Thibaut Houette)

There are ten huts, in three different sizes, from 20m to 28m in height, all interconnected by a footpath. Within the Cultural Centre these huts serve various functions. The first group comprises exhibition spaces whilst a second series of huts houses research areas, a conference room and a library. The last series of huts contains studios for music, dance, painting and sculpture. The tall curved iroko wood shields that form the pavilions have adaptable louvres that protect the Centre from the Pacific ocean weather but also let the local breezes naturally ventilate the spaces. Iroko wood was chosen because it is termite proof. The concept shows beauty in simplicity but it also displays practicality and functionality.

The façades of the pavilions are part of a passive ventilation system; they control environmental conditions in what is a humid, semi-tropical climate. The double outer walls allow air to circulate between the two layers of slatted wood. The apertures in the external shell have adjustable louvres to take advan-

ligent building. Not an easy question to answer; both the Notre Dame du Haut chapel by Le Corbusier (shown in Chapter 4) and the Fallingwater House[1] by Frank Lloyd Wright inspire me in various ways, but I often refer to the Jean-Marie Tjibaou Cultural Centre on the Tinu Peninsula in the Pacific near Noumea, built by the Renzo Piano Building Workshop Studios (RPBW). It is a low-tech and low-maintenance building in which the culture of the Kanak people of former times served as a starting point to the design because they knew and understood how to deal with the regional climate and the moods of the Pacific Ocean nearby.

The Centre is located on a spit of land surrounded by water on three sides. The site's lush vegetation is cut through with trails and paths, amongst which there are 'villages' with clusters of huts or small pavilions with strong ties to their context, Kanak culture arranged with a semicircular layout so defining open communal areas.

Fig. 1.3 Model of a pavilion for the Jean-Marie Tjibaou Cultural Centre shown at the Royal Academy Exhibition in London, September 2018.

12 Sustainable intelligent buildings for people

Fig. 1.4 The Jean-Marie Tjibaou Cultural Centre in Nouméa, New Caledonia. © RPBW – Renzo Piano Building Workshop Architects © ADCK – Agence de Développement de la Culture Kanak (Jean Pipite) © Fondazione Renzo Piano. (a) Aerial view of the 'huts' (photo: Pierre Alain Pantz); (b) aerial view (photo: John Gollings); (c) exterior view (photo: John Gollings); (d) interior (photo: Michel Denancé); (e) detail of the textural quality (photo: William Vassal); (f) people visiting the Cultural Centre (photo: William Vassal).

Sustainable intelligent buildings for people 13

14　Sustainable intelligent buildings for people

Fig. 1.5 (a) Exterior of Edge Olympic (photo: Ossip van Duivenbode); (b–d) interior (photos: Ronald Tilleman); (e) health and wellbeing at EDGE Headquarters. (Credit: EDGE Technologies; photos: Horizon Photoworks)

tage of winds to circulate the air around the building using the natural buoyancy of the air.

In contrast, EDGE Olympic[2] in Amsterdam is a high-tech building, but is also focused on user wellbeing and being environmentally sustainable. The building minimizes its environmental impact but also creates inspiring spaces for people to work. It uses a digital infrastructure to connect everything and everyone to a single cloud platform. Energy consumption is 72kWh/m^2, largely supplied from solar panels. It has a green accessible rooftop and uses a lot of glass for its façade. 15,000 sensors measure the quality of the inside environment in the building. The carefully planned spaces are rich with greenery, filled with natural daylight and offer circadian artificial lighting, which closely mimics the daylight spectrum throughout the day that affects the human circadian rhythms.

d

e

Some practical realities

Building maintenance has had little status except where safety is compromised and yet preventive maintenance not only costs less than repairing building failures, it also reduces human wear and tear. Occupants become frustrated by systems that continually break down; buildings become non-sustainable and wasteful.

Commissioning is another stage of the design process that is often neglected. Post-occupancy evaluation and continual commissioning are spoken of but too often not done, although this is now improving with the more recent emphasis on the health and wellbeing of occupants. Darryl K. Boyce, President of the American Society for Heating, Refrigeration and Air Conditioning Engineering (ASHRAE) in 2019–20, writes about achieving operational excellence in a paper emphasizing the need to recognize the close performance relationship between the building and people (*ASHRAE Journal*, 2019, 61, 14–18). He calls on us to think and act differently (an opinion I share in Chapter 7 in reference to creating sustainable, liveable buildings).

Buildings take a long time to plan, design and construct, and in some ways it is easy to understand how things can go wrong, bearing in mind all the stakeholders involved in all of these processes. As an example of the difficulties that often arise in planning buildings, Brand (1995) quotes the Sydney Opera House, finished in 1973 and universally recognized as a symbol of Australia. It cost $120 million with a cost overrun of about 1,700 per cent. The magnificent roof shells were designed to last 300 years and yet the waterproof joints between them were sealed with mastics that have a projected life of twelve years with no sensible provision made for inspection, maintenance or repair. In 1989, it was estimated that the Opera House would need $100 million to replace them. Why did that happen? Probably for several reasons. Was there a lack of systems and long-term thinking, or was it that the innumerable changes that inevitably take place during a building project could not be accounted for by the existing quantitative and qualitative processes? The design of the curved shell structures was complex and took time, so perhaps minds were concentrated on that (the result was brilliant) and maybe some practicalities were overlooked.

The three things that change a building most are economic and fashion markets, money and weather (temperature, moisture, water, frosts). To protect a building over a long period one needs to protect it from markets and weather by maintaining it. Money should be sufficient to maintain the building so that it can run efficiently and effectively for its intended purposes and to provide for renovation; sadly, all too often the maintenance budgets are viewed as an opportunity to reduce costs in the short term.

The facilities manager has an essential role: covering the planning and design related to construction and renovation; coordinating changes of facilities and relocation; developing facilities policies; long-term planning; building operations, maintenance and engineering; furnishings, equipment and inventory management; real estate procurement, disposal, reuse or recycling; and post-occupancy evaluation and continual commissioning.

Offices are a good building type to exemplify how buildings learn to take change continually. Open-plan and landscaped offices were developed in the 1960s, followed soon afterwards by a second wave of innovation in office furniture. Purpose-built partitions were easily linked; purpose-made work surfaces and storage devices became common and were suited to the open office environment. The nature of the open office environment was emphasized by the arrival of information technology which needs replacement practically every three years. This and sociological changes have altered the concept of the workplace, as discussed in Chapter 4.

The fuel crisis in the early 1970s started off an ever-increasing interest in energy and its consumption in buildings as well as in other sectors. New office buildings were sealed tightly with tinted windows or were double- and triple-glazed; tighter control was enforced by building management over lighting, ventilation and air temperature. Money was saved, public credit was taken for energy conservation but people became feeling unwell owing to being sealed in spaces with insufficient ventilation and exposed to chemicals – so called volatile organic compounds (VOCs) – outgassing from the carpets and building materials, a problem which can still occur today in tightly sealed buildings. Considerations such as water, waste management, pollution, and health and wellbeing are just as important as energy (as highlighted in Chapter 6). According to varying attitudes to climate change amongst all the cultures across the world, different priorities have been given to sustainability but a united global effort is needed to fulfil the challenges it gives nations and us as individuals.

The 'intelligent' building became dominant in the 1980s. Integration of climate control, fire services, security, lighting, heating, ventilation, air-conditioning and communications were all managed by a computerized integrated network. But vernacular architecture (as featured in Chapter 2) makes us pause and think. In all the increasing complexities of technology and changing social expectations we have to remember that simplicity is reliable, durable, gracious, elegant and natural.

Human values are always overwhelmingly important, however sophisticated the technology. It is the people who use the space who understand best how it can be altered to be conducive to the work being undertaken. Materials and structural systems can be used which invite change and allow changes to accumulate. According to Becker in *The Total Workplace* (1990), adaptability can be over-specified and cites the City of London Lloyds building (1985) as a case of this. The cost was £157 million and it was reckoned in a 1988 survey that 75 per cent of its occupants

Fig. 1.6 Lloyd's of London.

wanted to move back to their old 1958 building. The building was high-tech on a very large scale but took no account of the individual worker and work group needs, according to Becker, even though workplaces had a high degree of control. The building's services were installed on the outside of the building, as they had been in 1976 for the Centre Pompidou in Paris, in order to open up interiors for flexible space planning, but this led to an attractive but expensive exterior with high maintenance costs. In contrast, the Chrysler building (1930) and the Empire State Building (1931) in New York have proved adaptable, although it is not clear that this was originally intended. Their high ceilings, shallow floor depth and openable windows allowed flexibility in subsequent replanning of the interiors. More recent upgrading of the Empire State Building has led to a more energy-efficient building.

Brand (1995) gives many examples where buildings at the Massachusetts Institute of Technology (MIT) in Boston have proved flexible. Here there is a recognition that an abundance of natural daylight, controlled ventilation, good fire control and low energy consumption gave added value, an issue which is only more recently coming to be appreciated. Providing healthy environments should be seen as an investment, not as an expenditure. Good design and management of buildings with low energy demands tend to produce healthier buildings, for example. Capital cost outlooks do not respect these approaches and yet we know the flow of natural light through a building has a fundamental effect on health and a sense of wellbeing, so windows are very important for this and a range of other reasons. More fundamentally, sustainability means planning for future generations, which can only be achieved with a long-term outlook.

Brand believes scenario planning leads to a more versatile building because it takes advantage of the information developed by programming (detailed querying of building users) and offsets the common tendency to over-specify without properly understanding user needs. Buildings are treated in a strategic way and scenario planning and programming stimulate the design process so that a strategy can be formulated. This intent is conducted through the design and construction phases and ultimately through to the occupancy of the building.

I have emphasized that there has to be a common vision. Priority issues have to be understood. Integrated logistic support systems are common in naval architecture, aerospace, nuclear and defence industries; a lot can be learnt by studying them and applying some of the principles to buildings in order to reduce waste streams in the design and construction processes. The value of virtual reality is that designers and users can enter and walk round and view arrangements generated by computer modelling so that alternatives can be quickly reformed and different arrangements put into place. These processes can be helped considerably by feedback from post-occupancy evaluations.

Coda

James Gleick in his book *Chaos* states that simple shapes are inhuman. Mandelbrot was the inventor of fractal geometry (*Fractals: Form, Chance, and Dimension* (1977), and *The Fractal Geometry of Nature* (1982)) and wrote an explanation about this. Simple shapes fail to resonate with the way in which nature organizes itself or with the way that human perception sees the world. Physical architecture has immense detail; different scales draw one's attention and stir the imagination. The architectural composition changes as one approaches the building and sees details in which new elements of the structure come into play. People appear to be happiest in a building where change occurs at every scale in space and time. There is a resonance with human reactions if these layers of scale can be felt. The analogy with the onion is appropriate: peel back the layers and reveal simplicity and depth simultaneously. The layers in the built environment created by the building designed and operated *by* people *for* people affect our outer and inner selves in more subtle ways than perhaps we have realized previously.

Recommendations: a summary

- Plan and design with an integrated team so that there is a commitment to the project from all stakeholders.
- Set a clear vision and mission which increases the motivation of the team.
- Apply a holistic approach with systems thinking.
- Consider the impact of the built environment on occupants and communities.
- The occupants' behaviour has a significant effect on the consumption of energy and water besides the generation of waste, so it is important to increase the awareness of occupants to their impact on resources.
- Aim to increase the build asset value by designing for sustainable operation, flexible and agile spaces; health and wellbeing.
- Monitor using smart metering and wireless sensor technology.
- Develop data management systems to give feedback on the performance of spaces in the building.

- Measure the interaction between the building, the systems and the occupants using the latest wireless sensor systems (including wearables).
- Design for a degree of personal control of the environment.
- Use a whole life value approach to economic evaluations.
- Use technology as an enabler but aim for simplicity rather than over-complicated systems, and ensure interoperability is in place as connectivity is vital to effect smooth continuous operation.
- Remember efficiency does not guarantee effectiveness: you need to consider both when designing systems.
- Design beyond the expectations defined in codes and regulations.
- Keep abreast of relevant fields of knowledge and innovation which may be occurring in other sectors. Learn from other disciplines across sectors.
- Think of an intelligent building as an organism responding to human and environmental needs. Bio-façades are emerging where living and non-living elements coexist.

Futures

Now and in the future we must consider the influence that buildings have on society, the local community and future generations. For this we will need to consider the environmental, social and economic impacts of buildings throughout the total process of design, construction and operation – whether the buildings are new or old. Whole life value, in which quality and whole life costs are assessed, is paramount if we are to think long-term and meet growing sustainability demands. Emerging technologies (discussed in Chapter 5) can help in the process. However, this does not mean a project has to be starved of human considerations; after all, improving the quality of life is a primary basis for sustainable development. Chapter 7 seeks to encourage a change in the way we think and make decisions about designing and managing buildings.

END NOTES

[1] The Fallingwater House was designed by Frank Lloyd Wright for the Kaufmann family around 1936 and is a fine example of organic architecture.

> It has served well as a house, yet has always been more than that, a work of art beyond any ordinary measure of excellence. Itself an ever-flowing source of exhilaration, it is set on the waterfall of Bear Run, spouting nature's endless energy and grace. House and site together form the very image of man's desire to be at one with nature, equal and wedded to nature.
>
> Edgar Kaufmann, Junior

See also Percy Wong's 2011 essay: 'Fallingwater House: A design icon?'.

[2] EDGE Olympic and Deloitte Buildings: a smart phone app lets users personalize their workplace with the possibility to customize the lighting and temperature, continuously measuring noise levels and air quality to inform choices. The same technology allows users access to the building and enables them to locate their colleagues or find meeting rooms or workplaces. This sophisticated digital infrastructure is flexible, making it future-proof. Extra services can be added to meet changing needs. This enables the buildings to continuously update their systems and contribute to user comfort, productivity and creativity.

Chapter Two

Vernacular architecture

If we look at all the major concerns of humanists and environmentalists today: balanced ecosystems, recycling of waste products, people's participation, appropriate life-styles, indigenous technology, etc. we find the people of Asia already have it all... The old architecture – especially the vernacular – has much to teach us as it always develops a typology of fundamental common sense.

Charles Correa

MANY LESSONS CAN BE LEARNED by studying vernacular architecture (Oliver, 2003)[1]. The term 'vernacular' has been used since the 1850s by architectural historians to refer to the native architectural language of a region. Vernacular architecture has evolved from early humans living in caves or trees, to nomadic peoples using wood, wool and plant materials to make portable tents or yurts. And there are animals who make their homes in a myriad of ways to suit their needs, however hostile the environment. Vernacular architecture blends buildings into their specific settings, so that there is a natural harmony between the climate, architecture, and people. It features natural ventilation and controls air quality with the careful design and placement of indoor pollutant sources like stoves and commodes. Three examples of effective vernacular architecture are described in this chapter: wind towers, courtyards and igloos – each integrating the conditioning power of natural ventilation to give unique responses to local climate.

Some new buildings imitate the best of mature buildings; they increase in sophistication while retaining the simplicity that is a hallmark of vernacular architecture. Lim Jee Yuan describes in his book *The Malay House* (1987) how it creates a nearly perfect solution for the control of climate, with a multi-functional use of space, flexibility in design and a sophisticated prefabricated system which can extend the house with the growing needs of the family. There are many examples worldwide of how humans have ingeniously designed buildings to respond to climate; the principles upon which they were conceived are still relevant today.

People in countries throughout the world have shown that there are many ways of creating buildings that not only provide an enduring practical utility but also an aesthetic; Islamic architecture is one example that is renowned. Currently there is a danger that as the economy of nations becomes more reliant on the rapidly advancing technologies, lessons enshrined in the heritage of world architecture will be neglected and a solely modern technological approach adopted. The basis of this chapter is to argue that human and sustainable development are the main priorities. Buildings should enrich the lives of people and for this they need to be in harmony with the climate, the purposes for which they are built, and the culture that has evolved in their region.

One strength of vernacular architecture is that it blends buildings into various settings, so that there is a natural harmony between climate, architecture and people. In countries such as Iran, Iraq and Egypt, buildings have evolved which not only demonstrate this harmony and unity between people and their environment but also combine engineering and architecture with functional and aesthetic qualities.

Over the ages people have used their ingenuity to make habitats safe, warm and weather protected: the troglodytic architecture sculpted out of the hillside landscapes of Morocco; the igloos of the Inuit people; African courtyard houses; the Malaysian tree-dwellings; the English thatched cottage – and many more – are designed such that the inhabitants can withstand the hot or cold, the dry or humid rigours of the regional climate. Besides their orientation, the mass, built form and materials chosen for these habitats play an important role in vernacular architecture and characterize its style to suit the culture and local climate with an economic use of resources.

Buildings in cold climates must offer protection against wind, cold and snow; curved igloo shapes present the minimum surface area for the largest volume and use few openings at right angles to the wind direction. At lower latitudes the climate moderates and summer heat as well as rain becomes significant. Thus windows are designed to admit the winter sunshine whilst excluding it in the summer using overhangs or various shading arrangements; insulation is used to minimize heat loss, and ventilation helps to counteract heat gain. Heavy mass buildings with shaded courtyards are common in hot, dry tropical regions which usually have a large diurnal temperature range; advantage is taken of evaporative cooling from pools and even the soothing sound qualities of running water in fountains; sand and dust are further factors requiring consideration. Hot humid tropical areas are most demanding on the human system because evaporation from the body by sweating tires the body; every opportunity has to be taken to allow cross-ventilation currents to flow through the roof space and through preferably high rooms. In Malaysia, timber homes on stilts, with many openings to collect every breeze, are common; this relieves the effects of the high levels of relative humidity.

Iranian (or historically Persian) architecture displays a lot of evidence showing how ingenuity can combine planning, building shape, materials and systems design to produce simple but effective solutions to environmental control problems (beautifully illustrated in *Architecture of the Islamic World* edited by George Michell (1978)). Although the control is coarse there is an inherent flexibility which allows the buildings to be in rhythm with the natural cycles of temperature and sunshine. Buildings were closely clustered, partly to aid defence but also to reduce the impact of solar radiation and dust. Tall

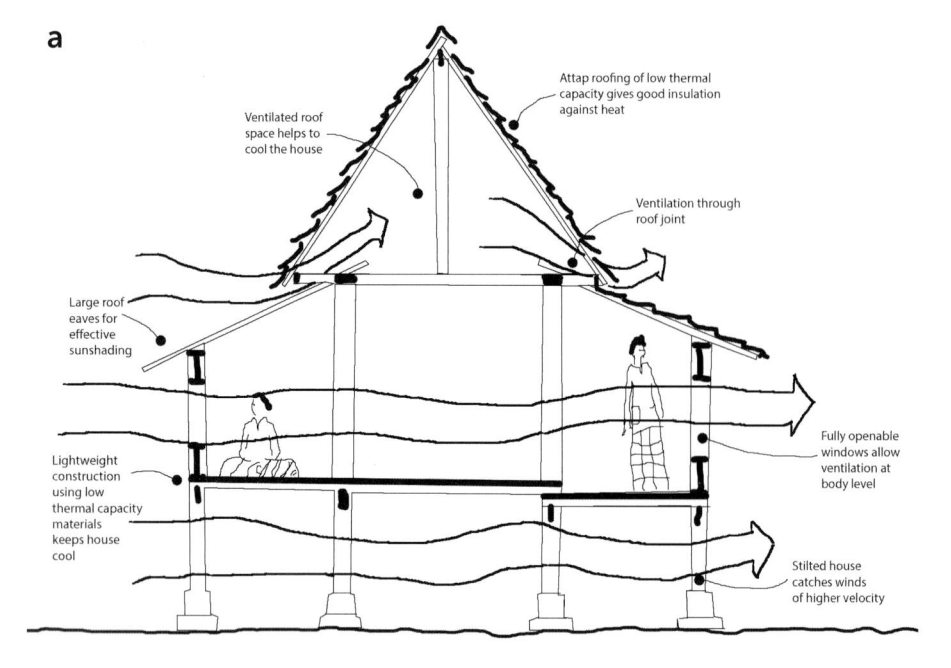

Fig. 2.1 A traditional Malay house. (a) Natural ventilation and stack effect diagram of Selangor traditional Malay house (Ramli, 2012, available via licence: CC BY-NC-SA 4.0); (b) Malaysian traditional architecture. (Photo: http://davidvso.blogspot.com/2012/09/east-coast-trip_20.html); (c) Fenestration design of the Selangor traditional Malay house. (Ramli, 2012, Available via licence: CC BY-NC-SA 4.0)

walls and narrow streets provided shade for pedestrians. Curved roofs were incorporated into buildings as early as 3,000 BC. The curvature accelerates the rate of airflow over the surface so that the consequent decrease in pressure induces any hot air which is stratified on the underside of the roof to flow out through air vents. Thick adobe walls retain the heat and release it to the interior and to the night sky as the cooler evening descends. Landscaping has always played a role in shielding walls from solar heat and courtyards are used to entrap cool night air for several hours.

Air-conditioning is often thought of as having emerged in the nineteenth century, but there are many examples of what one might term air-conditioning in the truest sense of the word in much earlier times in Egypt and India. Wind scoops are prominent features of the Lower Sind District in West Pakistan. The air-conditioners of Hyderabad are in reality the *badgirs* (wind catchers) that channel the wind breezes into each building. They are installed on the roofs, so that temperatures of 50°C which are experienced in summer are lowered by the breeze to what is felt to be a pleasant 35°C.

WIND TOWERS AND WIND CATCHERS

Wind towers (in Arabic called *badgir* and also *malqaf*) are often referred to as wind catchers (*bad* means 'wind' and *gir* means 'catcher') or wind scoops, and they harness summer breezes. Examples of wind towers can be found throughout the Middle East, Pakistan, and Afghanistan and now are sometimes incorporated into Western architecture.

They are an ideal example of a natural ventilation system which relies on a combination of features: the mass of the thick adobe walls; flexible openings at the top of the tower; doors and windows in the living spaces; and the wind pressure differentials on each side of the tower.

Wind flowing around a building causes a separation of flows which creates a positive pressure on the windward side and a negative pressure on the leeward side of the building. Due to its height, the wind catcher enhances the positive pressure on the windward side; it is then

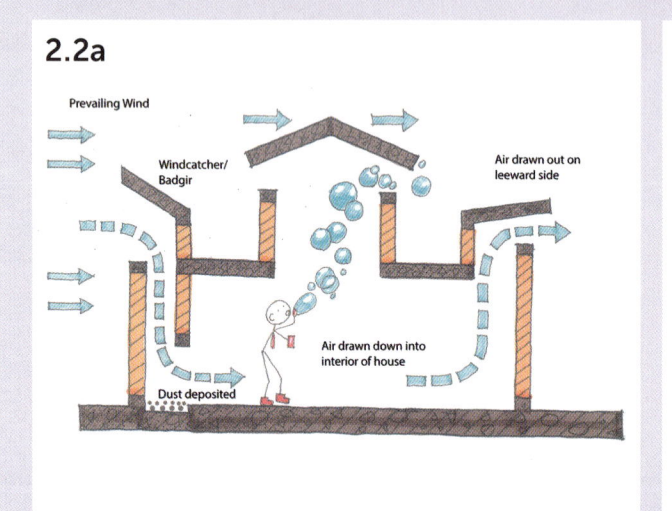

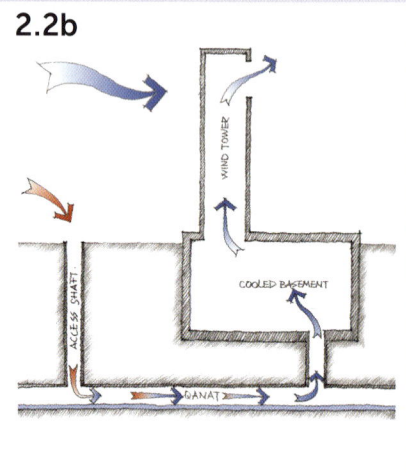

Fig. 2.2 (a) Wind catcher operation; (b) a wind catcher and *qanat* used for cooling (Yang Chen, FINC Architects); (c) paintings of chimneys acting like wind towers in Santa Luzia, Portugal (painting: Maxine Relton).

directed through the tower into the building. Airflow follows the pressure gradients within the structure and exits through purposely designed openings and through the leeward side of the tower. The size and location of openings (e.g., windows, doors, etc.) and distribution of internal party walls have a great impact on encouraging cross flow and mixing of the indoor air.

In addition to the pressure-induced flows, the principal factor in wind towers is buoyancy: in the day solar heat absorbed by the walls of the tower warms the air which then rises but at night there are often clear skies and the temperature drops significantly, cooling the tower walls; hence the air inside is cooler, so moves downwards. Doors and windows can be opened to assist any upward air movement on warmer nights; if there is a breeze at night the flow is downwards and the air warms slightly but still allows some cooling. When there are no daytime breezes air can flow through openings in the side of the tower.

Sometimes use is made of a fountain or an underground stream placed at the basement of a tower in a channel called a *qanat* to permit cooling by evaporation with some increases in moisture content. Ice can be produced during winter nights and stored in deep underground storage pits for summer use.

Fig. 2.3 (a) Tabatabael House, Kashan, Iran; windtower; (b) gardens at Tabatabael House. (Photos: Narges Felavarsoon)

vernacular architecture are built to meet specific needs, accommodating the values, economies and ways of living of the cultures that produce them. They may be adapted or developed over time as needs and circumstances change.

Oliver (2003)

Many would say Paul Oliver was a guru in respect of vernacular architecture and his beliefs are echoed in many of his written works (in 1987, 1997 and 2006, for example). Trying to understand built environments as dynamic systems that change over time causes us to consider how people have adapted to Earth's various climates. Europeans are familiar with architecture that has evolved in temperate climates, but there are good lessons they can learn from buildings intended for very cold and very hot climates. There are increasingly more examples of some aspects of Islamic architecture being adapted for use in a European context.

Some aspects of Islamic architecture have been used in modern Western architecture, such as the design for the School of Architecture at Yale University, which incorporates a wind catcher in the façade of the building. At De Montfort University in the UK, solar chimneys have been used to provide natural ventilation (Yang and Clements-Croome, 2013).

People in different countries have adapted to different levels of temperature, but their buildings alone without mechanical services systems allow a variation in indoor temperature of only some 4°C in climates where the diurnal range may be of the order of 17°C. In building, humans have adapted to the climate in many ways, whether by using the covered streets commonly found in hot countries, by arranging streets so that buildings are close together or by using cloisters or verandahs to provide shade around courtyards. In every case there is an attempt to balance basic needs in a simple way, with a style that is pleasing to the eye.

In desert regions, mud constructions can maintain fairly steady inside temperatures in spite of very

Fig. 2.4 (a) Basement entrance showing air inlets; (b) using spring water for a calming environment. (Photos: Narges Felavarsoon)

Lessons from vernacular architecture

Vernacular architecture comprises the dwellings and other buildings of the people. Related to their environmental contexts and available resources they are customarily owner- or community-built, utilizing traditional technologies. All forms of high air temperatures and solar radiation. Cross-ventilation is important in humid climates, but in the hot, dry regions of the world, shade and protection from solar glare and high temperatures are vital. Measurements have shown how the high thermal capacity of thick adobe walls and mud roofs give pleasant conditions of 24–30°C with midday external air temperatures of 40°C and roof temperatures of 60°C (Fitch, 1976).

Nature's architecture

> To my mind architecture is like the shell of a snail, the soft part secreting calcium carbonates, and by natural forces making the form by movement and surface tension.
>
> Hassan Fathy

A lot can be learnt about the response of buildings to their environment by considering the animal world. Termites are ingenious animal architects; more than 2,000 species of termite live in tropical and sub-tropical regions and this diversity is reflected in the variety of dwelling styles that have evolved. But they have a unifying feature: they can all maintain an equilibrium between the heat that the ants release as a community living inside their mound (described as a castle or termitary) and the heat gain and loss due to the surrounding climate.

In Australia, compass termites build large castles or termitaries in the shape of huge, flat chisel blades, always with their long axis pointing north–south. This arrangement exposes the minimum possible area to the midday heat but allows the castles to catch the rays of the early morning and late evening sun, when the termites need warmth, especially in the cold season; peak temperatures can be lowered by about 7°C with such orientation and thus maintain a preferred temperature for termites of 30–32°C.

Some termitaries have chimneys; others have rain roofs. Some of the most interesting termitaries are found on the Ivory Coast of Africa. A mound might reach a height of 3–4m and contain two million termites. Their oxygen consumption is considerable and without ventilation they would be suffocated within a few hours, yet the mound's solid outer surface shows no sign of openings. These insects have evolved an ingenious ventilation system that cuts vertically through the centre of the mound. There is a royal cell in the centre with many chambers and passages. Between it and the thick, harder outer walls are ridges with narrow air spaces, very much like capillaries in the human blood system. Below it is a larger air space called a cellar; another air space above reaches a long way into the centre of the nest like a chimney. Channels as thick as an arm radiate from the upper air space into the ridges, where they subdivide into many small ducts; these come together again to form channels as wide as those leading to the cellar. The ventilation system is completely automatic and maintains a temperature of about 30–32°C in the nest. The air in the chambers is heated by the fermentation processes taking place there, with the termites causing a rise in temperature. Hot air rises and is replaced by a stream of air from the ridges. The exterior and interior walls of these ridges are porous and allow diffusion of carbon dioxide outwards, while oxygen permeates inwards. The ridges with their system of ducts act as the lungs for the colony.

Another species, *Apicotermes gurgulifex*, builds an oval nest about 200mm high, which is embedded in the soil but is insulated by a mantle of air. In this nest, saliva and excrement are used to fashion an elegant structure. The surface is pierced by ventilation slits, each surrounded by a raised ring. So precise is their pattern and spacing that the slits appear to have been made by a machine. From each ring, circular passages lead into the exterior wall of the nest, which is in turn connected with the rooms inside. There is much debate today about air quality in buildings and the amount of fresh air that is required for healthy working conditions, but these insects mastered the art of ventilation many centuries ago.

Nature's landscapes

Vernacular architecture has lessons for all of us. The work of Bernard Rudofsky (1964) concerning what he termed 'non-pedigreed' architecture is fascinating. Perhaps the most durable and versatile examples

Fig. 2.7 Bamboo cathedral, based on a photo by Uli Johannes König (*Anthroposophy Worldwide*, March 2018; Credit: Yang Chen, FINC Architects)

Fig. 2.5 Castle at Uchisar in Cappadocia (Kapadokya Uçhisar Kalesi). In the Cappadocia region of Turkey, people have lived in the natural volcanic tufa formations and some still do. (Photo: Ilhan Aksit Kultur Turizm Ltd. Sti, 2000)

of this vernacular architecture are the troglodytic towns, such as those in the rocky landscapes of Cappadocia in Turkey or those found in Pantalica in Sicily or again those in Vardzia in the Erusheti mountains of Georgia. Other examples are at the oasis of Siwa in Egypt, where burial grounds have been converted into living quarters, and underground villages in parts of China, where rooms can even have ceilings carved into the soil. Occasionally people have carved entire towns out of rock above the ground. Perhaps the most spectacular example of this is the volcanic formations in Turkey's Anatolian valley of Göreme, in which the volcanic tufa cones have been sculpted by nature through wind and water erosion. Such sites appealed to people with a desire for seclusion. There are examples during the seventh century of as many as 30,000 people living as a monastic community in these tufa formations, for example.

Lightweight structures

Not all buildings are massive in construction and in recent years there have been many designs of lightweight structures which really owe their origins to nomadic architecture, such as the tents used by the Hadendana nomads of Eastern Sudan and tents made of black goats' wool used by the Bedouin tribes

Fig. 2.6 An over-thousand years old baobab tree in Senegal. (Patrut *et al.*, 2015)

that live on the Ajdir plateau of the Middle Atlas mountains.

Lightweight structures may be used in very cold or very hot climates. For example, in Mongolia the mean January temperature is −40°C. The yurt, or more properly called the *ger*, is a warm and well-insulated tent-like structure that protects against the cold, is streamlined against the wind, is stable and yet easily transportable and over the ages has been used by peasants and royalty alike. The *ger* is adjustable to suit the weather. The top felt can be moved to control light, smoke or ventilation, or closed to exclude dust and rain; felts can be raised in summer to allow the air to flow in at the base and in winter the layers of felt are increased and a foot felt is wrapped around the base to exclude drafts. The streamlining of its shape and its low profile make the *ger* well able to withstand severe winds, in a similar way to the igloo; the lack of corners helps to prevent cold spots. Even now many of the Mongolian population still own *gers* and improvements in their design are continually being made.

The idea of using lightweight structures was adopted on a grand scale in the twentieth century. Buckminster Fuller's proposal in the early 1960s to cover Manhattan with a transparent dome and the work on Arctic City in the 1950s by Frei Otto and Ralph Erskine are famous examples (Fitch, 1976). The development of materials in recent years has meant that lightweight fabrics can be selected that have enormous strength to withstand wind and snow. Frei Otto was a pioneer in this field (Drew, 1976). Even more importantly, fabric can be selected to meet any requirement of light transmission, so that the internal environment can be tuned to match heat gains and losses with lighting quality.

Two examples of lightweight structures in modern times (both designed by Buro Happold UK and involving Frei Otto) include one in 1982 for a township in the Alberta province of Canada that can experience temperatures lower than −40°C in winter, with severe wind chill. The design was for a 35-acre pneumatic or tent township in which 2,000 people would live and another 8,000 would work during the day, so that the meso-climate would ensure that the external environment around the normal dwellings was more like a European winter than one experienced in the severe conditions of that region (Croome, 1985). The other example is in Saudi Arabia, which has a very hot and mostly dry climate attaining tempera-

Fig. 2.8a, b and c   Diplomatic Club, now Tuwaiq Palace, Riyadh. (Photo: BuroHappold Engineering)

Vernacular architecture   29

tures of 45–50°C in the hottest seasons, and yet tents have been used over the centuries. The Diplomatic Quarters in Riyadh show contrasting building structures: one is a very massive, fortress, snake-like wall with a huge thermal inertia built of local stone; the other consists of five lightweight rosette-like tent structures which are attached to the high mass wall.

Architects such as Hassan Fathy had the ability to inspire teams who design and construct buildings that have a simplicity and yet are also functional (Steele 1988; 1997). Examples of Fathy's work include the air inlets for the souk at New Bariz in Egypt, the Dar Al-Islam mosque in New Mexico, constructed in 1980, and the Mit Rehan house built in Egypt during 1980. Many more are described in *Hassan Fathy: Earth and Utopia* by Salma Samar Damluji with Viola Bertini (2018). All these examples let the buildings blend into the surroundings; they soften the extremes of the climate for the people living or working inside; they allow natural ventilation; they are durable, long lasting and need little maintenance.

> Culture is the outcome of the interaction between man and his environment in satisfying his needs both spiritual and physical. So, architecture is one of the most important elements of culture and the result of this interaction.
>
> Hassan Fathy

Courtyards

Courtyards are one of the oldest plan forms for dwellings going back thousands of years and appearing as a distinctive form in many regions in the world. Examples exist in Latin America, China, the Middle East, Mediterranean, and in Europe. Preserving the basic typology of the courtyard, local climate and culture has created a unique style for each region.

The courtyard house, called a *siheyuan*, is a typical form in ancient Chinese architecture. It offers space, comfort, quiet, and privacy. A *siheyuan* consists of a

Fig. 2.9 A typical courtyard house in southern China. (Beifan Yang, Tianjin Weland Landscape Architecture Design Co., Ltd.)

rectangle with a row of houses bordering each side around a courtyard, normally with a southern orientation and having the only gate usually situated in the southeast side. Walls protect the houses from the harsh winter winds and from the spring dust storms that frequently occur in Northern China from the Gobi Desert in Mongolia. The house's deep eaves provide cooling shade and protection from the summer rains while allowing the winter sun's warmth to be captured in the rooms. Their design reflects the traditions of China, following the rules of *feng shui* and Confucian tenets of order and hierarchy.

All the rooms around the courtyard have doors and large windows facing onto the yard and small windows high up on the back wall facing out onto the street. Ridged roof tops provide shade in the summer and retain warmth in the winter. The verandah divides the courtyard into several big and small spaces that are closely connected, providing a common place for people to relax whatever the weather. The courtyard is an open-air living room and garden with plants, rocks, and flowers, for family members to chat and gather. In cold Northern China, courtyards are built broad and large to increase the exposure to sunlight, and there are more open areas inside the courtyard walls for daylight, fresh air, and rainwater capture for plants and gardens. In hot Southern China, the courtyard houses are built with multiple stories to encourage cross ventilation flow incorporating natural cooling effects. The orientation of houses is not strictly north–south aligned, but follows the local topology of hills and easy access to water sources.

Igloos

In contrast to the hot arid regions of Iran the people living in the cold frozen Arctic evolved a curved structure called the igloo[2]; although the ice block igloo has a short life it provides a satisfactory thermal control which opposes the rigours imposed by the climate (Fitch, 1976). The Inuit people build igloos as shelters from the extreme weather conditions in the Arctic. The igloo has excellent thermal performance without mechanical equipment (Cañizares and Bahamón, 2013). The hemispherical shape of the igloo provides the maximum resistance to winter gales from all directions, while simultaneously exposing the minimum surface area to heat loss. The dome uses packed snow blocks, some 500mm thick, 1,000mm long, and 150mm wide, which are laid in a continuously sloping pile so the finished dome is strong and windproof. Effectively, the shape encloses the largest volume with the least material, so it can be heated by a blubber lamp. The interior surface coated by a glaze of ice on the interior surface, is also draped with animal skins and furs to prevent radiant and convective heat loss to the cold floor and the walls. According to Fitch (1976) measurements have shown that with no heat source apart from the small blubber lamp, internal temperatures are held at levels of −6 to −4°C with external temperatures ranging from −24 to −40°C. Fitch shows in a similar way how houses in hot climates constructed with adobe walls and mud roofs attenuate the very hot temperatures of those regions.

The value of vernacular architecture

Eugène Viollet-le-Duc probably wrote the first book emphasizing vernacular architecture – *The Habitations of Man in All Ages* (1876) – although glimpses of its basis can be read in the works of others, such as Vitruvius. Vernacular architecture needs not only the involvement of architects and engineers but also the local people who work and live in the locality if it is to have real meaning and satisfy their environmental needs derived from their cultural heritage (Özkan *et al.*). There can be a mismatch between professional knowledge and that of the local people. This lack of direct experience has, in the stark words of Fitch (1961), '… made the citizen into an ignorant consumer, the designer into an isolated powerless special-

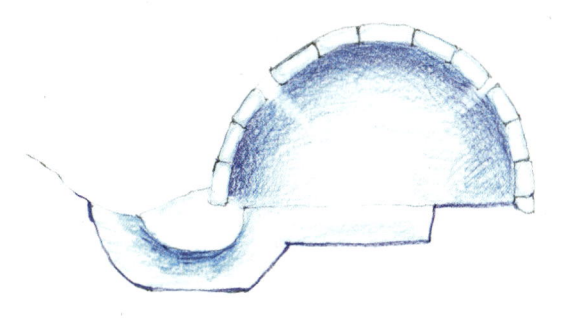

Fig. 2.10a and b   Illustration of an igloo. (Bin Zhang, Tianjin Weland Landscape Architecture Design Co., Ltd.)

ist,' and contrasts strongly, he believes, with history before the Industrial Revolution when direct involvement came naturally. Times have changed since 1961 but the words of Fitch are relevant to an integrated team working with the client, which is becoming so much more evident today. Building a shelter to house their families was and still is in some parts of the world a natural skill that tribes have inherited over aeons of time. The shaping of a socially acceptable and individually satisfying environment demands participation with the people as well as with the environment and there are many examples around the world that reveal how people under given environmental, social and technical limits have striven to create the most suitable living conditions in accordance with nature (Rapoport, 1946; Knowles, 1974). Good purposeful design of anything has intended meaning which blends form, function and human values. There is a coherent unity or wholeness, which is difficult to define except by a phrase like 'it feels just right'. Environmental adequacy has three essential attributes: flexibility in environmental control, identification of need, and economy of material and manpower resources (Özkan, 1979). These surely are key essentials for sustainable design.

Conclusions

History as reflected in the patterns of vernacular architecture has shown that orientation, shape, materials and mass are key starting points in building design for any climate. Moreover, the experience and participation of local people give a richness and depth to their architecture within the context of regional development and ensure that intended meanings and environmental needs are interpreted to fulfil social, technical and economic visions and objectives.

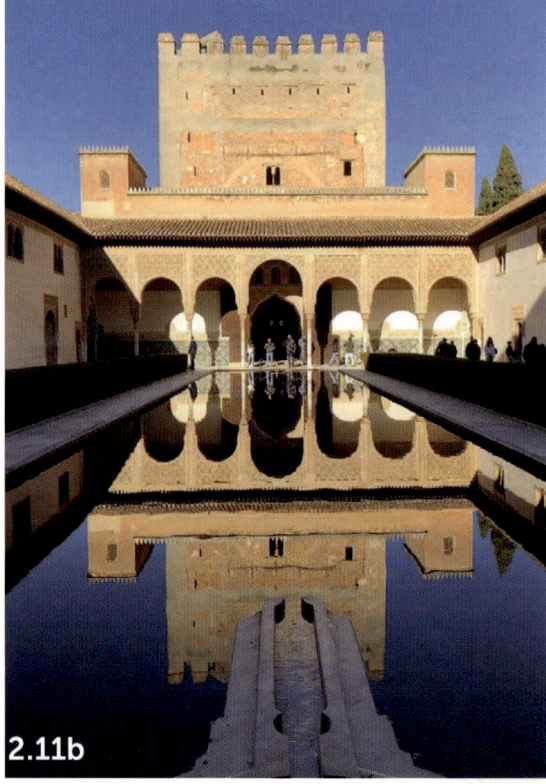

Fig. 2.11a, b and c   Nasrid Palaces. El Alhambra, Granada, Spain. (Photos: Andrea Sargeant Branca)

The principles that produced the traditional solutions must be respected. This is the only way modern architecture can surpass, in human and ecological quality, the achievement of vernacular architecture in the hot arid regions of the world.

Fathy et al. (1986)

The essence of these words by Hassan Fathy are of course true for all regions of the world. Environments that have a high cultural and social quality do not become obsolete. The present arrives from the past and moves forward to the future. Bio-diversity, social diversity and cultural diversity guarantee a long-term stable equilibrium. Vernacular architecture provides many exemplars for the sustainability agenda whilst respecting the culture, natural resources and people of the region.

Let us finish this chapter in the calm atmosphere of the El Alhambra in Spain, where Arabic influences are evident in these photos by Andrea Sargeant Branca.

END NOTES

[1] Neveen Hamza presents an interesting perspective on the value of vernacular architecture. See Hamza, N., 2019, 'Contested legacies: vernacular architecture between sustainability and the exotic', in Sayigh A. (ed.) *Sustainable Vernacular Architecture: How the Past Can Enrich the Future.*

[2] In the Arctic context igloos are intelligent buildings. See *Igloo: Contemporary Vernacular Architecture* by Cañizares and Bahamón (2013). See also 'Optimal environments: CFD analysis of an igloo' by D. Woolf (2000).

2.11c

Chapter Three

Lessons from nature – biomimetic and biophilic architecture

An interdisciplinary exchange between behavioural ecologists, evolutionary biologists, cognitive scientists, social scientists, architects and engineers can facilitate a productive exchange of ideas, methods and theory that could lead us to uncover unifying principles and novel research approaches and questions in studies of animal and human collective behaviour.

Pinter-Wollman et al. (2018)

Architecture has always been an interdisciplinary pursuit, combining engineering, art and culture. The rise of biomimetic architecture adds to the interdisciplinary span.

Penn and Turner (2018)

Evolution in biology follows guiding principles that have the potential to push architecture and building technologies towards a (more) sustainable direction: the efficient utilization of scarce natural resources and their efficient conversion into physiological performance is one of the main selection criteria of biological evolution.

Knippers et al. (2016)

GEORGE DE MESTRAL was returning from a hunting trip with his dog in the Swiss Alps in 1941 and he noticed that burdock burrs kept sticking to his clothes and his dog's fur. He became curious as to how it worked so he examined them under a microscope, and saw that hundreds of hooks became caught on anything with a loop, such as clothing, animal fur, or hair. He saw the possibility of binding two materials reversibly in a simple fashion and then it took several years to develop the innovative idea into a production process; he finally submitted a patent in 1951. This was the birth of Velcro, a name de Mestral gave his invention taken from a portmanteau of the French words *velours* (velvet) and *crochet* (hook).

This is a well-known case showing how by observing nature we can discover ideas that can contribute in various ways to everyday life. As I write this in February 2019 I read how the microstructure on the abdomen of the firefly has inspired Professor Chen and his research team at Pennsylvania State University to see a way to increase the light extraction efficiency of LEDs from about 50 per cent to nearer 90 per cent (Chen et al., 2019). It is possible that the microstructure of other insects could lead to similar effects.

Many published books and peer-reviewed papers describe architectural engineering applications inspired by nature: the natural mollusc shell nacre is many times stronger than the calcium carbonate from which it is made, so making it a paradigm for a new family of composites; the Atlantic hagfish has its body covered with special glands that can emit a sticky slime which are keratin fibres forming threads as strong as those from spider dragline silk, so giving an alternative for bulletproof vests, suspension cables or artificial ligaments; the first artificial leaf to use sunlight to split water into oxygen and also hydrogen which could be stored in a fuel cell and used to generate electricity (Nocera, 2012); the camel's nose acting as a humidifier and a dehumidifier thus conserving some 70 per cent of the moisture produced in the breathing cycle (Schmidt-Nielsen et al., 1981); adhesives inspired by the hair-like setae on the toes of geckoes; water repellent (hydrophobic) leaves of many plants and trees (the surfaces of the wings of dragonflies are hydrophobic too). These are just some examples but illustrate how biomimetics can lead us towards a more adaptable and sustainable architecture. Gorb and Gorb (2018) describe in great detail how some of the main challenges facing architecture such as multi-functionality and sustainability have been solved by insects in their evolution.

Kellert (2016) defines biomimetics – *bio* (life) and *mimesis* (to imitate) – as the examination of nature, its models, systems, processes and elements to emulate or

Fig. 3.1 Levels of biomimicry (adapted from Zari, 2007).

Fig. 3.2 These images and quotations are extracts from the book *Built to Grow: Blending Architecture and Biology* by Barbara Imhof and Petra Gruber (2016). (a) Oyster mycelium grown in a cylindrical mould (Thomas Speck); (b) designing a grown building envelope made of a mycelium material (Laura Mesa Arango; image: Ivana Sinica, based on a collaborative design with Jiri Vitek); (c) oyster mycelium grown in a 3D printed mould from organic plastics with extending fruiting bodies (Rafael Sanchez Herrera).

Biological solutions are cost- and energy-efficient, multi-functional, long-lasting and environment friendly and with several billion test runs, they have stood the test of time. Their combination of properties allows living beings to interact with their environments very efficiently. It also makes them fantastic role models for a new bio-inspired architecture in which living and non-living matter may eventually be combined.
Thomas Speck

take inspiration from. Biomimetics is the abstraction of design or inspiration from nature. It is important because nature optimizes the use of materials and energy hence shows a way to fulfil some of the sustainability objectives. Vincent (2016) further points out the advantages of biomimetics in being multi-functional and adaptable to local environmental conditions. Fauna and flora have evolved and by natural selection ensured only the best adapted forms survive[1]. Vincent (2016) describes how the byssus thread of mussels is incredibly strong but also watertight. Biological materials are tough: silk is the strongest and stiffest fibre we know; leather is best for oil seals; wood is comparatively lightweight but can support heavy loads; mother-of-pearl is one of the toughest ceramics.

Kellert (2016) defines biophilia as people's connection to the natural world, which evolved aeons before the Industrial Revolution, when people hunted and gathered their food from the fields, walked through woodlands and lived amongst nature. With increasing urbanization this connection has diminished but now we realize how nature provides calming and soothing environments in which to lead our lives, away from technology noise with its fast-flowing, high volumes of information[2].

The idea of combining nature with architecture is deeply interesting; the idea of pushing forward the limits of both in order to make them interact in such a harmonic way. Architects can design organic and unimaginable shapes and this makes me envisage an amazing future.
Laura Mesa Arango.

b

Designing an architecture which is linked to the analysis of patterns found in nature will enable us to live in a more harmonious and sustainable manner. It is possible to establish a symbiotic system where humans, nature and architecture create a new pattern in the design of existing settlements.
Rafael Sánchez Herrera

Patterns in nature

The Fibonacci numbers (1, 2, 3, 5, 8, 13, 21, 34, 55, 89, 144 etc.) frequently occur in nature. Sunflowers and daisies have spiral patterns; daisies have twenty-one clockwise and thirty-four anticlockwise spirals for example. According to Hersey (1999), the Italian architect Piranesi (1720–78) compared marine shells with features of architectural ornamentation. The shell of the nautilus and the florets of Romanesco broccoli are examples of a logarithmic growth spiral (sometimes called an equiangular spiral) and reflect the natural growth curves of plants and seashells. The Archimedean spiral is less prevalent in nature. The logarithmic spiral can be distinguished from the Archimedean spiral by the distances between the turnings, which for a logarithmic spiral increase in geometric progression, while for an Archimedean spiral these distances are constant. Both types of spiral can be found in architecture.

Hersey (1999) shows how architecture has its roots in the various forms which distinguish the natural habitats of plants and animals. Climate has been a major driver but so has the diversity of animal and plant life. A striking example of geometry in natural forms at various scales is the florets of the cauliflower, in which you can see ever smaller spirals, following the Fibonacci sequence. The forms of leaves, flowers, shells, insects and birds have inspired human architecture in various ways. Sometimes it just seems to be about aesthetics but nowadays it seems that these natural forms lead to economical use of materials and even water through the channels for transpiration. These features suggest that

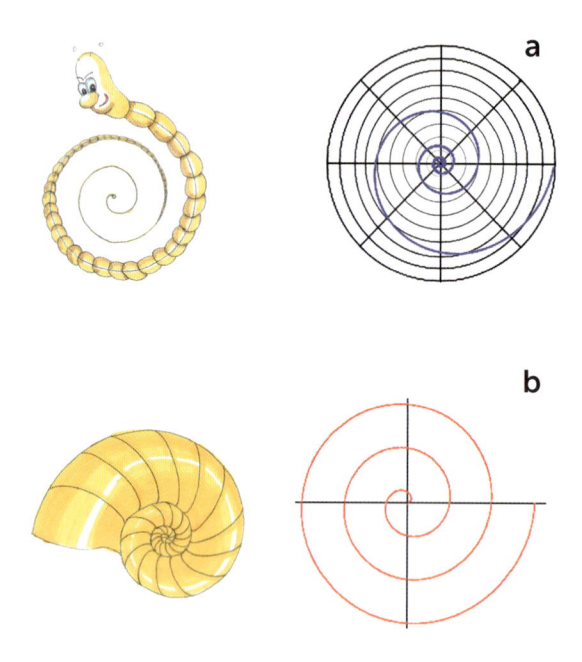

Fig. 3.3 Geometric patterns in nature. (a) Logarithmic spiral (drawing: Desislava Veleva); (b) Archimedean spiral (drawing: Desislava Veleva); (c) fossil ammonite.

nature is an ideal sustainable system from which we can learn. Furthermore nature has an innate response to change which always seems to result in an optimized economy of scale and use or reuse of materials to match environmental conditions.

If you take Fibonacci numbers as successive ratios (8/5, 13/8, 21/13 etc.) then the ratio value approaches 1.618, which is the golden number (Stewart, 2010) associated with the golden ratio which features in aesthetics of art and architecture. The golden logarithmic spiral uses the golden number as the geometric ratio. Le Corbusier based his Modulor on the golden number but it is also seen in the work of painters such as Vermeer, Mondrian, Seurat and others (Bullock and Trombley, 1999). Fibonacci numbers also occur in the rhythms of music sequences. Stewart (2011) believes phyllotaxis (the arrangement of leaves on a plant stem) is probably the only context in which the golden number can be associated with the natural world; nevertheless it continues to fascinate minds in many fields.

Mathematics helps us to reveal form patterns in nature which we respond to innately when we see objects, paintings and buildings. But do we have some inner response to things we cannot see in detail? Chaos theory and in particular the fractal patterns first described by Mandelbrot in 1974 show that perhaps we do. The famous example is the snowflake, whose beauty is fully revealed by analysis using the curve first mentioned by the Swedish mathema-

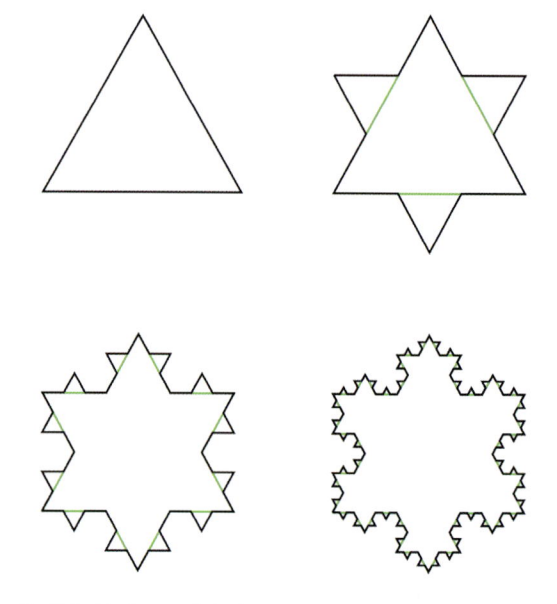

Fig. 3.4 Koch snowflake (drawing: Desislava Veleva).

38   Lessons from nature – biomimetic and biophilic architecture

tician Helge von Koch in 1904 before fractal patterns had been defined as such. Once again nature appears to be made up of shapes and structures in a random manner but on closer inspection shows patterns of regularity.

Fractals are composed of smaller-scale copies arranged in layers of repeating patterns from a larger to an infinitely small scale. Broll (2010) illustrates this vividly via electron microscopy images. In many practical applications, temporal and spatial analysis has been used to characterize and quantify the hidden order in complex patterns. Fractal patterns are characterized by a fractal dimension which can be defined by a ratio providing an indicator of complexity which compares how detail in a pattern changes with the scale at which it is measured. The fractal dimension D is defined as $D = \log E / \log N$ for magnification E and N number of identical layers. Hosey (2012) illustrates the nature of D. So for a complex thick jungle $D=2$ whereas for a simple flat line $D=1$. Taylor (2011) has carried out a series of perception experiments using various patterns which showed that mid-D fractal dimension around 1.3 to 1.5 was found to be more aesthetically pleasing and also, by using skin conductance tests and EEG brain scans, was found to reduce stress by as much as 60 per cent. Our sense of aesthetics perhaps goes beyond what is visible, as the work of Taylor suggests. It as though objects have layers of detail which are interrelated by an underlying sense of order which perhaps we can sense in some sort of subconscious way.

Fractal geometry and architecture

Fractal geometry is the language of nature (Mandelbrot, 1982) and therefore it is natural to assume that this could play a role in developing new forms of design for sustainable architecture and buildings. The geometry of nature has inspired many architects. Gaudí used the helicoid or helix shapes found in tree trunks for the columns at his Teresian School; the hyperboloid is the shape of the femur, forming the columns at Sagrada Família; conoids are typical shapes in the leaves of trees and Gaudí uses similar roof forms at the Sagrada Família; the porch domes of the church crypt in the Güell Estate are based on the hyperbolic paraboloid which describe the tendons in the fingers and hand (Nonell, 2000). At the beginning of the twenty-first century, increasing concerns about sustainability have added new challenges in building architecture design and called for new design and management responses. Fractal analysis can deepen our understanding and is leading us to better solutions.

Lu *et al*. (2012) describe how the idea of buildings in harmony with nature can be traced back to ancient times, with examples from Egypt, China, Greece and Italy. Fractal patterns are found in Mayan settlements, twelfth-century European buildings, Gothic cathedrals, Persian decorative art forms and many examples in Eastern architecture; some even speak of fractal Venice. Fractals have inspired many notable modern designers such as Zaha Hadid, Daniel Libeskind, Frank Gehry and others including Frank Lloyd Wright before them. Yessios (1987) was among the first to use fractals and fractal geometry design in architecture by developing a computer programme to aid architecture using fractal generators. Wen and Kao (2005) established a fractal dimension relations matrix table analysis to classify design style patterns for the masterpieces of three modern architecture masters: Frank Lloyd Wright, Le Corbusier and Mies van der Rohe (Clements-Croome, 2013).

Lu *et al*. (2012) conclude that fractal geometry has important implications for buildings. The representative review shows that architecture design is not made to be isolated but to anticipate changes in the environment. More specifically, sustainable development in a building can be looked upon as adaptability and flexibility over time when it comes to responding to changing environment. Chaos and many other nonlinear theories have explained that deterministic and linear processes, which currently predominate our thinking, are very fragile in maintaining stability over a wide range of conditions, whereas chaotic and fractal systems can function effectively over a wide range of different conditions, thereby offering adaptability and flexibility. In this context, fractal geometry theory offers deeper insights for architecture design.

Biophilic design

> Biophilia offers a healing environment and allows people to draw emotional support from their settings. This psychological vitality of built space depends on the high number and the high quality of visual and intuitive sensory interactions among elements of a space and its users. Such interactions provide a multi-sensory experience. How the elements that construct a space together with the openings to the outside world and the air within it govern how people respond to the whole design. Physiology and psychology reactions govern interactions between structural elements, the space and human beings.
>
> Salingaros (2015)

> When we have learned how to listen to trees, then the brevity and the quickness and the childlike hastiness of our thoughts achieve an incomparable joy.
>
> Hermann Hesse

As mentioned earlier, the human race has lived and worked in rural settings throughout history until about the last 300 years. We were hunter gatherers. With the Industrial Revolution, people dashed to towns and cities to work, unaware of the disconnect with nature that they were experiencing.

Biophilia means a love of life or living systems (Wilson, 1984) whether they be flora or fauna. Now we see the advantages that biophilic design can bring to environments in terms of freshness and aesthetics but above all it can help to improve health and wellbeing (Browning, 2012; Gillis and Gatersleben, 2015). The Japanese recognize the health benefits of forest bathing (*shinrin-yoku*): not just the visual impact but also the fragrances and essential oils that trees emit, making walking in natural settings calming to the mind. This can also lead to increased levels of the protein hormone serum adiponectin for example, which aids the regulation of glucose levels and the breakdown of fatty acids. The fractal patterns in nature awaken our inner aesthetic senses responding to the visual richness and diversity. All these factors can affect cortisol levels, pulse rates, blood pressure, glucose levels, and the balance of serotonin and melatonin, which in turn can affect mood and energy levels[3, 4, 5].

These effects can easily be measured today with a variety of wearables. A research team at Harvard University led by Yin *et al.* (2018) using wearables with twenty-eight subjects showed that biophilic environments can decrease stress. Blood pressure, skin conductance and negative emotions decreased whilst short-term memory and positive emotions increased. This evidence supports that gathered by Cooper and Browning (2015) in their extensive survey of over 7,500 subjects. In the 2015 Human Spaces Report, *The Global Impact of Biophilic Design in the Workplace*, their research showed that those who work in environments with natural elements, such as greenery, natural materials and sunlight reported 15 per cent higher level of wellbeing, 6 per cent higher level of productivity; and 15 per cent higher level of creativity, when compared with those occupants with no connection with natural elements in the workplace (www.humanspaces.com/2015/ Cooper and Browning).

Much research shows that we can prevent stressful conditions by providing and enriching physical and social environments[6]. We are beginning to understand how architecture and urban environments can act therapeutically on human minds and bodies. There is now much evidence showing how the use of biophilic design can produce calming and soothing places, which can relieve stress and encourage positive moods besides impacting health, wellbeing,

Table 3.1 The fourteen Biophilic Patterns and the ways in which they support cognitive performance. (Adapted from Browning *et al.*, 2014 and as shown in Turner *et al.*, *Creating the Productive Workplace*, 2018)

Sensory Qualities of Nature's Elements	Sensory Patterns in Nature	Sensory Perceptions from Nature
1. Visual Connection with Nature A view to elements of nature, living systems and natural processes. Cognitive Performance: Improved mental engagement and attentiveness.	**8. Biomorphic Forms and Patterns** Symbolic references to contoured, patterned, textured or numerical arrangements that persist in nature.	**11. Prospect** An unimpeded view over a distance, for surveillance and planning. Cognitive Performance: Reduces boredom, irritation, fatigue.
2. Non-Visual Connection with Nature Auditory, haptic, olfactory, or gustatory stimuli that engender a deliberate and positive reference to nature, living systems or natural processes. CP: Positively impacted	**9. Material Connection with Nature** Materials and elements from nature that, through minimal processing, reflect the local ecology or geology and create a distinct sense of place. CP: Blood pressure and creative performance.	**12. Refuge** A place for withdrawal from environmental conditions or the main flow of activity, in which the individual is protected from behind and overhead. CP: Concentration, attention and perception of safety
3. Non-Rhythmic Sensory Stimuli Stochastic and ephemeral connections with nature that may be analysed statistically but may not be predicted precisely. CP: Attention and exploration	**10. Complexity and Order** Rich sensory information that adheres to a spatial hierarchy similar to those encountered in nature.	**13. Mystery** The promise of more information, achieved through partially obscured views or other sensory devices that entice the individual to travel deeper into the environment.
4. Thermal and Airflow Variability Subtle changes in air temperature, relative humidity, airflow across the skin, and surface temperatures that mimic natural environments. CP: Concentration		**14. Risk/Peril** An identifiable threat coupled with a reliable safeguard.
5. Presence of Water A condition that enhances the experience of a place through seeing, hearing or touching water. CP: Concentration, memory restoration, perception and psychological responsiveness		

Sensory Qualities of Nature's Elements	Sensory Patterns in Nature	Sensory Perceptions from Nature
6. Dynamic and Diffuse Light Leverages varying intensities of light and shadow that change over time to create conditions that occur in nature.		
7. Connection with Natural Systems Awareness of natural processes, especially seasonal and temporal changes characteristic of a healthy ecosystem.		

Note: The *Patterns of Biophilic Design* report also identifies the ways in which the patterns support stress reduction as well as emotion, mood and preference enhancement.

productivity and creativity. Ulrich (1984) showed how views out from hospital windows onto greenery improved patient recovery rates.

Mangone *et al.* (2014) studied the effects on the environment of incorporating a substantial number of plants into office spaces and found that they had a positive, statistically significant effect on thermal comfort. Interior plants can reduce buildings' operating energy consumption rates because the set temperatures for winter and summer can be lower or higher respectively so decreasing heating or cooling loads. Mangone's experiments showed that the presence of greenery had a psychological influence on peoples' perceptions of the environment. Various research studies have shown that plants can lower CO_2 levels and alter humidity enough to give a feeling of freshness, but the results are variable in the degree of significance. There are also significant differences between the types of plants and how they react to environmental conditions. However, interior landscaping has to be properly designed to be effective; the odd plant here and there looks pleasing but will not be effective as a restorative therapy. Knight and Haslam (2010) describe how plants and artwork make spaces more interesting to occupants.

A walk outside in nature has the ability to calm and soothe and refocus the mind, by restimulating and rebalancing our sensory receptors. The research by Roe *et al.* (2013) uses mobile electroencephalography (EEG) to measure the emotional experience of walkers in different urban environments and showed that urban green space enhances mood.

Turner *et al.* (2018) describe biophilic patterns and the ways in which they support cognitive performance. 'The 14 Patterns of Biophilic Design' (*see* Table 3.1) has been developed for designers from a review of over 500 publications relating to biophilic responses in order to identify flexible and adaptive design patterns (Browning *et al.*, 2014). This offers a powerful tool that can be used by built environment professionals for interiors and exteriors to reconnect the human sensory systems to the biophysical reality and the meaning that these natural elements conjure up. For instance, the rustling of leaves, the fragrance of flowers, birdsong, the sound of flowing water, the spaciousness of landscapes (particularly horizons between earth, sky and water), a light breeze and fresh, cool, clean air are all details that are remembered in terms of the emotional response they provoke.

The location of the building with respect to nature is important. I have already mentioned the work of Ulrich (1984, 1991), which showed how views out from hospital windows onto greenery improved patient recovery rates. The poet Walt Whitman (1819–92) suffered a severe stroke and it took him two years to recover – his convalescence aided greatly, he believed, by his immersion in nature and its healing power which he expressed in these words: 'How it all nourishes, lulls me, in the way most needed; the open air, the rye-fields, the apple orchards.' Alvarsson *et al.* (2010) showed that the sounds of nature aid physiological stress recovery. Greenery and still or running water refresh the body and spirit in any climate. There is growing evidence that landscape surrounding buildings can relieve occupants' stress (Beil and Hanes, 2013; Rainham *et al.*, 2013).

Urban parks care for the environment – storm control, CO_2 conversion, wildlife diversity, softening the raucous quality of noise, offsetting city pollution – and public health in terms of improving mood, mental and physical wellbeing, according to Jane Owen (*Financial Times*, 2016). Owen goes on to report Natural England's findings that if everyone had access to green space this would save the UK healthcare system £2.1 billion a year. The economic case is vividly demonstrated by Browning (2012) in terms of attendance rates at schools, reduction in crime, increases in worker productivity and quicker recovery rates in hospitals. Property values for homes or commercial buildings in nature landscape settings are higher than those that are not. Green space lets children play with friends and also encourages people to walk or cycle more. Housing estates in natural settings with trees and greenery have social and healing values. Loneliness, crime, stress and isolation are lessened but walkability, sense of community and sensorial beauty are increased. These qualities inspired the Garden City idea of Ebenezer Howard and Patrick Geddes in the early twentieth century for Letchworth Garden City in the UK (Welter, 2002). Now we see the Garden City concept reborn as a vital ingredient of new or regeneration schemes for cities in Europe, US and China, for example, and these are supported by Beatley (2011, 2016) who argues strongly that we need biophilic cities worldwide.

The UK Parliamentary Office for Science and Technology (POST) has issued a series of information guidelines called POSTnotes on biodiversity. POSTnote 538 (2016) is entitled *Green Space and Health* and states that there are challenges to providing green spaces, such as how to make parks easily accessible and how to fund both their creation and maintenance. However, parks, woodlands and allotments do provide habitats for wildlife as well as being used for recreation. Key points in this POSTnote are given which echo many of the arguments in this chapter; they show that the UK Government is taking the benefits of biophilia seriously and realize that it is very beneficial to individuals and the community in terms of health, wellbeing and reducing pollution:

- Physical and mental illnesses associated with sedentary urban lifestyles are increasing economic and social costs.
- Areas with more accessible green space are associated with better mental and physical health.
- The risk of mortality caused by cardiovascular disease is lower in residential areas that have higher levels of 'greenness'.
- There is evidence that exposure to nature could be used as part of the treatment for some conditions.
- There are challenges to providing green spaces, such as how to make parks easily accessible and how to fund both their creation and maintenance.

Bio-inspired sustainability

Listed below are just a few examples of the many ways in which biomimetics can lead to more sustainable outcomes.

The lotus leaf effect

The leaves of the lotus flower are difficult to wet because of their ultrahydrophobicity; also the micro-

and nano-architecture of the leaf surface is such that any dirt particles, once they have landed on the surface, can be removed by falling water droplets. This self-cleaning effect has resulted in the development of treatments, coatings, paints, roof tiles, fabrics and other surfaces that can stay dry and clean themselves by replicating the self-cleaning properties of plants such as the lotus flower.

The *Salvinia* effect

The *Salvinia* effect, inspired by the floating fern (*Salvinia*), describes the permanent stabilization of an air layer upon a finely structured surface submerged in water. Salvinia surfaces are used as drag reducing coatings and when applied to a ship hull for example, the coating allows the vessel to float on an air-layer, thus reducing energy consumption and emissions.

Other examples

Other applications that help to map out sustainability pathways include: self-healing materials; highly solar reflective materials being developed in photonics which can leave surfaces cooler; and the use of titanium dioxide in conjunction with the ultra violet part of the light spectrum to break down dirt particles.[7,8,9]

Here I want to conclude by highlighting research on two types of solarleaf system: (1) the artificial leaf, a development that could lead to a hydrogen-generating bionic façade (Bensaid *et al.*, 2012; Liu *et al.*, 2016), and (2) an algae facade as demonstrated by the Bio-Intelligent Quotient (BIQ) building in Hamburg.

BIO INTELLIGENT QUOTIENT BUILDING (BIQ), HAMBURG

This is a pilot residential building in Hamburg designed and completed in 2013 by Arup Berlin and Splitterwerk in Graz, who together formed a design and construction team. It has a bio-reactive façade called SolarLeaf to generate renewable energy from algal biomass and solar heat. The 129 glass photobioreactors containing algae are installed on the south-west and south-east faces and provide dynamic shading, besides acting as insulators for thermal and sound energy. The thermal heat and algae are collected in a closed loop to be stored and used to provide hot water for the apartments.

Compressed air is introduced periodically into the bottom of the reactors to generate a water flow which stimulates the intake of CO_2 and light by the algae. Sunlight acts as a catalyst in the photosynthesis process. The result is a carbon-neutral building with reduced CO_2 emissions.

Fig. 3.5 Bio-facade of BIQ building. (Credit: Fondazione Eni Enrico Mattei, FEEM (www.feem.it); Arup (www.arup.com/projects/solarleaf.aspx)

44 Lessons from nature – biomimetic and biophilic architecture

CASE STUDY: BEYOND BIOMIMETICS: THE BIODIGITAL AND GENETIC RESEARCH OF PROFESSOR ALBERTO T. ESTÉVEZ

Fig. 3.6a Sporopollenin for architecture. Alberto T. Estévez, Sporopollenin houses, Barcelona, 2009–10: biological and genetic architecture project about genetic research on growth control which makes live cells grow for architectural material and habitable spaces. Sporopollenin, coming from the growth of living cells, is the most durable material of the known universe.

We know that nature is the answer to our planetary problems. We are exploring this, through interdisciplinary endeavours, involving fields such as genetics, biology, digital, computation, art, architecture, civil engineering, design. We are exploring the frontiers of knowledge. And a main interdisciplinary cross-point for really arriving at these frontiers is where genetics meets biology and the digital as applied to architecture and design. For these reasons the Genetic Architectures Research Group & Office and the Biodigital Architecture University Master Program was founded at the School of Architecture of Universitat Internacional de Catalunya (UIC) in Barcelona in 2000 which is now organized as the iNSTITUTE FOR BiODiGITAL ARCHITECTURE & GENETICS (iBAG-UIC Barcelona). We work to create architecture and design together with geneticists that is focused on architectural objectives, and involves researching the fusion of biological and digital techniques. Within that framework, many projects have been born, such as the Genetic Barcelona Project in which genetic creation of bioluminescent plants for urban and domestic use is one example among many other biodigital architecture projects that use the concept of biolearning. This takes us beyond biomimetics.

Alberto T. Estévez

Fig. 3.6b Dandelions, trees and other flowers fractality. Alberto T. Estévez – GenArqOffice, Telecommunications building, Santiago de Chile, 2013–14: biodigital architecture project about biolearning, learning from nature, discovering the secret laws of the universe. Developed digitally and fractally, it is at the same time a 'purifying air machine' (below left). Following the fractality of nature: dandelions (above left), trees (below right), and other flowers (above right).

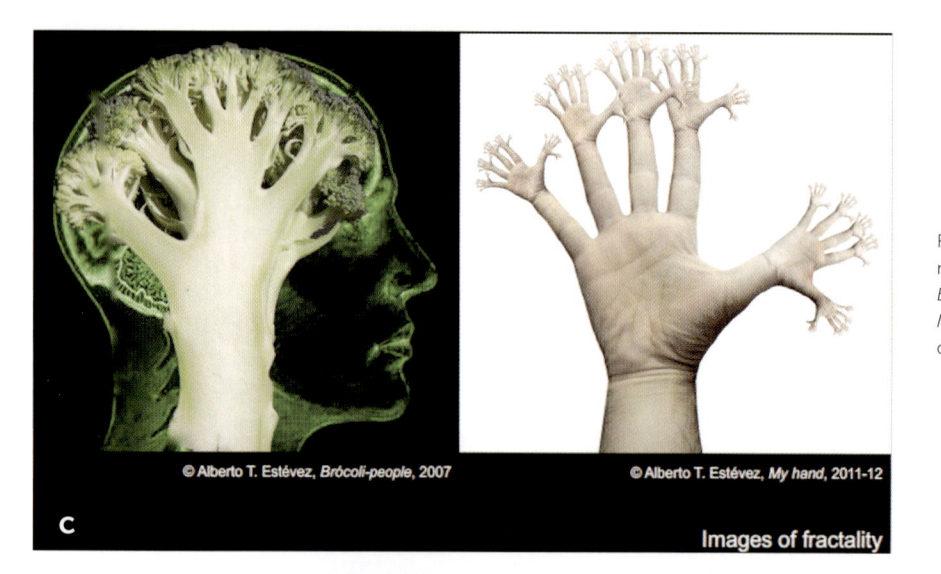

Fig. 3.6c The fractality of nature. Alberto T. Estévez, *Brocoli-people*, 2007 and *My hand*, 2011–12. Images of fractality.

Fig. 3.6d Bamboos and sea sponges fractality. Alberto T. Estévez. Above: bamboos (×1, ×1, ×200, ×400, ×3000) and, below, sea sponges (×1, ×100, ×400, ×3000, ×7000), 2008–09. Photos taken with scanning electron microscope, which allows us to appreciate the structural fractality.

Fig. 3.6e Aster, roses and dragonflies Voronoi patterns. Alberto T. Estévez – GenArqOffice, Park and multifunctional building, Hard, 2014: biodigital architecture project about biolearning, learning from nature, and discovering the secret laws of the universe. Below left: scanning electron microscope photo (×1600) of aster pollen grains. Below centre: scanning electron microscope photo (×800) of rose petal, which shows the structural similarity to a Voronoi diagram, which partitions the space based on the minimal distance to each point.

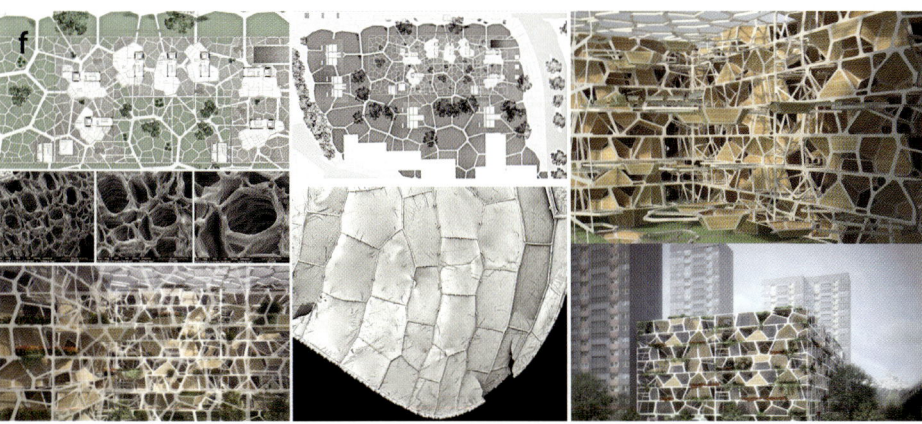

Fig. 3.6f Cactus and dragonflies Voronoi pattern. Alberto T. Estévez – GenArqOffice, Solar passive biodigital housing, Innsbruck, 2014–15. Above left and centre: park and entrance floor organized in different levels of Voronoi diagrams. Below left: scanning electron microscope photos of a cactus section (×1600, ×3000, ×6000), which allows us to discover its structural approach to Voronoi diagrams, in three dimensions: they appear also in the walls. Below centre: dragonfly wing detail (×91); photo taken with scanning electron microscope. Above right and below left: interior patio of floating green platforms organized in different levels of Voronoi diagrams. Below right: general view of the building.

Fig. 3.6g Lilies curvatures. Alberto T. Estévez – GenArqOffice, Market, Casablanca, 2012. Above left: overall view; below: curvature diagrams and lilies; above left: set of Moroccan carpets; above right: Flora on Sand by Paul Klee; below right: its respective pixellation; below centre: creation of the market pavement.

Lessons from nature – biomimetic and biophilic architecture 47

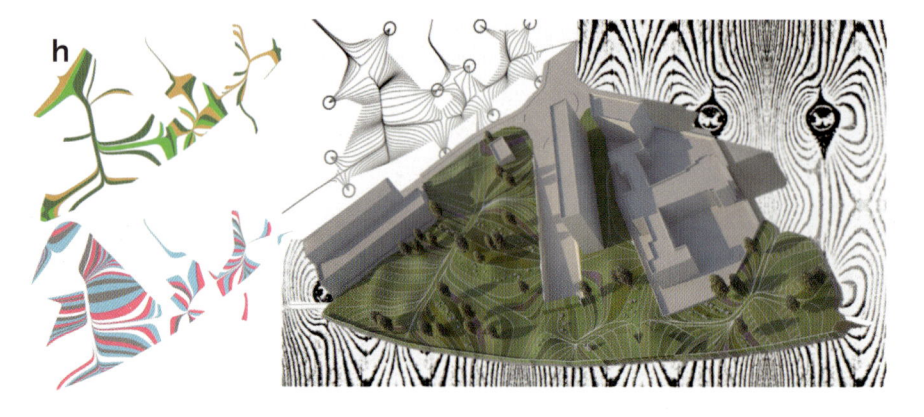

Fig. 3.6h Wood lines. Alberto T. Estévez – GenArqOffice, Park, Cornellà, 2013. The digital strategy of 'force fields' and attractors is applied in this project of a park. The fields follow the daily flows of people and define bands with separate uses – green areas, flowerbeds, activities, and parking. This case is informed by structural organization in nature, for example, the lines of wood.

Fig. 3.6i Wood lines. Alberto T. Estévez – GenArqOffice. Solar passive biodigital housing, Innsbruck, 2016–17. The digital strategy of 'force fields' and attractors is applied in this housing complex project, which is a compact building with several floors, surrounded by a park.

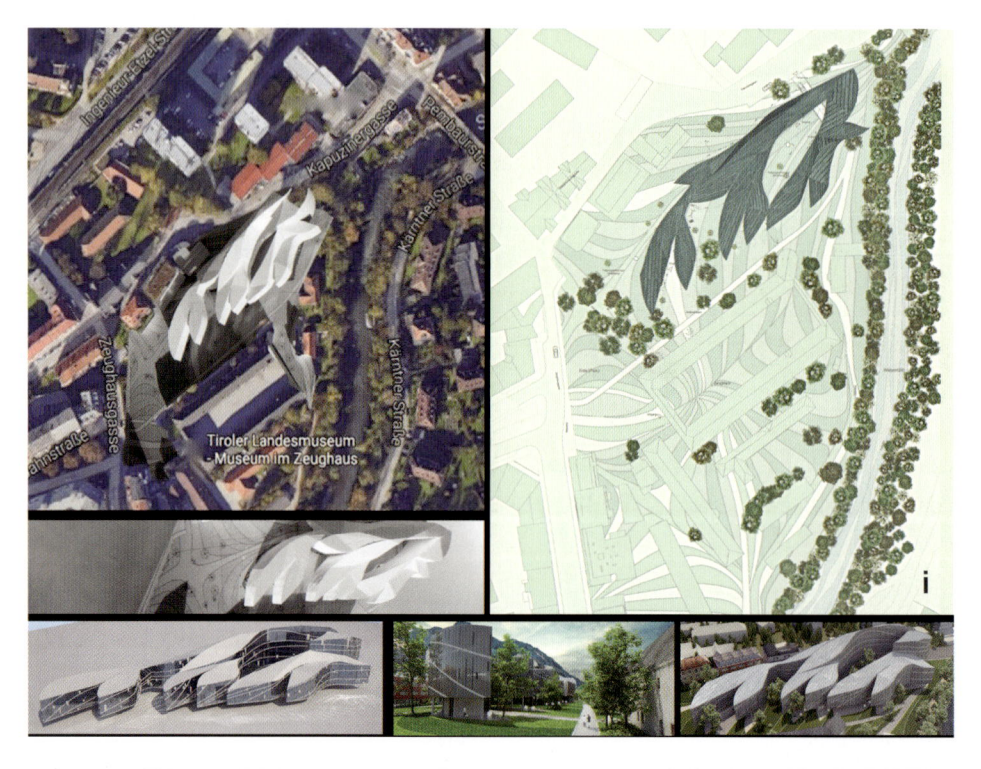

Fig. 3.6j Lichens. Alberto T. Estévez – GenArqOffice, Urban door, Castellón, 2011. Biodigital architecture project for an urban door. In the centre, views of lichens of different colours to be applied on the surface of this structure, prepared for it. Following a way of non-horizontal architectural elements that can be covered with life without requirements of irrigation facilities, which add complexity.

48 Lessons from nature – biomimetic and biophilic architecture

Fig. 3.6k Urban nature. Alberto T. Estévez, Green Barcelona Project, Barcelona, 1995–98. Biological architecture project for the creation of a huge interconnected urban park on the roofs of the buildings.

Fig. 3.6l Genetics and bioluminescence. Alberto T. Estévez, Genetic Barcelona Project (first phase), 2003–2006: genetic creation of bioluminescent plants for urban and domestic use. Left: image of the magic light of the GFP lemon trees. Centre: image of a possible world. Right: real comparison between a lemon tree leaf with GFP and another without GFP from the same tree type (top photo taken with conventional reflex camera; bottom photo taken with special UV camera). Below: images of *Aequorea victoria* jellyfish, from which the gene responsible for GFP comes. (Note: GFP is Green Fluorescent Protein.)

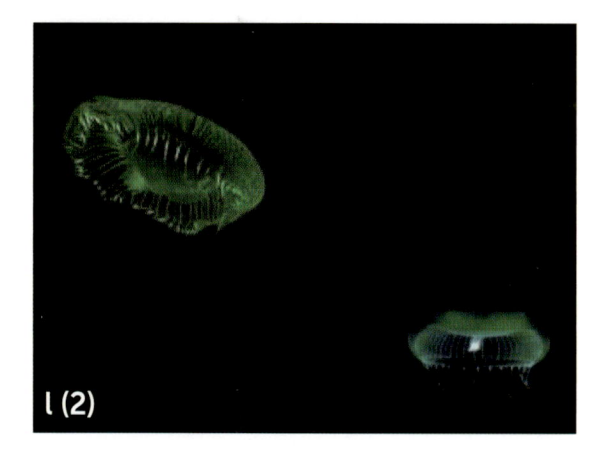

Fig. 3.6m and n Genetics and bioluminescence. Alberto T. Estévez, Genetic Barcelona Project (first phase), 2003–2006: genetic creation of bioluminescent plants for urban and domestic use. Image of a possible world: streets and highways with bioluminescent lighting.

Fig. 3.6o Genetics and bioluminescence. Alberto T. Estévez, Genetic Barcelona Project (second phase), 2007–2010: genetic creation of bioluminescent lamps for urban and domestic use. Above: biolamps in the first systematically fully illuminated apartment with living light (human-eye view photos by the author, taken with a conventional reflex camera).Below: images of *Vibrio fischeri* bacteria and *Euprymna scolopes* squid, from which this kind of bioluminescence comes.

Lessons from nature – biomimetic and biophilic architecture   49

CASE STUDY: A BIOPHILIC CLASSROOM BY CLARE BOWMAN (RCZM)

The value of using bio-technology solutions can be assessed. Horn *et al.* (2018), for example, present the bio-sustainability assessment (BiSA) method based on a life-cycling approach to evaluate the value of using bio-inspired systems in sustainability design. The integration of bio-inspiration into sustainability and its assessment can lead to new insights and a better connection to development processes in practice.

The value of nature in a learning environment: background

> We live through our senses. What we see, touch, taste and smell affects us physiologically and psychologically.
>
> Professor Derek Clements-Croome

> The value of nature in a learning environment study looks at the benefits of biophilic design through the role of nature in a space, nature of the space and nature's analogue patterns.
>
> Gillis and Gatersleben (2015)

Nature in a space is tangible, from the presence of a stimulating view of nature; or by using plants, water features, natural air-flow or breezes, sounds and scents. By mimicking the finer details of natural analogues with textiles, artwork, light, shapes or patterns, designers can re-create the biophilic human connection, and therefore the healthy responses.

Objective

The biophilic classroom study is based on the theory 'The Flourish Model' of calming the mind in order for the imagination to thrive. The theory promotes creating a natural and harmonious environment

Fig. 3.7 The Biophilic English Classroom, benefits of nature in a learning environment, Putney High School GDST (Girls' Day School Trust, Clare Bowman, RCZM). (Photo: Matt Cattell Photography)

which will stimulate the alpha brain waves (high relaxation) and lower the high beta brain waves (high stress), with the aim of calming the mind to improve attention and creating the space for the imagination to thrive (Clements-Croome, 2018).

The purpose of the study was to carry out an objective and subjective examination of the impact of biophilic design within physically and demographically similar sixth-form classrooms at Putney High School GDST (Girls' Day School Trust). 'Nature in space' was introduced in the form of plants and a 'natural analogue' in the form of a woodlands photo mural. The classrooms were analyzed in comparison with a third un-changed classroom.

Method

Occupant comfort of the classrooms was monitored

for temperature, relative humidity and CO_2, formaldehyde (CH_2O), total volatile organic compounds (TVOC), and particles of sizes 2.5 and 10 microns referred to as PM2.5 and PM10. Building user surveys were undertaken to understand perception of the classroom design, occupant comfort, health, attention, cognitive and emotional wellbeing. Further observational studies of attention were also undertaken using the Leuven scale for wellbeing, developed by Professor Ferre Laevers.

Summary of findings

The classrooms are located adjacent to a busy road; however, they all benefit from views of mature trees which create a natural boundary to the school. Throughout the study internal and external air quality surveys revealed that the 15m deep mature landscape setting within the campus improved external air quality by an average of 23 per cent above the adjacent road and the internal air quality with the use of plants and a passive ventilation system set at 750ppm improved air quality by an average of 58 per cent.

The impact of the photographic mural of a woodland setting demonstrated change to a more animated environment, with students choosing to move to a seat with a view of the mural; the teacher stated, 'I love teaching in this room'. The impact of plants in the Maths classroom demonstrated a change to a calmer environment with students describing the lessons as 'so relaxing now'. A student survey found that overall 65 per cent of students are content and 78 per cent feel healthier.

GALLERY OF BIOPHILIC SCENES

Fig. 3.8   Pinacoteca Ambrosiana, Milan. (a) Courtyard; (b) author at Pinocoteca Ambrosiana. (Photos: Andrea Sargeant Branca)

Fig. 3.9   Broadgate, London.

Fig. 3.10 Tree, London.

Fig. 3.11a–b The author at Tianyi Ge, Ningbo, China. (Photo: Tong Yang)

52   Lessons from nature – biomimetic and biophilic architecture

Fig. 3.12a–c Scenes in the Ardèche region of France. (Photo: Stefanie Eigenmann)

Lessons from nature – biomimetic and biophilic architecture 53

Fig. 3.13a–c   London Wall.

France.

Croydon, UK.

Spain.

Balham, London.

Fig. 3.14   Projects by Alexander Bond of Biophilic Design. (a)–(b) GSky Plant Systems, Inc. Versa Wall®; (c) Vegetal i.D.®; (d) GSky Plant Systems, Inc. Versa Wall®; (e)–(f) Versa Wall®, located at Embassy Suites in Chicago, Illinois USA. (© GSky Plant Systems, Inc.)

Lessons from nature – biomimetic and biophilic architecture   55

END NOTES

[1] In his book *Nature's Palette* David Lee explains how plants in shade adapt to optimize their efficiency of energy capture using colours and textures that are different from those plants growing in direct sunlight. Another example of adaptation is the compass termites that orientate their chisel-shaped mounds to minimize solar heat gain.

[2] Bio-digital design: Dennis Dollens explains bio-algorithms which can be used to design buildings based on nature in his book *The Pangolin Guide to Bio-Digital Movement in Architecture* (2010).

For a useful resource for architectural design incorporating some of nature's characteristics using bio-algorithms, visit www.xfrog.com

[3] Joy Lo Dico (2019) writes about the Bosco Verticale in Milan, where each residence has fully planted and treed balconies that reduce pollution, and reduce the impacts of high summer temperatures on residents at all levels as well as giving them much pleasure and happiness. Bringing nature to city people, as do architects Ken Yeang in Malaysia, Vincent Callebaut and Patrick Blanc in Paris and Stefano Boeri in Italy, working with landscape agronomists like Laura Gatti in Italy, has many benefits. Other examples are now evident in London, Singapore and China, for example.

[4] Contact with nature improves health and wellbeing; lowers CO_2 emissions; offers shading to buildings; and increases biodiversity. A study by University College London, in association with London Wildlife Trust, Green Biodiversity Strategy and Action Plan by UCL, 2013, suggests that on old housing estates there is a £2 benefit for every £1 invested. Other work shows loneliness and crime rates are reduced in green urban space (Burton, 2015).

[5] Research into the beneficial effects of biophilia on stress and cognitive function are being carried out at the Department of Environmental Health at the Harvard Chan School of Public Health in Boston. The work uses virtual reality, eye tracking and wearable biomonitoring sensors. See Yin, J. *et al.*, 2019. Similar research but in real environments using wristbands, EEG and face recognition has been conducted in 2019 by Joyce Chan at Loughborough University in UK.

[6] The importance of nature on wellbeing is reviewed in White (2019) and Ward-Thompson (2012).

[7] Bioluminescence is a form of chemiluminescence in which a light molecule luciferin, which is exposed to oxygen, and an enzyme luciferase interact producing a light emission as observed in fireflies for example. See Edith Widder (2002; 2010).

[8] Geckoes, snails and slugs have inspired research into adhesives that are very strong. The gecko foot has numerous tiny hairs that interact with surfaces through molecular attraction (known as Van Der Waals forces). Snails and slugs crawl along on a mucus layer so they can climb vertically. Various forms of robots are being developed using these natural behaviours as the focus so that micro-robots can access and climb around hidden spaces easily. (*China Daily*, 16 August 2019, page 7.)

[9] 'A Moment of Convergence: How nature innovates through agents, swarms and algorithms' is a thirty-minute documentary by Professor Rupert Soar on YouTube channel Phenotech. This is an enlightening film showing biomimetics in action.

Chapter Four

Buildings for health and wellbeing

There is a power in eternity, and it's green.
Hildegard of Bingen (c. 1100AD)

Let the sunshine into our workplace, brains and hearts
Put desks in the forests
Olivia Dodd (@thehaikuguys 28 November 2018)

The quieter I became the more I heard.
Erling Kagge (2018)

WHETHER OUTDOORS OR INDOORS we live through our senses, stimulated by the environment around us[1,2]. Our existence is enlivened every waking moment by a symphony of stimuli from people, objects, building spaces, task interest and nature. This rich array of inputs to the mind and body generates the multi-sensory experience which can colour and enrich the environment for people to live and work in. Like in music the notes of melodies, harmonies and rhythms magically combine in a myriad ways to inspire the mind so too in multi-sensory design which weaves a tapestry and diversity of experience for people to flourish in.

The idea of taking into account the senses of a building occupant has extended our thinking into how we smell, touch, hear and see things in the built environment, as well as our psychological interactions with the stimuli it provides[3]. Architecture deals not only with materials and form but also with people, their emotions, the environment, space and relationships between them. This makes a rich tapestry of stimuli which touch the human body and mind.

The senses not only mediate information for the judgement of the intellect, they also ignite the imagination. This aspect of thought and experience through the senses is stimulated not only by the environment and people around us but by the architecture of the space which sculpts the outline of our reactions[4]. The French philosopher Merleau-Ponty wrote that the task of architecture was to make visible how the world touches us.

Buildings must relate to the language and wisdom of the body. If they do not, they become isolated in the cool and distant realm of vision. However, in assessing the value of a building, how much attention is given to the quality of the environment inside the building and its effects on the occupants? The qualities of the environment together with the people within it affect our human physical and mental performance and these qualities should always be given a high priority[5].

Buildings should be a sanctuary not just as a place of security and protection from the weather but (as noted in Chapter 1) should also provide a multi-sensory experience for people and uplift their spirits[6]. A walk through a forest is invigorating and healing due to the interaction of all the senses but we need to see that the indoor environment is stimulating too. This array of sensory impressions and the interplay between the senses has been referred to as the 'polyphony of the senses'. Architecture is an extension of nature into the person-made realm and provides the ground for perception, a basis from which people can learn to understand and enjoy the world.

The interaction between humans and buildings is more complex than we might imagine. In addition to simple reactions that we can measure, there are many sensory and psychological reactions that are difficult to understand and quantify but we must recognize they happen. This is what might be considered an invisible aesthetic and together with the visual impact these make up a total sensory aesthetic. Visual beauty is important but it is only one aspect of what we mean by aesthetics. We respond to beautiful smells, tastes and sounds which are invisible.

Our vocabulary in the field of health and wellbeing is changing to embrace a wider span of meaning. Recently the Danish word *hygge*, meaning 'cosiness' or 'snug', and now the Japanese word *ikigai* (*iki* – 'life' and *gai* – 'value'), expressing a reason for being or a life with purpose, have made their presence felt in Western languages too. To feel *ikigai* you need to recognize the value of things that make life worthwhile. Life is worthwhile if you love what you do and are good at doing it and it contributes to the values you cherish. You need time to reflect and think and nowadays the value to one's wellbeing of mindfulness, yoga, meditation and simply walking in the countryside are being realized to offset this world of increasingly fast communication, which can freeze the mind.

The philosopher Heidegger believed people were sacrificing their freedom to use new technology (*The Question Concerning Technology*, 1977). Are we becoming slaves in an AI world? How is technology changing our behaviour? We can see every day, wherever we are, people of all ages absorbed in their mobile screens – not only when they are sitting but also when walking along, bumping into one another. The screen can even trump a beautiful rural or seaside view. We are social creatures but this is virtual socializing. However how many times do we hear

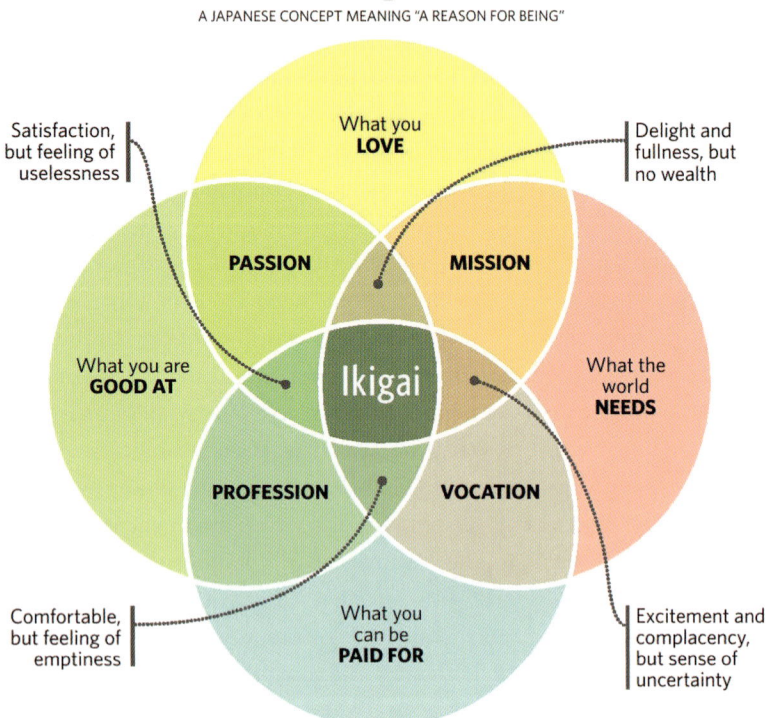

Fig. 4.1 A reason for being.

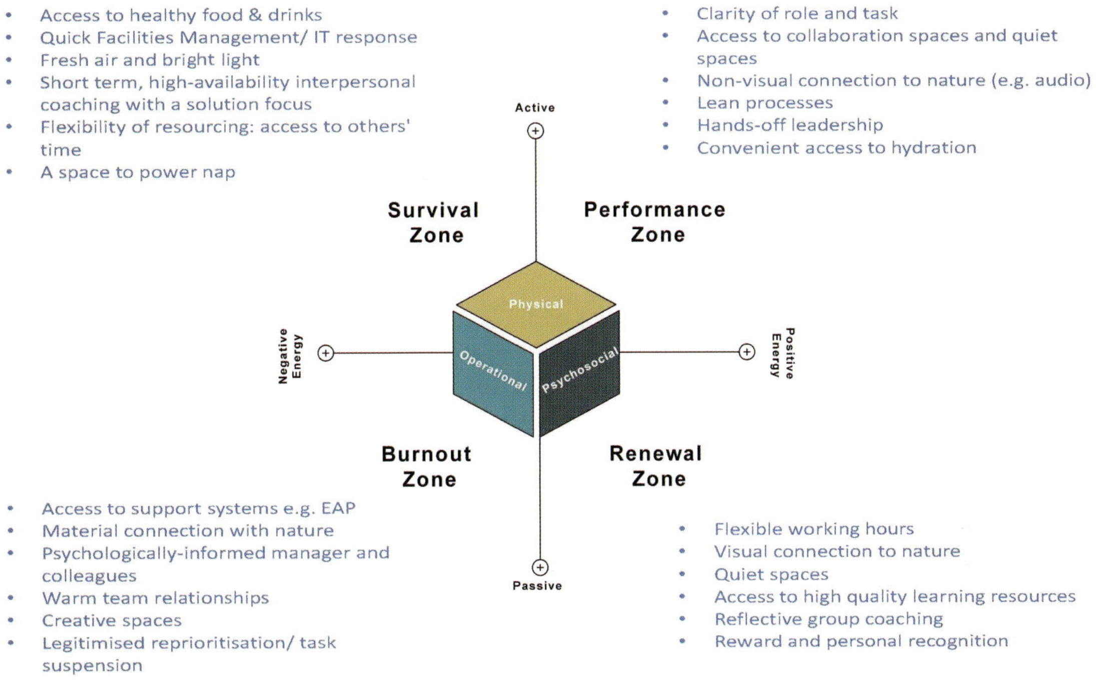

Access to healthy food & drinks
Quick Facilities Management/ IT response
Fresh air and bright light
Short term, high-availability interpersonal coaching with a solution focus
Flexibility of resourcing: access to others' time
A space to power nap
Clarity of role and task
Access to collaboration spaces and quiet spaces
Non-visual connection to nature (e.g. audio)
Lean processes
Hands-off leadership
Convenient access to hydration
Active
Survival Zone
Performance Zone
Physical
Operational
Psychosocial
Negative Energy
Positive Energy
Burnout Zone
Renewal Zone
Passive
Access to support systems e.g. EAP
Material connection with nature
Psychologically-informed manager and colleagues
Warm team relationships
Creative spaces
Legitimised reprioritisation/ task suspension
Flexible working hours
Visual connection to nature
Quiet spaces
Access to high quality learning resources
Reflective group coaching
Reward and personal recognition

Fig. 4.2 The energy and emotion management zones as proposed by Loehr and Schwartz (adapted from Emotional Intelligence Map by Arup).

that 'face to face' is the best way of enjoying social interaction? Silence and mindfulness are ways of turning technology off and avoiding mental obesity.

Health and wellbeing

The World Health Organization states: 'Health is a state of complete physical, mental and social wellbeing and not merely the absence of disease or infirmity' (WHO, 2001). The mind and body are intimately connected via biochemical systems which themselves are interconnected, hence medical evidence covers physiological and psychological issues in a range of disciplines covering medicine, occupational psychology, environmental psychology and others[7].

The body and mind depend on three main systems that ensure their health. The immune system is the body's defence system and if it is weak then bacteria and viruses can invade the body more easily and reduce a person's energy. The blood circulatory system distributes oxygen to nourish all the organs of the body; low levels of oxygenation will affect the body's health. The nervous system communicates messages from the brain to all parts of the body; if this deteriorates in some way then the connectivity is impaired and this can result in slow responses to demands or in extreme cases dementia can result.

Loehr and Schwartz (2010) describe an energy–emotion map. Negative energy is a characteristic denoted by anxiousness, frustration or burnout whereas positive energy leads to good human performance with periods of renewal, as happens when we power nap, meditate or contemplate.

Engagement

Tony Schwartz and Catherine McCarthy, in an article entitled 'Manage Your Energy, Not Your Time'

(*The Harvard Business Review*, October 2007), describe how one can maintain high energy levels and hence focus on work objectives. Physical energy can be frittered away so easily on activities with little real purpose or trying to do several things at once with no central focus. Of course a poor night's sleep or skipping an energy-fuelled breakfast or a tortuous journey to work can make the start to the day very fatiguing. Healthy food and physical activity can help to raise and maintain energy levels. Work breaks help to restore high energy levels after the cyclical troughs in energy which we experience throughout the day and which are known as ultradian rhythms. The breaks can be naps, walking around in fresh air preferably in areas with nature or one's personal preferences for disengaging from work to refresh the brain.

Emotions can upset one's energy levels. Generally people with a positive outlook handle emotions more effectively than those who are more negative in outlook. Deep breathing in contrast to shallow breathing is recommended but also simple things like giving appreciation to others or a smile showing a happy countenance can benefit one's wellbeing.

Concentrating can be difficult in busy environments. The need for quiet space away from emails, babble of voices, phones and other interruptions is essential. But also giving priority to the most valuable tasks in terms of mental reward is another way to manage one's time more effectively. This is also a pathway to nourishing the spirits by undertaking worthwhile work in which you also feel effective.

The WHO European Charter on Environment and Health 1989 states:

> Good health and wellbeing require a clean and harmonious environment in which physical, psychological, social and aesthetic factors are all given their due importance.

Wellbeing is only one aspect of mental health; other factors include personal feelings about motivation, one's competence, aspirations and degree of personal control. Wellbeing is connected with overall satisfaction, happiness and quality of life; it depends on the management ethos of the organization, the social ambience and personal factors, but the physical environment also has a major role to play (*see* Clements-Croome, 2018). For example, warm stuffy conditions can sap one's energy; a lack of daylight can be depressing.

A building with a stimulating environment can help people produce more creative work and hence they are happier and more satisfied because their minds are focused and concentrated; good building design together with other factors can help to achieve this[8]. At very low (sluggish) or very high (nervousness) levels of attention, arousal or alertness, the capacity for performing work is low; at the optimum level the individual can concentrate on work while being aware of, but not distracted by their surroundings. Different types of work tasks require different environmental settings for an optimum level of arousal to be achieved.

Achieving wellbeing

Mental wellbeing can have two perspectives: a hedonistic one defined by the subjective experience of happiness and life satisfaction; a eudaimonic one described by positive psychological functioning through positive social connections and self-realization and often referred to as human flourishing.

The term 'wellbeing' reflects one's feelings about oneself in relation to the world and is reflected in the hierarchy of human needs proposed by Maslow (1943) which covers physical, social and mental needs. Maslow spoke of a good wellbeing feeling as a deep, complete correspondence between the inner state and the outer landscape interpreted as a kind of 'spiritual ecology'. People are happier in more scenic locations in general which can be true in rural environments and built-up areas with plenty of green space (Seresinhe *et al.*, 2019).

Fig. 4.3 Maslow's hierarchy of needs.

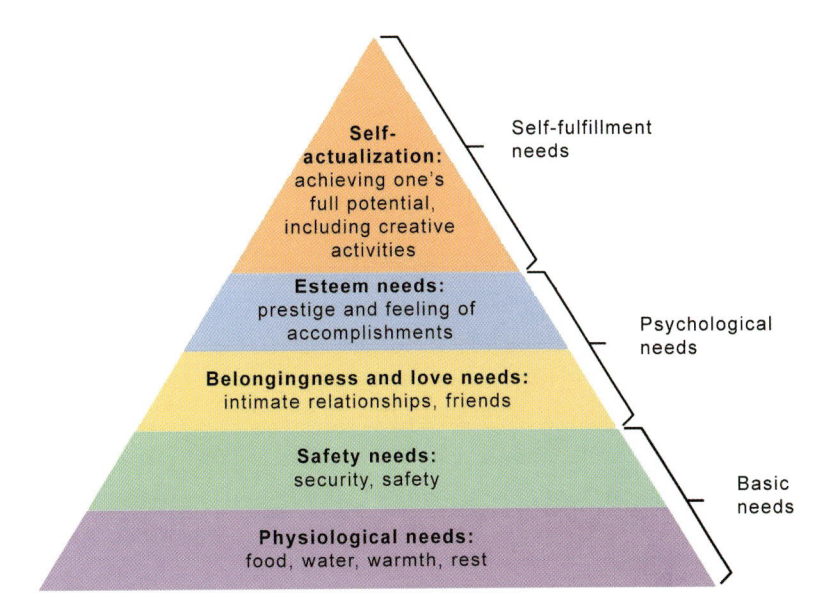

International evidence has been collected to measure wellbeing and demonstrates how this field has now emerged as a rigorous discipline (Steemers, 2015; Huppert and So, 2013). Professor Emeritus Felicia Huppert of the Wellbeing Institute at Cambridge University and her team carried out a study on the meaning of wellbeing across Europe (Huppert and So, 2013) and concluded there were ten principal features that distinguish wellbeing which enable people to flourish. These included competence, emotional stability, engagement, meaning, optimism, positive emotion, positive relationships, resilience, self-esteem and vitality. Wellbeing is a multi-dimensional construct and questionnaires to assess wellbeing have been designed to recognize this.

In his book *Happiness by Design* (2014) Paul Dolan shows how we can increase the possibilities of designing happier places for people to live and work. He proposes the SALIENT mnemonic, which identifies seven important elements that can be used to explore the design of built environments for enhancing wellbeing: Sound, Air, Light, Image, Ergonomics, Nature and Tint.

'Image' refers to positive factors like the use of artwork to give interest but not too much to result in clutter. Tint refers to colour[9]. He describes and presents evidence on how these factors affect wellbeing (Dolan *et al.*, 2016).

In her book, *The Shaping of Us*, Bernheimer (2017) proposes a BALANCED space checklist:

B   Biophilia – natural materials, views and patterns
A   Atmospheric – light, air quality, temperature and smell
L   Layout – space quality, circulation
A   Amenities – nutrition, movement, ergonomics
N   Noise
C   Cohesion – community, communication
E   Energy – resources and waste
D   Design – colour, shape, materials, proportions, detail and style

It is interesting to note how close these independent studies are to the WELL version 2 rating system for health and wellbeing, which has ten similar factors to consider for health and wellbeing:

- Air
- Water
- Light
- Nourishment
- Movement

- Thermal comfort
- Sound
- Materials
- Mind
- Community

All these approaches are methods of evaluating and rating health and wellbeing using the indicators described. Other methodologies include Building User Studies (BUS), the Leesman Index and the evolving Flourish approach (discussed later). Currently the WELL (2015) and version 2 system (2018) originating from the US is now beginning to be used by designers in the UK but will undergo modifications, as most POE approaches do as our knowledge and understanding deepen.

Assessing health and wellbeing

Stressors can cause increased heart rate, vomiting, shallow breathing and muscle tension. They can affect brain rhythms and alter the alpha, beta and theta patterns, which are correlated with mood and affect which is a term used in psychology to denote the experiences of feelings and emotions. Affective states affect judgement, productivity, interpersonal relations, self-image, morale and aggression. So one can see the sequence of possible physiological and psychological reactions that may occur when exposed to the environment. There are clues here also as to how physiological measures may aid our understanding of human reaction to the environment.

The Warwick-Edinburgh Mental Wellbeing Scale (WEMWBS) originated in the Warwick University Medical School and is a well-known part of the wellbeing assessment within post-occupancy evaluation that has been used in the UK. The shortened form of WEMWBS (*see* Appendix) is a good way to find out about people's feelings and thoughts in different environmental settings. This can act as a background indication to see if the environment is a contributory factor to negative or positive well-being (Stewart-Brown *et al.* 2009; Tennant *et al.* 2007).

Wellbeing data is sourced and analysed by a range of methods used by scientists from epidemiology, occupational psychology, ergonomics and related disciplines. Until now this has been largely carried out through surveys and interviews, with the data analysed using rigorous statistical methods. But with advancements in technology this is changing.

Professor Rosalind Picard directs the Affective Computing Research Group at the MIT Media Lab. Her research is about connecting emotions, brain and behaviour using wearables like wrist bands which measure the changes in skin conductance that occur as arousal levels and hence attention fluctuate. Professor Elaine Fox in the Centre for Emotions and Affective Neuroscience at Oxford University focuses her research on the nature of human emotions and why there is such a wide variety of response to the same environmental situation. Her approach is to examine the subtle cognitive biases that are linked to emotional vulnerability on the one hand, and human resilience and mental wellbeing on the other. This work should deepen our understanding of why some people flourish and others struggle.

Neuroscience is making an in-road too in helping us to understand much more about the human response to the environment around us. For example, Catharine Ward-Thompson, Professor of Landscape Architecture at Edinburgh University has used brainwave headsets to study people's reactions to a variety of urban settings (Roe *et al.*, 2013). The use of brainwaves has also been used by Snow *et al.* (2019) to study the effects of CO_2 on drowsiness.

Environmental factors like temperature, ventilation, light levels, moisture and sound can be measured using traditional environmental measuring instruments. In addition personal sensors are becoming common in the form of wearables which allow the physiological, mood and stress states to be measured (Taub, Clements-Croome and Lockhart, 2016). Radio Frequency Identification sensors (RFID tags) have been used to study how organizational structure and spatial configuration of work environments combine to influence communication between employees (Brown *et al.*, 2014). This approach means we have an interconnected system linking the person to the environment in the building and the effectiveness of this system can be assessed. Some companies are issuing wearables to their employees and there is a growing number of examples of sensors being embedded in clothing and even the body.

Research by Yin and his team at Harvard University has measured the physiological responses to biophilia. This independently supports the findings of Cooper and Browning, whose work is described in the Human Spaces report *The Global Impact of Biophilic Design in the Workplace* (2015). They surveyed over 7,500 people and showed that those who work in environments with natural elements, such as greenery, natural materials and sunlight reported: 15 per cent higher level of wellbeing; 6 per cent higher level of productivity; and 15 per cent higher level of creativity compared with those occupants with no connection with natural elements in the workplace (www.humanspaces.com/2015/ Cooper and Browning).

These various assessment approaches are evolving and advancing. They will give us a deeper understanding about how the environment affects people whether working, sleeping or just carrying out everyday activities. Codes, regulations and design guidelines need to keep abreast of these developments so as to reflect the peer-reviewed outcomes and so help to achieve better health- and wellbeing-based architecture. Social wellbeing is referred to in the End Notes at the end of this chapter.

Creativity and productivity

> The real voyage of discovery consists not in seeking out new landscapes, but in having new eyes.
>
> Marcel Proust

> The most beautiful experience we can have is in the mysterious. It is the fundamental emotion which stands at the cradle of true art and science.
>
> Einstein (in Nelson, 2018)

Health and wellbeing are the roots of human work productivity as they set our energy levels to carry out physical and mental work. In his article entitled 'Groupthink', Jonah Lehrer (*The New Yorker* Volume 87, January 30, 2012) says there are two types of brainstorming – a free-for-all exchange of ideas in a structured environment, and a random, unplanned debate. He believes only the latter really works. However, some people prefer to work alone – often introverts – and they can be very creative. Composers and writers work creatively often in a one-person setting. Engaging work is important to individuals, to companies and to the nation but with the advent of artificial intelligence many routine jobs will disappear but this will open up many more opportunities for more creative work to emerge and so now we need to think more about creativity, not just productivity[10].

The layout and arrangement of spaces in buildings play an important role in easing communication between people. People like to be able to control and arrange their workplace in various interesting ways but diversity and connection with nature are important factors whether occupants have allocated workplaces or not. Diversity can be viewed in different ways. It may mean artwork on walls, views to the outside or colour tones – all are things that absorb one's attention, even though they are transitory, and engage the human sensory system; however, it can also mean a certain amount of 'creative clutter' or untidiness if not arranged in an orderly way.

Building 20 at Massachusetts Institute of Technology (MIT) was replaced in 2004 by the Stata Center designed by Frank Gehry. Building 20 had a reputation for being one of the most innovative spaces because it fostered brainstorming that threw up many creative ideas even though the walls were thin, the roof leaked, and the building was boiling hot in the summer and freezing cold in the winter.

Over time it housed many famous names like Noam Chomsky and Amar Bose and the space encouraged people with different diverse backgrounds to intermix. 'Mingle space' is so important. I have not been able to ascertain if the modern Stata Center benefits the people who work there in the same way that Building 20 did. One can argue that you can be creative anywhere but we also know that the built environment can attract people to work in attractive and engaging places. This can trigger the possibility of gathering a diverse working population in an organization.

Lehrer points out that the late Steve Jobs created a similar environment with Pixar's headquarters 'so that Pixar's diverse staff of artists, writers, and computer scientists would run into each other more often.'

E.O. Wilson, in his book *The Origins of Creativity* (2017), believes creativity is sparked when there is interplay between those professing either arts, humanities or natural sciences, rather than keeping them separate, thus not only enhancing their bodies of knowledge but encouraging intermingling imaginative threads of thoughts with unusual and unexpected pathways of connectivity.

So again this is another kind of diversity and one which mixes people from different backgrounds. Today, however, occupants do not always have a prescribed workplace. In offices like the EDGE Deloitte building in Amsterdam everyone uses an app to plan their day in the office which includes selecting a location to sit. Planning space in buildings has become more fluid and flexible.

What stimulates the mind not only to create compositions in music, paintings, sculptures, architecture and poetry, but also to originate new ways of thinking out problems, whether theoretical or practical? My candle holders at home are simply marrow bones that I have used in cooking; my dinner companions often say how creative that is but it was an idea that flashed across my mind in a completely unstructured way. This is an everyday happening but then I say to my friends, open the score of, say, Mozart's opera *Don Giovanni* and see real creativity on a colossal scale. But what was going on in the minds of Mozart, Beethoven, Goethe, Michelangelo and the many geniuses who inspire us today? They were not always happy people – do we need a certain amount of chaos in the mind to trigger creativity? They seemed to have a tap to switch on to deliver a

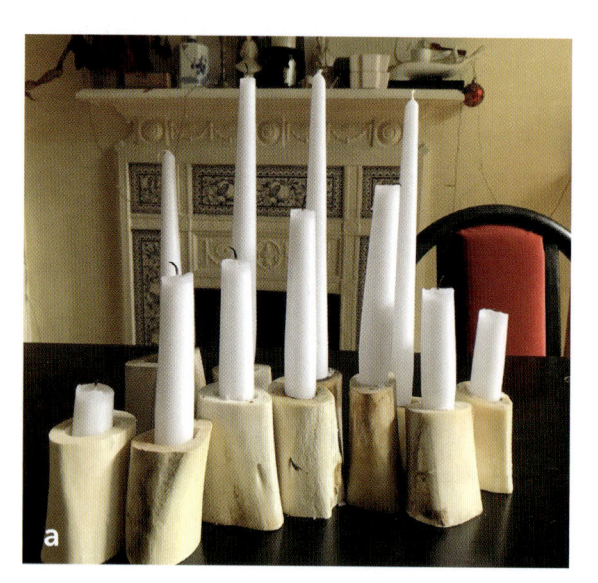

Fig. 4.4 Examples of creativity: (a) and (b) marrowbone candle holders; (c) and (d) scores of Mozart's operas *The Marriage of Figaro* and *Don Giovanni*.

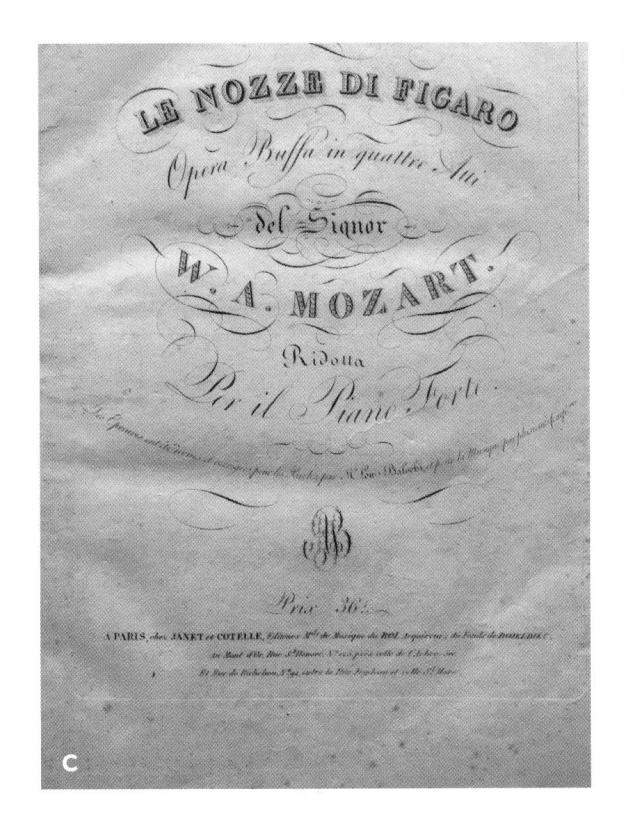

creative imaginative flow but sometimes it remained stubbornly off, as happens when authors get 'writers block'. Hopefully we do not have to be sad and unhappy always to be creative. We do learn from each other, for example Bach learnt from Vivaldi in writing some of his music. Leonardo da Vinci could be creative in several spheres, spurred on by his very keen sense of focused observation.

A chapter by Gorb and Gorb in *Biomimetic Research for Architecture and Building Construction* (ed. Jan Knippers *et al.*, 2016) entitled 'Insect-Inspired Architecture: Insects and other Arthropods as a Source for Creative Design and Architecture' shows that biophilia and biomimetics can indeed motivate and generate creative ideas. It is as if nature loosens up the mind and takes us away from fixed ideas and the strictures of regulations to a more visionary state of mind[11].

It is claimed that Einstein said, 'The true sign of intelligence is not knowledge but imagination.' Certainly a free-ranging imagination and perhaps a deep curiosity about the world and ideas plus a sense of discovery or invention are needed in order to be creative. Everyday activities like dealing with vast amounts of fast information via emails for example do not promote creativity but rather tire out the mind. We need to begin to understand more about creativity. What is divergent, intuitive and convergent thinking for example? How are people inspired? I believe ideas gestate in the sub-conscious in what is often referred to as an incubation period but at other times one gets a sudden Archimedean flash or eureka moment of inspiration.

Carson (2010) in her book *Your Creative Brain* argues for seven brain sets to maximize imagination, productivity and innovation.

Absorb – opening up the mind to new ideas and experiences
Envision – using imagination
Connect – divergent thinking to generate multiple solutions

Reason – the logical ordered mind
Evaluate – judging the value of and testing ideas and concepts
Transform – creativity that can spring from negativity
Stream – thoughts flow in a harmonious and systematic way

Our knowledge about the brain and mind is increasing rapidly so that our understanding about how we think, how we concentrate and how we get distracted is becoming more evident. Consciousness is the interaction of the world and the mind and so has remained elusive but the knowledge from neuroscience is already bringing greater insights into what is happening in our minds when we think and act in various ways. Salutogenic environments are ones that help to stimulate the mind. The intention is to design for producing ideation or creative environments. Csikszentmihalyi in his 2004 TED lecture advocated the concept of 'flow', which refers to a person being fully immersed with energized focus on an activity. Understanding these issues will increase creativity and productivity.

Creative minds have always been with us but are now needed more than ever to meet the challenges of the world we live in today and those we will live in tomorrow.

An example of a space designed to nurture and encourage creativity is the Rawthmells Coffeehouse

Fig. 4.5a–d   Rawthmells – a creative space at Royal Society of Arts, London. (Credit: Richard Caldecourt and Kavya Menon)

66   Buildings for health and wellbeing

at the Royal Society of Arts in London, opened in 2018. The coffee-house culture is not new and has been prevalent in Paris, Vienna and Budapest or centuries. The intention is to foster creative thinking and collaboration by providing spaces which make it easy to meet and share ideas. All-day din- ing, various patterns of spaces, changing wall displays on which one can write ideas, and a programme of events to stimulate participation are all features intended to make a vibrant space which has vitality. Spaces can energize people.

Fig. 4.6 Chapel Notre Dame au Haut, by Le Corbusier in Ronchamp. (a) The chapel in April 2019; (b) an anonymous historic picture bought at the chapel; (c) the chapel interior; (d) author in light opening channels (photo: Marcel Croome); (e) celestial light on side altar.

Physical wellbeing: Environmental factors

A survey of 2,000 office workers described in a report entitled *What Workers Want* by BCO (2016) showed the factors which are important and those found to be irritating. Occupants reported preferences for lots of natural light; access to outdoor spaces; contemplation spaces; support from colleagues; and private as well as collaborative spaces. The main irritants were noise in open-plan areas; lack of natural light; lack of colour, greenery and artwork; lack of fresh air; no personal control of temperature; lack of privacy; clutter; and inflexible space. Later surveys broadly reiterate most of these findings.

Users are generally dissatisfied when building and systems are over-complicated with poor usability rendering personal control too complicated and unreliable. Adaptive control based on relating the indoor temperature to outdoor temperatures for naturally ventilated and air-conditioned buildings has become the preferred way to set basic thermal comfort levels.

However, it has to be remembered that other factors such as air movement, relative humidity and air quality all contribute to thermal comfort, which is not governed solely by temperature.

Personal control is important. There is much evidence showing that comfort, perceived health and self-assessed productivity are related to occupants' perceived control through simple means like knowing that one can open a window. Central control for items such as security and fire is sensible, but people in general prefer to have some degree of control over their immediate physical environment. Using data from the European HOPE (Health Optimisation Protocol for Energy-Efficient) Buildings Project it has been shown that occupants with a high degree of personal control over their thermal and indoor air quality environment feel they are more healthy and productive than those with a low amount of control (Boerstra *et al.*, 2013, 2014; Bluyssen, 2014; Roulet *et al.*, 2006). The increase in productivity between no control to full control was reckoned to be at least 6 per cent. In addition occupants were more thermally comfortable and suffered less severe sick building symptoms.

The effects of the environment on emotions and cognitive function

Our life inside buildings is related to that outside[12]. Natural light, smells, sounds, greenery and other environmental factors can enhance mood, but if lacking can disturb, distract or irritate the mind, causing lapses in concentration. These negative effects can be transitory or be more long-lasting and give rise to stress. There are a host of factors that affect mental health of people, whether at home or in the workplace: cold or hot conditions; lack of fresh air; spatial layout; overcrowding; air and noise pollution; damp conditions; lack of green space; lack of access to public transport; and work or management issues can all lead to a sense of frustration leading to irritation and stress which in turn can result in negative emotions. Planning and design around the outside of the building as well as inside it are important. I found the atmosphere of many twinkling bright lights and over-crowding on the gaming floor of the hotel in Las Vegas where I stayed in 2017 intensely stressful, sapping all my energy, but for others the prospect of winning was exciting and overcame any possible stress.

In her book *Thermal Delight in Architecture* (1979) Lisa Heschong describes not only the necessity of a compatible thermal environment to suit the body's physical needs but the delight, affection and sacredness offered by warmth in various settings, which affect our emotional needs. Emotions can be stirred by other factors too, like the look and feel of a space, daylight, views, colour, sounds, tastes and smells. The look and feel of a space give an immediate impression and this perception is transposed to how we feel in a space[13].

> Beauty is nothing other than the promise of happiness.
>
> Stendahl

Aristotle believed the three essential components of beauty were wholeness, harmony and radiance. Mathematics, art, language and music light up different parts of the brain and we need from a young age to study across this range of subjects to ensure our brain and mind are stimulated in a holistic way. Currently there is much debate about the impact on the brain of music and why it should be a much more important part of the school curriculum than it is now. From education to everyday life, cultural activities and opportunities are so important for creating flourishing communities. This can also be said for life inside offices, schools or hospitals where storytelling, poetry readings, art and music can feature and be a creative stimulus in the daily work life. Breakout spaces should not just be for coffee but for creative activities.

It is probably true that most research and surveys about environmental conditions and their effects on human physical performance have been concerned with temperature and indoor air quality. Less work has been carried out on how thermal conditions affect our emotions and mental wellbeing.

Cao and Wei (2005) investigated the question, 'Do temperature variations cause investors to alter their investment behaviour?', which is highly relevant to the banking sector. They hypothesized that lower temperature leads to higher stock returns due to investors' aggressive risk-taking, and higher temperatures can lead to higher or lower stock returns as aggression and apathy become competing effects on risk-taking. Their work offers evidence to suggest that low temperatures tend to cause aggression, and high temperatures tend to cause aggression, hysteria and apathy. Here we begin to see how the environment may affect decision-making evoking responses coloured by emotion. Tanabe and Nishihara (2018) describe their research on how the thermal environment affects fatigue and satisfaction.

The effects of light on health is reviewed by Veitch (2018). Daylight has a strong psychological effect on people, but reactions are linked with sensing the views out of the building, colour, shadow and spaciousness. Daylight has a primary role in setting the mood tone of the building. Steven Holl said in his Studio 360 Interview (2 April 2015) entitled 'The Pantheon: A Lesson in Designing with Light':

> Someone asked what my favourite material was and I said light. I really believe in a certain sense you can sculpt with light [compare Le Corbusier's words with reference to the Notre Dame du Haut Chapel in Ronchamp]. I think architecture should connect, like the Pantheon does, to the atmosphere, the seasons, to the sunlight, to the air, to the wind.

Science helps our understanding about the nature of light but then there is the emotional impact that daylight has on us all, as is well illustrated by the Notre Dame du Haut chapel at Ronchamp in France designed by Le Corbusier[9] (see Fig. 4.6). In his words:

> I have created a place of silence, prayer, peace and internal joy. These things are sacred. I compose with light.
>
> The key is light and light illuminates forms. And these forms take on an emotive power through the proportions, through the interplay of unexpected, stunning relationships. And also through the intellectual challenge of the reason for living; their authentic birth, their ability to last, structure astuteness, boldness even brazenness, play – who are essential beings – the constituents of architecture.
>
> Le Corbusier, quoted in Bouvier and Cousin (2015)

Light defines the forms. Le Corbusier sculpts with light. The South façade has openings of various shapes which act as light channels. The French call the openings vitrages. They are not windows in the conventional sense of the word. Le Corbusier was agnostic not a catholic and yet he created a holy place, one of contemplation which is very special and touched the spirits of many people who go there whether religious or not.

Bouvier and Cousin (2015)

What we see in the diversity of colour outdoors leaves its imprint on the brain when considering colour inside a space. Wright (1995) demonstrates vividly the importance of colour psychology. The sense of smell and the visual impact of colour affect us in many subtle ways, perhaps rooted in what we experience in nature. In his book *Nature's Palette* David Lee (2010) gives the following quotations:

> The world in which we live is teeming with colour: the sky, earth, water and fire all have distinct colours. From time immemorial, we who delight in such perceptions have tried to reproduce these colours in our day-to-day surroundings.
>
> François Delamare and Bernard Guineau in Lee (2010)

> Colour rings the doorbell of the human mind and emotion then leaves.
>
> Faber Birren, quoted in Lee (2010)

We talk a lot about light and sound being present but much less about the absence of them, as in shadow or silence. As artists know so well, shadow is so important in articulating shape and form. Silence in music is powerful, too. Just listen to the opening of Beethoven's *Eroica* symphony where the simple one-beat chord is followed by two beats' rest. Of course in some contexts shadow and darkness can awaken fear and fright; silence can be lonely. However, silence can also offset the brutality of noise in cities for example. Silence can calm and soothe the spirit and soul. Intrusive sounds from phones, air systems, and chatter can be distracting. However, offices can be too quiet, so one has to relate the sound level to the type of work being undertaken within the building and the culture of the organization. The effects of sound on cognitive function are described in papers by Jahnke (2011), Schlittmeier (2008) and Sorquist (2015).

The effect of ionization on human health has long been debated. It is reckoned that the negative ions in the air are good for us and the positive ones less so – but scientific evidence is still patchy. Shu-Ye Jiang and his team give an up-to date account of the knowledge in this area in the *International Journal of Molecular Science* ('Negative Air Ions and Their Effects on Human Health and Air Quality Improvement', 2018, 19, 10 2966). Similarly the effects of electromagnetic radiation on health are still in contention (see the End Notes for this chapter, in which recent research is highlighted)[16].

There is a lot of evidence emerging showing the restorative power of nature (*see* Chapter 3) and David Lee highlights this in his book *Nature's Palette*. Spengler and his team at Harvard University researched the cognitive performance of twenty-four participants over six days in November 2014, and compared those working in green, low-polluting environments and enhanced ventilation with those who worked in conventional environments where greenery is absent and pollution levels can be high. On average, those in the green and low-polluting environments had double the cognitive test scores of those who were not. Measuring nine cognitive function domains it was found that the largest improvements occurred in the areas of crisis response, strategy and information usage. MacNaughton (2019) and Yin (2018), also at Harvard, show the effects of greenery on relieving stress in their laboratory research studies.

In addition, when researchers looked at the effect of CO_2 they found that for seven of the nine cognitive functions tested, average scores decreased as CO_2 levels increased to levels commonly observed in many typical indoor environments.

Ventilation, carbon dioxide (CO_2) and drowsiness

The French physiologist Xavier Bichat in 1800 described how CO_2 poisons the mind and befuddles the brain, but over 200 years later we still debate and research this issue. EEG testing used to measure brain rhythms showed that even short exposures to raised CO_2 levels and also temperature showed a progression towards drowsiness (Snow *et al.*, 2019). Further work is necessary to verify this but the earlier research by Vehviläinen *et al.* (2016) reached similar conclusions[14]. The work by Snow *et al.* at Southampton University also presents evidence which suggests CO_2 levels in the range 2,000–3,000ppm can induce difficulties in thinking clearly due to increases in the transcutaneous (passing through the skin) CO_2 level which can lead to sleepiness during cognitive work. Other factors like stuffy conditions due to warm temperature, low humidity and a lack of air movement can also induce drowsiness.

These CO_2 levels are commonly reached in UK primary school classrooms where high CO_2 levels in the range 1,500–5,000ppm are commonly experienced and have been found to affect learning performance. Other research in offices demonstrates that CO_2 levels as low as 600ppm can affect decision-making in companies. Without doubt the physical environment affects human performance (Bakó-Biró *et al.*, 2012; Wyon and Wargocki, 2013; 2018; Wargocki *et al.*, 2006; Satish, 2012).

Air quality is a combination of CO_2 and contaminant levels, temperature, relative humidity and air movement. A danger of sealing buildings to reduce their energy consumption is that there will be insufficient fresh air, so it is important to build in a controlled clean air supply such as trickle ventilators or properly located windows that can be opened a little or a lot depending on the seasonal weather. Often occupants complain about stuffy conditions whereas we should be aiming for freshness. It should be added that cleanliness, colour, greenery and sense of space also contribute to fresh and airy environments.

Space layout, active working and ergonomics

Before the Industrial Revolution people led active

lives and sat much less than today. Today office workers can sit for 7 or even as much as 15 hours per day (Levine, 2015). Add to this sedentary home life then add on 8 hours sleep and it means we walk around for only 1–4 hours a day. The human body needs to move around otherwise muscles become slack, blood circulation is sluggish and generally we are less healthy. As a result alertness and attention drop and hence productivity is lower. Walking helps us to keep lean by burning off the calories we eat; if we do not, then fat accumulates.

Today we are encouraging people to develop a habit of active working, for example by using the stairs more than they have been in the past. Colour, greenery, music and art work have been used to attract people to use the stairs more. The layout of our spaces can also contribute towards encouraging active working besides providing active space areas such as gyms or roof gardens for example. Sit-stand desks are also now becoming available so that people can balance sedentary working with standing. The Alexander technique improves posture and this in turn reduces the stresses on the body caused by poor posture that often we are unaware of. Nowadays we can be reminded about bad posture by simple wearable technology.

Excessive sitting contributes to many chronic diseases such as obesity, heart problems, cancer, diabetes and this can be explained by the alterations that occur in physiological and molecular mechanisms (Levine, 2015; Ekelund, *et al.*, 2016). We need offices to be designed to allow active working. In addition we need to select furniture which is ergonomically designed (Hermans, 2016, 2018; Bowden, 2018). Musculoskeletal problems are a principal reason for absenteeism and presenteeism which is a big cost to companies and one which is much more than paying a higher cost for ergonomic furniture. Moving about leads to another advantage in that we mingle more and this aids informal or formal face-to-face communication. Marmot and Ucci (2015) edited a series of papers on physical activity, sedentary behaviour and the indoor environment, which discuss the evidence on the effects of sedentary working on health[15].

Planning for mindful work spaces

Some guiding ideas are listed below:

- Plan spaces where one can be quiet, alone and contemplate
- Plan spaces to allow walking around
- Plan spaces connected with nature
- Manage spaces to be clean
- Plan spaces to have social character where people can be kind and compassionate to each other

Break-out spaces for contemplation
Break-out spaces can take many different forms, like sensory roof gardens, calm indoor spaces or places

---

SHARD REGENERATION PODS

DaeWha Kang Design were commissioned by outsourcing company Mitie to make these iconic Regeneration Pods as part of their mental health and wellness initiative. They provide a tech-free meditative moment within the workday, creating a sense of shelter and refuge while also maintaining beautiful views to the outside. The visual language of these bamboo structures reflects their function but also creates an anchoring identity for this corner of the Shard floorplate at Mitie HQ. After sitting down in the pod, a bell rings three times and bathes one in a sound- and lightscape for fifteen minutes. The pods are currently the subject of a wellbeing study to evaluate the effects of the design and the experience on worker stress levels where a few people can share ideas about their hobbies, for example. In South Korea periods in some school timetables are devoted to meditation.

Improved concentration and focus in daily life can help people reduce stress, worry and anxiety, irritation, anger and frustration. It can also bring more inner peace and happiness, confidence and self-esteem, mental and physical wellbeing, better relationships and a more positive outlook on life.

Due to the now ubiquitous use of mobile phones, computers and other electronic equipment there is increasing electromagnetic pollution. However, as mentioned earlier, the effects of this on health are still not well understood (some recent research is listed in the End Notes for this chapter[16]. Computers can cause eye strain, repetitive strain injuries, poor posture and associated aches and pains, so work patterns need to include 'breaks' for users to walk, stand and move around besides having a break from screen time (Clements-Croome, 2000a, 2004b; Hermans, 2016).

'Techno stress' caused by such things as email overload are spoken of but not well documented. Some surveys show that on average people spend nearly an hour a day sorting out problems with IT systems (Stich *et al*., 2019a and 2019b).

Health and wellbeing in practice

Surveys of office occupants in the UK by the British Council for Offices (BCO) show that many occupants requested more contemplation spaces. The BCO (2018) has published a major report entitled *Wellness Matters*, written by a team of professionals from practice and academia. (*Wellness Matters: Health and Wellbeing in Offices and What to Do About It*, British Council for Offices, 2018 http://www.bco.org/HealthWellbeing/WellnessMatters.aspx). It is in fact a roadmap that has been developed over the year 2017–18 in which 55 outcomes have been pruned from a vast array of factors

Fig. 4.7a–b Regeneration pods provide a space for mindfulness in the middle of the day. Activating the pods creates a sound and lightscape for fifteen minutes. (DaeWha Kang. Photo: Tom Donald for Aldworth James & Bond)

that influence wellbeing and health and that were researched internationally.

To engage with the roadmap throughout the processes of planning, design, construction and post-occupancy performance there should be interventions by health and wellbeing specialists, as knowledge in these areas is rapidly evolving and it is difficult to keep up to date. We need to monitor and collect data. We also need to use the metrics described in the various UK Green Building Council Reports issued from 2014 onwards to aid the process so each building becomes a learning experience. Human Resources departments need to provide data such as medical absenteeism rates, staff retention and attraction rates, medical illnesses, staff reported issues, physical space environmental measurements, people's physiological measurements, and post-occupancy surveys.

The present state of research reveals an underlying basic need to balance our lives between our use of machines and natural things like meeting people face to face and nature itself. Questions are debated about our long hours spent on phones, looking at emails and screens and generally squeezing out human interaction time and screen-less activities inside or outside the home or workplace. In the past there used to be often a lady (in those days) bringing drinks around the office and is now sorely missed as she has been replaced by a vending machine; the social interactive moments she brought to the office have disappeared. Vending machines cannot smile. So many things are decided by cost cutting, which usually seems to mean ridding systems of people and substituting them with inhuman replacements. The real social health and wellbeing values of things are not usually assessed. There is hope though. In July 2019 I visited the Mitie company on the twelfth floor of the Shard in London and there was a big, buzzy social space by the reception for people to meet, to chat, to drink; besides, it created a welcoming atmosphere for visitors, as my photos here show.

Absenteeism and presenteeism

The roots of productivity in the workplace are health and wellbeing. We need energy and motivation to work; if the mind and body are not in harmony then these suffer and our work output will be less. Productive and creative workplaces need to be healthy and engaging, as well as having efficient and effective support systems. The look and feel of the space which engages the sensory system; the IT systems; the ancillary services; the employer–employee relationship – all of these contribute to establishing a stimulating and caring climate in an organization.

People can be absent because they are ill and that can be supported by evidence from a doctor so as to distinguish it from home working or holidays. The major reasons for illness absence are musculoskeletal conditions, mental health and other ailments like building sickness syndrome. The costs of absenteeism and presenteeism (include staff turnover costs) vary from year to year but in the UK they are over £100bn

Fig. 4.8a–b   Social space in the Mitie company on the twelfth floor of the Shard, London.

per year. Information from a collection of sources as at 2019 suggests that the overall costs in the UK for absenteeism and presenteeism are £42bn and £98bn respectively, which accounts for about 12–15 per cent GDP – more than the cost of the NHS in the UK. The exact figures are less important than the fact that this financial waste affects the overall productivity of the nation. It is important that in designing indoor environments governments are aware of the impact of health and wellbeing on national productivity. Each 1 per cent gain in productivity is worth about £20bn to the UK economy and more productivity is gained by a healthier workforce, which means that NHS costs are ultimately reduced. Healthy environments can be part of a 'prevention is better than cure' philosophy for the national health policy of a country.

The Deloitte Monitor in 2017 reported on mental stress, which represents about 10–12 per cent of total workplace illnesses and their analysis estimated the cost breakdown to be £8bn for absenteeism and £17–26bn for presenteeism plus costs for staff turnover of £8bn. Interestingly mental stress is least evident in the agriculture, forestry and the fishing sectors; this could be due to the health benefits of the outdoor life compared with the inside conditions the majority of workers have to experience. Mental stress covers difficulties in concentrating, lack of self-esteem, lack of resilience to deal with everyday stresses, emotional and social relationship problems and sluggish productivity.

The most common problems which lead to illness absenteeism include:

- Musculoskeletal problems
- Mental stress
- Building sickness symptoms (respiratory ailments, nose, sore eyes, headaches, dry skin)
- Heart problems
- Migraine
- Stomach disorders

These can be due to a number of causes but the environment is a significant factor. We know with certainty that environmental factors can act as negative stressors as well as positive motivators. Odours, sound, air quality, temperature and light affect the human body through four different mechanisms: physiological, psychosomatic (body and mind), affective behaviour (moods, feelings, attitudes), and emotional stress. Here are a few basic features that are characteristic of a healthy environment:

- A fresh thermal environment (ventilation rates sufficient to provide clean, fresh air with effective distribution and good air movement together with acceptable levels of CO_2 and low levels of indoor pollutants such as particulates, allergens, VOCs, NO_2).
- Plenty of daylighting.
- No glare.
- Views out and on natural settings if possible.
- Acceptable acoustic climate.
- Spatial settings to suit various individual or team working needs.
- Flexible space layouts to allow for active working, human interaction and breakout spaces including ones for contemplation.
- The 'look and feel' – visual interest using colour and a variety of artwork, for example.
- Ergonomic workplaces that have been designed to minimize musculoskeletal disorders.
- Landscaped surroundings inside and around buildings should be properly considered (referred to as biophilic design).
- Minimum pollution from external air and noise.

Every company should have a 'wellness' policy and for this to be effective there needs to be:

- A commitment to wellness at Board level by electing a Health Wellbeing Champion executive. Employees need to feel sincerely cared for.
- There should be a coherent and up-to-date monitoring system in place that aims to assess whether conditions in the workplace are caring, healthy and conducive to wellbeing.

- Management should encourage occupants to be aware of their environmental conditions by using wearables and by setting up health and wellbeing focus groups, for example.
- HR departments should provide up-to-date information on absenteeism, presenteeism, medical records, and staff retention rates.

The Institute of Occupational Safety and Health (IOSH) published in 2015 *Guidance on Promoting Health and Wellbeing at Work* (www.iosh.co.uk/freeguide), which every company should be aware of and contains useful advice on setting a policy; this should be read in conjunction with the BCO Wellness Matters Report 2018.

Flourish

The word 'comfort' is perhaps overused. It has a neutral quality, usually seen as a pleasant or relaxed state of a human being in relation to their environment. Surely, however, that is only part of what we need for stimulating and concentrating the mind? After all, comfort can be more soporific than stimulating. The 'flourish' approach takes us beyond comfort.

Our experience of the environment is the result of an interplay of physical, psychological and social factors. Buildings create an environment and, together with people, provide a multi-sensory experience. The senses need stimulation to react to, otherwise boredom sets in. One response to this type of thinking has been air systems which give random air pulsations, rather than a steady flow of air, because of its stimulating nature. The atrium in the Kajima Headquarters in Tokyo has periodic flows of fragrances and bio-music (which is based on heartbeat rhythms) into the space. Occupants appreciate the variety of stimulation this offers their senses. Comfort is a backdrop but human beings also need sensory change from the stimuli around them. There is a complex balance between steady state and transient patterns that needs to be achieved. We seem to need variety to give contrast to our sensory system.

Research is improving our depth of knowledge all the time. What we can conclude from this work is that comfort alone is not enough. We need to continue to develop a more comprehensive view about the effects of the environment on people and widen our scope of design to produce more stimulating places for people to work in and enjoy (Bluyssen, 2014; Gou et al., 2014; Barrett, 2010; 2012; 2018). As Malnar and Vodvarka (2004) point out:

> The problem with most of the research on the thermal environment is that it has centred on thermal comfort or thermal neutrality.

Gou and his team have carried out research on the gap between comfortable and stimulating illuminance settings. Levels of 400–500 lux were felt to be neutral and comfortable whereas some periods with levels above 900 lux were perceived as more stimulating for the task being undertaken.

Barrett believes that there is no real understanding of the holistic impacts of built spaces on people, despite the huge amount of knowledge there is on individual aspects like heat, light and sound. The outcome of his HEAD (Holistic Evidence and Design) project is the SIN Model which has three main dimensions: stimulation level; individualization; and naturalness.

Stimulation arises from the amount of information in the setting in which triggers such as colour,

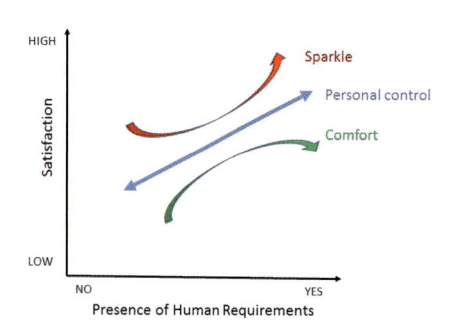

Fig. 4.9 Basis of Flourish approach.

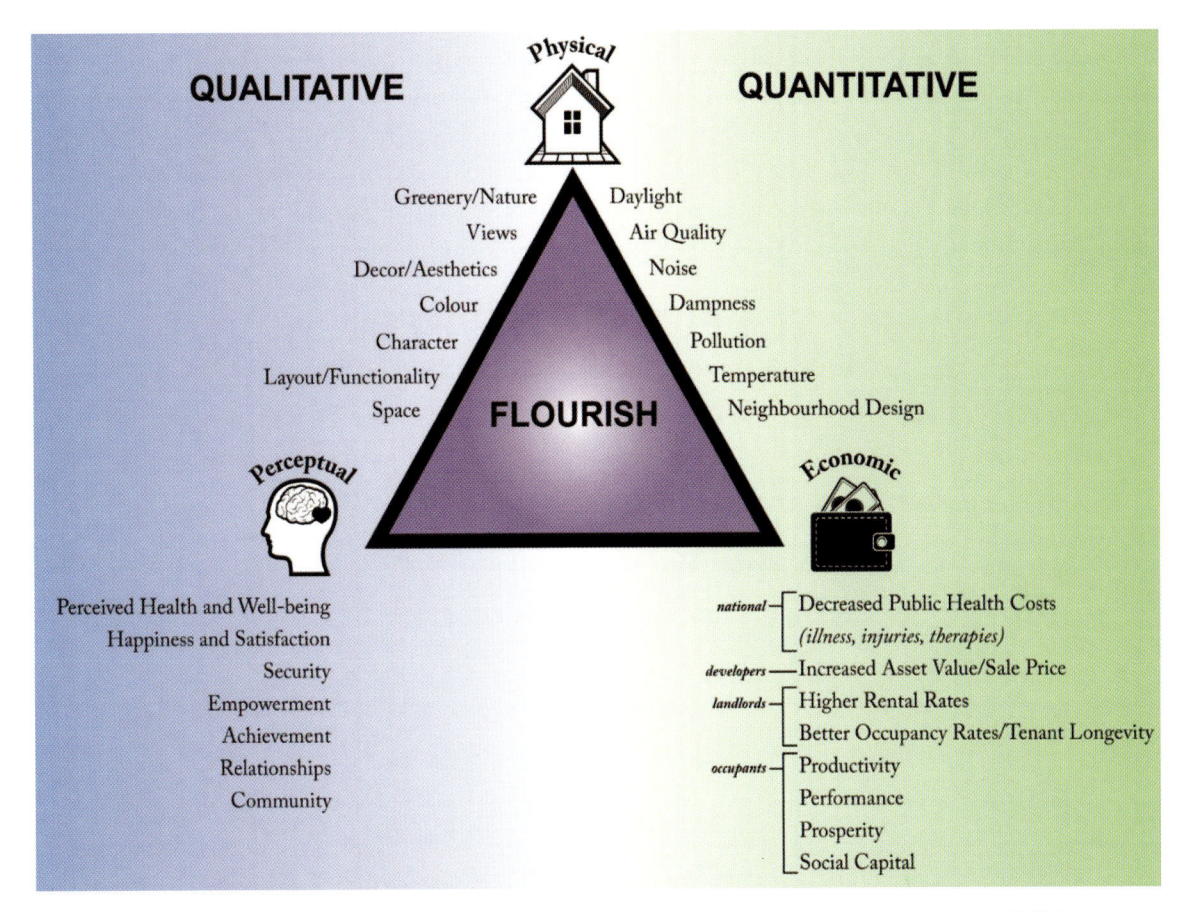

Fig. 4.10 The Flourish Model Assessment Method as an early design and POE assessment tool (Clements-Croome, 2018). It comprises environmental factors (objective and subjective); perceptual factors (feelings and emotions); and economic factors, which embrace the impact of the environment on value to users and owners.

aromas, greenery, or things that are changing – such as formal or informal social contacts or changes in the natural setting – give variety, context and interest. I call this the 'sparkle' layer. Complexity, colour and texture, for example, give contrast and make the environment more interesting. Over-stimulation can give confusing and hectic signals which can increase stress levels, whereas too little stimulation can be boring.

Individualization is the occupant's personal environment and includes factors like personal control, flexibility and one's identity with a space. This can be seen as a 'personal control' layer.

Naturalness is the basic environmental setting and this is where the 'comfort' backdrop forms an important foundation.

The holistic experience is the interplay between these three layers of 'sparkle', personal control and comfort. Together these three layers constitute 'flourish'[17] (see Fig. 4.9).

The three pillars that form the basis for this model are classed as environmental factors (both subjective and objective), feelings, and economic factors. Undervalue the environment and there will be a detrimental impact on feelings and economics (Clements-Croome, 2018). Fig. 4.10 shows the Flourish model, which can be used at the early design and POE stages.

We need to continually monitor buildings using occupants' data, in order to develop a deeper understanding about the effects of the environment on the health and wellbeing of people and to widen our

Buildings for health and wellbeing 77

scope of design to produce more flourishing, stimulating, creative and productive places for people to work in and enjoy.

Each quadrant of the Flourish Wheel shown in Fig. 4.11 can be detailed using a combination of measuring methods, such as questionnaires and interviews with individuals and focus groups, standard measurements of environment, and wearable sensors to assess physiological and psychological factors covering a variety of bio-markers and indicators like patterns of heart beats, skin conductance and even brain waves. The economic quadrant

The FLOURISH WHEEL
An assessment tool for health and well-being

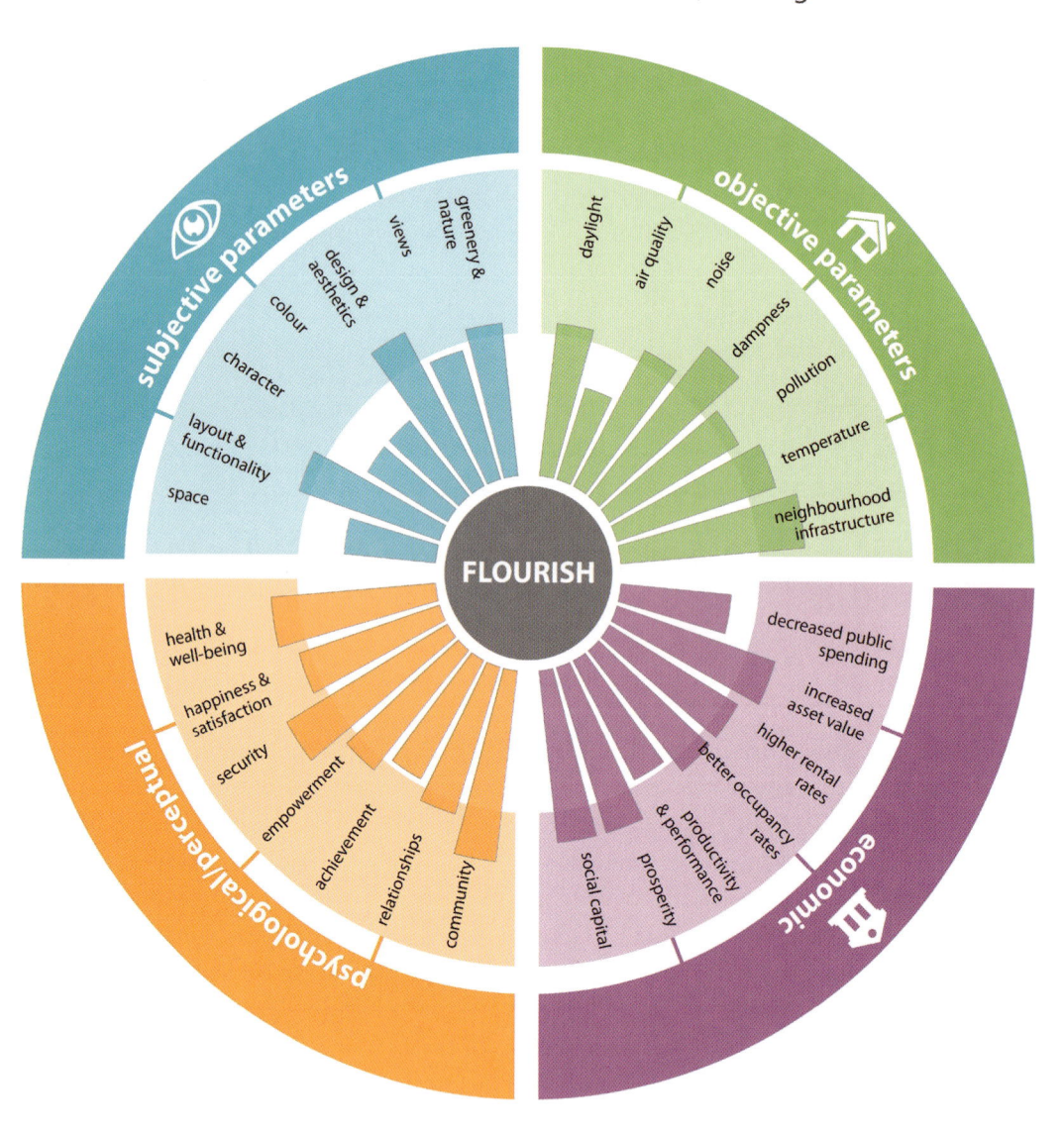

- **subjective parameters**: greenery & nature, views, design & aesthetics, colour, character, layout & functionality, space
- **objective parameters**: daylight, air quality, noise, dampness, pollution, temperature, neighbourhood infrastructure
- **psychological/perceptual**: health & well-being, happiness & satisfaction, security, empowerment, achievement, relationships, community
- **economic**: decreased public spending, increased asset value, higher rental rates, better occupancy rates, productivity & performance, prosperity, social capital

© Derek Clements-Croome and Marylis Ramos

Fig. 4.11 The Flourish Wheel (Clements-Croome 2018).

requires data to be obtained from Human Resources departments.

Flourish can be used in the following ways:

- Working with occupants to map their needs with the Flourish Wheel;
- Using a sample survey of occupants using questions based on Flourish factors;
- Working with HR on economic data;
- Analysing results to get a pre-design Flourish map;
- At POE stage, collecting data from environment and people;
- Providing analysis and recommendations;
- Plotting a Flourish Chart indicating weak/strong areas; problems; advocating solutions.

As we have seen, buildings and their effects on occupants need to be monitored to provide feedback which we can share and learn from, providing a deeper understanding that can lead to improvements in building performance and provision of healthier workplaces. In addition, basic information should be collected using an interview approach about:

- Organization culture – management/ethos;
- Types of work undertaken;
- Location – city/rural; connection with nature; accessibility;
- HR data on absenteeism for medical reasons, staff turnover and acquisition rates, medical problems;
- Physical data plus facilities management experience – by comparing all the physical factors with each other and prioritizing them. Obtain feedback from occupants using focus groups;
- Any other factors mentioned by users.

Some questionnaires that may be used in the survey are shown in the Appendix.

Health, wellbeing and sustainability

In this section, two examples are given showing how the health and sustainability agendas are loosely interconnected. The first piece of research, undertaken by MacNaughton *et al.*, (2017) at Harvard University, used 109 subjects from ten high-performing buildings, of which six were green certified and four not. The subjects in the LEED-certified buildings had 26.4 per cent higher cognitive function scores, better environmental perceptions and fewer building sickness health problems than those in the high-energy performing non-certified buildings.

Another paper by MacNaughton *et al.* (2019) in the *Journal of Exposure Science and Environmental Epidemiology* shows that in LEED-certified buildings in six countries, energy savings and emission reductions are accompanied by health co-benefits resulting in reduced days off work and school, mortality rates, hospital admissions, and asthma or other respiratory problems. (LEED is the acronym for Leadership in Energy and Environmental Design which originated in the US to certify sustainable – often referred to as 'green' – buildings.)

The relationship between health, wellbeing and sustainability is not absolute but rather a loose association. However, it is likely that sustainable buildings increase the probability that they will also be healthy ones too.

Rating systems

The WELL version 2 (WELL, 2018) is a recognized performance-based system for assessing the features of the built environment which impact human health and wellbeing. BREEAM, LEED and NABERS are examples of sustainability rating tools originally intended to deal with energy and efficient use of resources but which include sections on some aspects of traditional comfort parameters and are now changing towards a more dynamic health and wellbeing approach. (BREEAM is the UK certification scheme Building Research Establishment Environmental Assessment Method and the Australian one is National Australian Built Environment Rating

Fig. 4.12a–b Well certified offices. (a) Second Home uses biophilia and curved designs to create a natural environment, where people are encouraged to explore the workplace and interact with each other (credit: office of Rohan Silva; photo: Jeremy Myerson); (b) the Vortex in the Bloomberg Building, London, is a literal and metaphorical 'twist' on the classic timber-panelled lobbies that define many London buildings. Olafur Eliasson's No Future is Possible without a Past sits above (photo: Nigel Young/Foster + Partners).

System. BREEAM, LEED and NABERS certification schemes are used internationally.)

The WELL version 2 and its predecessor are based on feedback from the public, medics, building designers and other professionals. It has ten primary factors which cover fresh clean air, water, light, comfort (this includes ergonomics and thermal comfort), sound, materials, community, nourishment, fitness and mind (including the effects of nature, colour, role of artwork, and contemplation spaces). There are subtleties here, like recognizing the need to pay attention to circadian lighting and not just systems determined by lighting and glare levels alone, as well as the need to support mental and emotional health in the various ways[18]. However good the built environment is, people are still required to have some responsibility, by eating, drinking, exercising healthily and not smoking.

Health and wellbeing futures

Integration is not just about working together, but is also about developing language and frameworks in order to think differently about the problems and opportunities we encounter.

… The attention to sensory design is not separate from but, in many ways, arises with the desire for a sustainable, thriving existence on Earth.

Barbara Erwine (2017)

These words in a way thread together the principles of passive design drawn from vernacular architecture in Chapter 2 with those on sustainability in Chapter 6, a need for new approaches to decision-making in Chapter 7 and this chapter, which focuses upon the relationship between people and their environment.

A growing body of research opens up new avenues of thinking – not just to knowledge workers like health specialists, occupational psychologists and ergonomists, but to all of us – as the ways of measuring ourselves become simpler and cheaper. Sometimes the information we gain confirms what

Fig. 4.13a–e   The Victoria and Albert Museum extension, London – a design for people by Amanda Levete. (Photo: Hufton+Crow)

Buildings for health and wellbeing   81

82 Buildings for health and wellbeing

we have known from experience; sometimes it does not. Certainly in many cases it causes us to stop and rethink habits or simply learn to do things better. To ignore health and wellbeing is expensive, as people who are ill or not working at their full potential take time off work; besides this, their motivation is dented. The impacts on the national health costs and productivity performance have been mentioned. Health and wellbeing is not a luxury – it is an essential. In order to effect it, quite simple measures can be adopted, such as biophilic design for example. It should be viewed as an investment not a cost. The environment affects us in a much more subtle way than we have appreciated up until now and this needs to be appreciated when designing building or city environments. These powerful words by Amanda Levete are reflected in her architecture:

> To live in a great space inspires you and lifts your spirits. The environment in which you live and work has a tremendous capacity to change your mood and affect the way you live your life. Space, volume and natural light are vital for good living.
>
> Amanda Levete (2008)

END NOTES

[1] A call for 'sensorial urban futures' has been long postulated. Cities are inevitably 'sensescapes' – landscapes of sounds and sights, smells and textures, and the flavours of its characteristic foods. As we rethink urban design within a context of ecological sustainability, we need to look for urban models that can fruitfully sustain our sensory lives.

Constance Classen (2013)

[2] The complexity and multiplicity of sensory experiences and perceptual affect, make them a challenging but also exciting subject to explore. In the urban interior, perceptions are shaped by the gradual articulation of meanings as we move through the environment to feel through our senses and experiences, and construct our perceptual knowledge. Perceptions are not only spatial but temporal and define the way we feel about our surroundings, whether a space becomes a place, whether we feel a sense of belonging.

Valerie Mace (2014)

[3] Simultaneously wall and window, our skin surrounds us physically but it is also an exquisitely psychological and social part of our being. Our skin is not just a marvellous material; it is a lens through which we learn about the world and ourselves.

Monty Lyman (2019)

[4] Between stimulus and response, there is a space. In that space is our power to choose our response. In our response lies our growth and our freedom.

Victor Frankl

[5] Money dominates too much of our decision-making at the expense of the value an investment can bring. How can we pay more attention to the values that can be created? Lizzie Trotter *et al.*'s 2014 paper 'Measuring the Social Impact of Community Investment: a Methodology' (Housing Associations Charitable Trust) proposes a wellbeing valuation approach that can apply not just to housing but any building project that impacts on the community. The analysis draws on the following four UK datasets: the British Household Panel Survey (BHPS); Understanding Society (U Soc); the Crime Survey for England and Wales (CSEW); and the Taking Part (TP) Survey.

[6] People are happier in more beautiful places which empower the senses. This is more about simplicity and certainly is not about expensive false adornment. These factors are repeated time and time again in responses to surveys of occupants about their responses to the environment (*see* Watson, 2018).

[7] The definition of health has been changing and now includes an awareness of the interrelationships between social and psychological, as well as

medical, factors. The way in which an individual functions in society is seen as part of the definition of health, alongside biological and physiological symptoms. Health is no longer simply a question of access to medical treatment but it is determined by a range of factors related to the quality of our built environment.

Koen Steemers (2015)

[8]Mental illnesses can have their root causes in home or work life. The workplace can be stressful for many reasons and we need more understanding about the contributory factors.

According to a recent WHO report, 615 million individuals suffer from depression and anxiety worldwide, costing about $1 trillion in lost productivity. Most people do not get any treatment and yet WHO believe that every dollar invested in improving access to treatment leads to a return of 4 dollars in better health and productivity. Break a leg and people know what to do, but mental illnesses remain elusive and a mystery to many. Impaired states of mind are too often seen as something personal and people simply need to 'sort themselves out'.

[9]Justine Fox of Calzada Fox on colour

The relationship between colour, light, interior design and architecture is one that transcends pure aesthetics. It has been found that we receive colour information through both visual and non-visual receptors in our bodies that stimulate biological responses and resonate with the emotional self. Developing research focuses the understanding of these connections to promote the wellbeing of users within a space, not just across the healthcare sector but through commercial, residential and public spaces.

Chromotherapy: the use of the varying vibrations within light to alleviate certain ailments is an ancient practice. Studies now suggest that the future benefits of using electromagnetic energy in complementary and alternative treatments are widespread. These attributes are being incorporated today within a range of daily wellness routines, initially driven by the millennial generation, through their interior spaces in waiting rooms, saunas and fitness.

ChromaYoga integrates specific frequencies within their yoga studios to promote alertness, healthy sleep cycles, productivity and to reduce anxiety also rebalancing clients from the influence of our overexposure to blue light from technology devices. Classes are colour specific to exploit the positive properties of each hue's vibrations; designed to precise length and timing for optimum psychological and health benefits.

It is important to take into consideration that these focused exposures of chromotherapy are too intense for long term use within an interior space. When designing colour for a 'well space' through coatings, materials and textiles the primary question to answer is what your outcome should be and how do you want people to feel?

Applied colour psychology recognizes the universal effects of the colour spectrum on us and its use in directing and supporting user behaviour through the built environment has grown exponentially in recent years. This acts as a foundation to your primary objectives for the space, be they calming, energizing or restorative. Integrating demographic and cultural insights with clear visual ergonomics centres the colour design on the person. Allowing users intuitive interactions with a space where the colour design is familiar and harmonized promotes feelings of reassurance and wellbeing. *See The Little Book of Colour* by Karen Haller (Penguin Random House UK, 2019).

The award-winning project The Chocolate Works Care Village reflects the positive effects of natural daylight in its Market Square with a palette that includes nuanced accents of a soft blue with green undertones in wall detailing and furniture against warm whites with yellow accents. These harmonious combinations interact with biophilia to enhance optimism and clarity.

Fig. 8.14 (a) PPG Comex Colorlife Trends 2020 by Calzada Fox; (b) The Chocolate Works Care Village, Springfield Healthcare, Norr Architects. (Image: PPG Voice of Colour)

[10]The tendency has been to focus on productivity which is an obvious economic indicator but creativity is just as important. Dr Robin Philipp, a consultant occupational physician, has conducted research into the health benefits of writing poetry and many said that writing poetry helped them to cope with the pain of bereavement, while others were able to stop taking antidepressants or tranquillizers. He suggests that other forms of creative writing, such as drama or biography, can produce the same effect. I suggest other art forms like music and painting can also help in focusing the mind on creative activities. *See* Magadly and Birdi, 2009; Balfe, 1998; Philipp, 2001; Philipp and Thorne, 2018.

[11]Sir Hans Krebs was a biologist, physician and biochemist. He developed the citric acid and urea cycles now referred to as the Krebs Cycle which explains the chemical reactions that take place in the cells of humans and other organisms. These reactions underlie the processes involved in generating and regenerating energy.

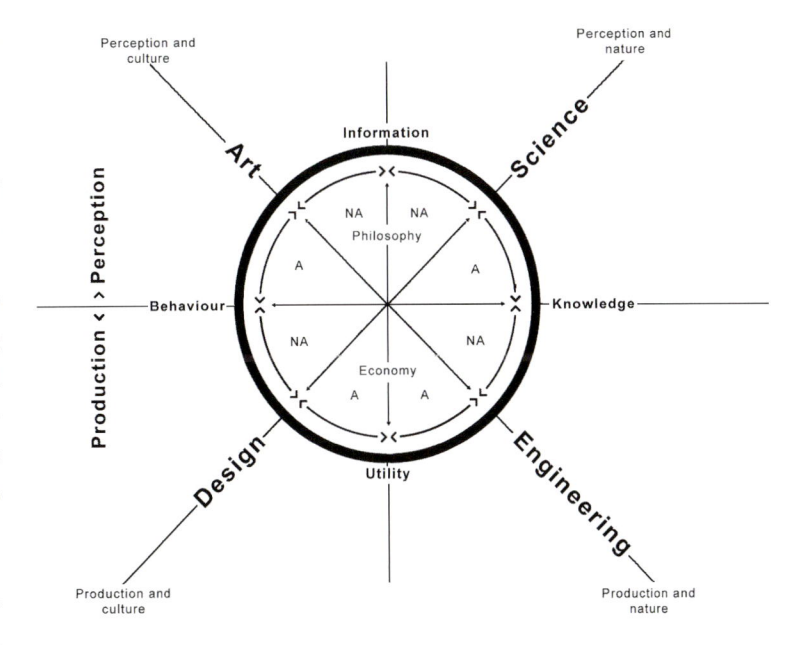

Fig. 4.15 The Krebs Cycle.

Buildings for health and wellbeing 85

Neri Oxman is an architect and designer at the MIT Media Lab. Her research and teaching is in the arts and sciences, combining design, biology, computing and materials engineering. She has adapted the Krebs Cycle to explain the interactions which can generate creative energy. She believes top-down form generation by 3D printing, for example, combined with bottom-up growth of biological systems, offers many opportunities such as bio-façades, 3D printed matter that repairs damaged surfaces and many other possibilities. So we now can see emerging dynamic design where products and structures and hence buildings will be able to grow, heal and adapt (Oxman, 2016).

[12]The environment should open up our senses, not close them down. Forest 404 is a project at Exeter University being undertaken by PhD student Alex Smalley, financed by the Wellcome Trust, which explores the value of natural soundscapes on people's wellbeing (Smalley, 2019). But not just sounds – the fragrances, dappled light or the rich diversity all create an atmosphere in a forest that can decrease stress levels and calm the mind. Measurements show people have lower levels of the stress hormone cortisol, decreased blood pressures and pulse rates. Similar effects can happen when walking by the sea (see Seresinhe et al., 2019).

[13]In her book *Wellbeing in Interiors* (RIBA, 2019), Elina Grigoriou describes many features that contribute towards our reaction to a space and thus affect our sense of wellbeing. These include not only factors like light, colour, sound, biophilia and air freshness, but also shapes, textures, volumes, proportions and ceiling heights. Our responses to the environment are much more subtle than we traditionally assume in design.

> [14]When people hear I work on the heart and how signals from the heart can shape how we think and feel, they might think it is a little light and fluffy. But I love the basic science of it. I'm all about scanning brains with concurrent autonomic monitoring and manipulation. I have shown that signals from our heart can interact with the brain to disrupt memories and alter decision-making.
>
> Sarah Garfinkel, Professor in neuroscience and psychiatry, 2019

Increasingly the measurement of brain rhythms (EEG) is being used to study the effects of different environments on people (see Nayak et al., 2018).

[15]Nelson and Holzer (2017) describe the use of activity trackers for assessing how subjects responded to 'healthy' areas compared with 'normal' ones with no special attention being given to environmental health needs. One group was located in healthy areas and each fitted with an activity tracker; a second group similarly but without trackers; a third group was a control. In 'healthy' areas attention was given to spaces respecting nature; circadian lighting; optional healthy choices regarding nutrition (less sugar and caffeine); more opportunities for active working and an attempt to provide conditions that would be less mentally stressful. The results showed subjects in the 'healthy' places felt:

More energized 65–76%
Improved performance by interviews 10–20%
Improved performance with objective measures 10–45%
Healthier 50–71%
Happier 36–78%

In general this supports the survey work by Cooper and Browning (2015), in which many people thought that simple features, such as biophilia; use of natural materials; daylighting and effective artificial lighting; fresh air, together with healthy choices by individuals on nutrition, exercise and mental balance – allowed people to be healthy and enjoy a high level of well-being.

[16]All living tissues have magnetic properties that

are affected to some extent by the existence of electromagnetic radiation in the environment. Therefore all living creatures including plants, microbes, animals and humans are environmental indicators of exposure to electromagnetic radiation (*see* Stein *et al.*, 2015). *See also* Consales *et al.*, 2012; Mitra and Pattanayak, 2018; Yakymenko *et al.*, 2016; Jibreal *et al.*, 2018; Parmar and Saini, 2018; Sallomi *et al.*, 2018, Miller *et al.*, 2019.

[17]Seligman in his 2011 book *Flourish* proposes the PERMA model – Positive Emotion; Engagement; Relationships; Meaning; Achievement for leading a way to a more enriched life. This, alongside work by Diener and Biswas-Diener (2008) perhaps covers the most comprehensive range of attributes that can contribute to happiness and wellbeing by including in their research a psychological flourishing scale which adds some aspects on accomplishment, moral character and citizenship. Diener's model for wellbeing is based on three issues – the environmental factors, the perceptions and feelings people have in various environmental settings and the economic consequences of the environments created. (*See also* UK Green Building Council, 2016.)

[18]Blue light boosts attention, reaction times and mood in daylight but at night it can suppress melatonin production and disrupt circadian rhythms. The importance of daylight and how it affects the circadian rhythms of our hormone system, especially in relation to melatonin, is now recognized. It is currently recommended that blue light (LEDs produce more blue light than fluorescent lamps, for example) from screens on phones, computers or televisions should not be viewed some two or three hours or so before we sleep. Blue light blocking glasses can now be bought cheaply to help overcome its effects (*see Harvard Health Letter* 13 August 2018).

Chapter Five

Technology as an enabler

Now is the time for an optimistic vision of life's destiny – in this world and perhaps far beyond it. We need to think globally, we need to think rationally, we need to think long-term – empowered by twenty-first-century technology but guided by values that science alone can't provide.

Martin Rees (2018)

Rates of change in innovation are rapid and making us reconsider how we design or refurbish buildings. Robotics, augmented reality, new materials, nano-technology, 3D printing and smart digital devices will influence design and the processes we use in the construction industry. New products too are appearing in the market place to offer the opportunity to design smart systems which respond to user needs.

Derek Clements-Croome (2017)

FOR CENTURIES, HUMAN BEINGS have been driven by curiosity and the passion to discover and make things, and to create technology. The time scales moved very slowly at first but then the pace gradually quickened towards today's high-speed, technologically driven world. In earlier times people observed the stars with their eyes but now with the aid of radio telescopes the world of astronomy reaches out to the galaxies and distant planets. But magnification works in the opposite direction too so we can search matter at sub-atomic levels and see the patterns in the microcosmic world with high-powered microscopes. The sciences of physics, chemistry and biology have become intertwined as we search for an understanding of how the world works at all scales. Mathematics help to unravel the relationships between one thing and another, helping us to handle and analyse data from which we can denote patterns and trends. Our world has become

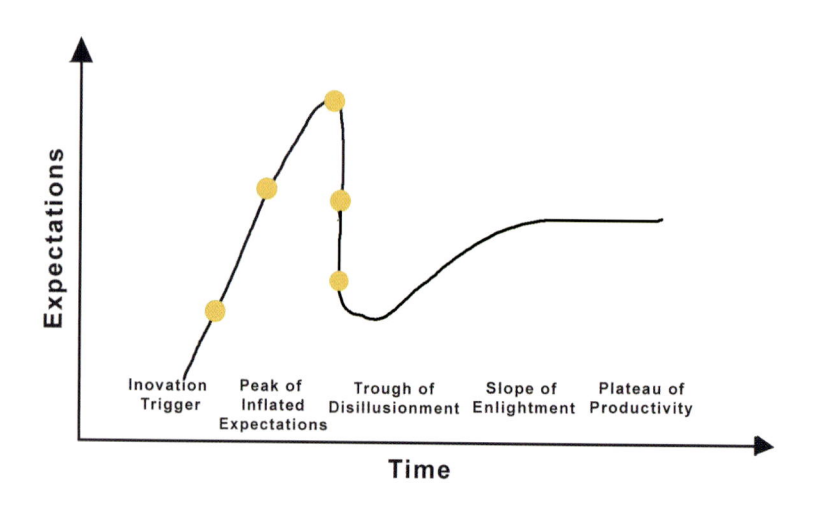

Fig. 5.1   Hype cycle for technologies (adapted from Gartner, 2019 by Desislava Veleva).

more interconnected. This means that in architecture we can monitor the performance of the building envelope or the building services, for example, at a detailed level and this will provide feedback data which can help to predict using fault diagnosis techniques and so improve or rectify conditions as necessary. Beyond this we can measure the atmosphere, and the people's reactions to it, so we can develop a complete data loop linking occupants to their environment and the building fabric.

In the hype cycle shown in Fig. 5.1 we see a high number of technologies populating the expectancy peak in the curve followed by disappointment as some innovations fall away, but then enlightenment appears as durable technologies make their mark. Keeping abreast of technologies, updating them and spotting the worthwhile ones is challenging. Curves like this change yearly, so soon become dated, but they show the need for discernment in choosing technologies that will have a lasting value for society[1].

Every year at the World Economic Forum in Davos, world thinkers from many sectors give their views on many things, including technology futures. Klaus Schwab, the Forum's founder, writes about how technology will change human progress in his book *The Fourth Industrial Revolution* (2017). The first Industrial Revolution was characterized by the steam engine, railways and mechanical production; in the second, mass production accelerated further with the advent of electricity. In the 1950s and 60s the computer took hold (this is the period often referred to as the third Industrial Revolution), rapidly taking over many parts of working and home life. The terms (artificial intelligence) 'AI' and 'machine learning' were coined in the 1950s. The two world wars had made their impact on technology in many fields, such as air flight, weaponry, cybernetics, communications, intelligence and ergonomics; the earliest computers were also developed during World War II for breaking enemy codes. This century (the 'fourth Industrial Revolution') is like an interconnected information age characterized by the Internet of Things and AI, together with many other technologies born from physics, biology and chemistry.

The explosion of information and instant virtual communication brings advantages in many ways but there are downsides too. Data speed and quantity bombard us daily and demand our attention to an extraordinary degree. Is it all too much? The desire for more calming, slower-paced environments has become evident in work and home life. Like all things it is a question of balance: in their quest for discovery, humans have developed and created the technologies like artificial intelligence that we now question. There is excitement in science as we try to understand living things, a unified field theory to explain matter, space research and many other mysteries and phenomena. In the end technology must be for the benefit of people – advances in medicine, for example, are so important – but often it can be difficult to make them available to the public at large. The impacts on health and wellbeing are not often considered at the discovery and development stages and in any case not always easy to detect, since some effects take a long time to become evident.

Schwab (2017) believes that the key megatrends (modified to include artificial intelligence) over the next fifteen years will be:

- AI
- 3D printing
- Robotics
- New materials
- Internet of things (IoT)
- Autonomous vehicles

Schwab goes on to discuss the positive and negative aspects of these technologies in various sectors[2].

To do any job well requires the use of head (cognitive skills), heart (emotions and feelings) and hands (practicality). How do we think and make decisions? Feelings are involved to some degree and we need a degree of practicality to carry out tasks. Technologies can extend our abilities in all these areas if used in a structured way. We can add to and extend the range of our senses by the use of wearable sensors and these are beginning to be embedded in clothing and even the body. The sensors can measure physiological factors like heart rate, skin conductance or brain waves. They can also monitor physical activity, sleep and calorie intake. Autonomous vehicles too depend on arrays of sensors so they can detect every situation influencing the drive and give more information than a human driver can manage.

In the excitement of technological discovery there is a cautionary note: we talk about the rapid changes in society and technology but are we going beyond the natural rhythms that our biological clocks are tuned for? The digital technology speeds communications in one sense, but sucks our energy levels with the speed and volume of emails, for example, that people have to deal with[3]. It also seems to produce more layers of administration, so it can result in slowing down the decision-making chain. Is all this good for our mental health, which is the biggest cause of why there is so much absenteeism and presenteeism? Screen time via phones, tablets and television is for many people several hours a day, comparable with their hours of sleep.

As Gillian Tett comments in *The Financial Times* (June 17, 2017):

> While our digital platforms create the illusion that humans are hyper-connected, in fact they divide us in subtle ways because people choose who they wish to be connected with and develop cyber tribes. Each tribe holds what they think is the truth although within it there are a range of views expressed. In some ways digital technologies are liberating and that can be good but makes it more difficult to agree solutions with so many competing and polarized views. This can lead to instability and uncertainty and perpetuate even more 'wicked' problems.

In an interesting essay written in 1908 by Arnold Bennett, entitled 'How to Live on 24 Hours Per Day' he recommends five principles (amongst others):

- Do not read newspapers
- Concentrate
- Reflect
- Do not waste non-work hours
- Avoid rushing

This was in times when office hours were more regulated to eight hours, leaving sixteen hours for other things, and they were not flexible like today where work and home hours have merged. Bennett's view was that one should spend these sixteen hours to cultivate the mind, sleep well, and exercise in fresh air at a calm, soothing pace (Clements-Croome, 2018).

Several surveys of office workers show that there is a demand for contemplation spaces at a time when therapies like pilates, mindfulness and yoga are becoming more widespread through society. According to the *Times Higher Education* (No. 2346, March 1–7, 2018), growing numbers of universities worldwide are introducing brief mindfulness periods into their curricula. Meditation periods have been in school timetables for years in South Korea, and forest bathing has been enjoyed for years in Japan.

Internet of things

The Internet of Things, big data analytics, generative adaptive algorithms and artificial intelligence are influencing all aspects of architecture and more widely the construction industry. These technologies can help us to analyse and study the trends for the future so we can monitor change as well as understanding the immediate impacts of the environment on the health and wellbeing of building occupants, the patterns of consumption and wider sustainability issues, predicting maintenance needs and patterns of failure[4]. These developments apply across the whole supply chain. 5G networks are emerging that will increase connectivity between devices with a faster response time and more reliability.

Artificial neural networks are a form of machine learning algorithm with a structure roughly based on that of the human brain. They can solve problems by trial and error without being explicitly programmed with rules to follow. As in the brain, the output of an artificial neural network depends on the strengths of the connections between its virtual neurons, which in this case are connected modules of a computer programme. Neural networks are good at matching patterns and finding trends in highly multi-variate data. This is useful for problems with solutions that are complex and poorly understood.

Neural networks are particularly well suited to deal with big data and they can also help to generate predictions based on imported data. But we need to appreciate that neural networks are not a substitute for good understanding of the problem. They offer blackbox solutions. Human judgement is still necessary to ensure that the networks are actually solving the correct problem. They are not a substitute for critical thinking and human expertise.

> Quantum computers are devices that use the quantum mechanical superposition principle to process information. These devices can solve certain computationally hard problems. Nature is fundamentally quantum mechanical and because of this quantum computers have the potential to solve problems concerning the fundamental structure and dynamics of solids, molecules, atoms or subatomic particles.
>
> *Physics World*, July 2018, page 5

Today more people are using wearables to raise their awareness of their physical and psychological state of being in different environments. Can these be integrated in some way to become a personal environment system that lets individual preferences be achieved? In this way the environment can then become a coexistence of many personal microclimates.

Researchers have developed a variety of wearable sensors in recent years including electronic skin coatings that can detect blood oxygen levels; contact lenses made from metal oxide thin films that can detect glucose levels in tears; and flexible integrated sensor arrays based on plastic and silicon integrated circuits that can detect glucose and other molecules in sweat.

Researchers at San Diego University of California and Taiwan University of Science and Technology have produced wearable ultra-thin sensors using a graphene nano-sheet based ink. These sensors can measure deformations in hand or face caused by hand motions or eye blinks. Recent research in haptic technology can not only alert you to new messages through your skin, but read them too.

Technology for architecture and buildings

Artificial Intelligence (AI)

Machines are good at crunching big numbers, remembering things, finding patterns, lifting heavy objects, and moving with precision, whereas humans are better at creativity, abstract thinking and dealing with uncertainty. People are good at perception, reasoning, communication and creativity whilst computers lack social intelligence and are not so good at putting together unfamiliar combinations of ideas.

Together, humans working with machines can enable more effective operations to be performed. Construction and maintenance operations can for example be done more reliably thus keeping buildings running efficiently. Filters will be changed as needed – a job that often is neglected – and so clean air supplies are continuous. Site safety will improve as the dirty and dangerous jobs are taken over by robots.

The challenge is to see how we can integrate AI into our lives and prepare for new job opportunities. This will require new developments in education and training at all levels. The impacts are already evident in sectors like medicine, aerospace and some parts of architecture. Self-learning algorithms will mean AI and humans will continuously learn and update their skills.

Human beings, as well the nature of work, are changing. Wearables are being embedded in clothing and even the body so one could imagine that eventually this symbiosis might lead to us becoming humanoids or cyborgs[5]. We can also expect that people will do several different types of work throughout their lives and so there will be a continual stream of education programmes which people can use to acquire relevant skills and so adapt to change. Machines can collect and analyse big data sets but human capabilities shine beyond this with curiosity, imagination, intuition, creativity and empathy. Of course it is these attributes that drive the motivation to discover and make technological progress, and often an advancement in one sector can have relevance to another one.

According to Gartner (*Top 10 Strategic Technology Trends for 2018*, 03 October 2017 ID: G00327329), planning for using technology involves:

- Devising new business scenarios using AI as the enabler.
- Creating a more natural and immersive user experience using conversational platforms together with virtual, augmented and mixed reality.
- Supporting Internet of Things (IoT) initiatives and using the cloud for data storage and possibilities for individual data capture on laptops, tablets or smart phones (called edge computing).
- Adopting an adaptable strategic approach for security and risk.

Computing will migrate out of laptops and into digital devices in our surroundings like walls and furniture. The human–computer interface in the future will be based on voice recognition and natural language processing. There are also developments in mind-controlled computer screens.

Computers and robots in the future might be made of soft materials like rubber and will come in many shapes, and eventually 3D printing will also make an impact on the production of robots[6]. We can expect systems that will soon analyse and synthesize masses of data on a big scale, which will help many professionals in areas such as medicine, law and other specialisms to make better-informed decisions. Already algorithms are helping us to generate key insights into some of the world's biggest challenges by analysing sets of data from various situations.

Can we seamlessly connect living and non-living physical states? A digital twin is a digital replica of a living or non-living state enabling data to be transmitted seamlessly between the virtual and the physical entities[7]. Again this points towards treating buildings as organisms, not lifeless objects.

3D printing

After vehicles, construction sites generate the highest levels of noise and air pollution. Prefabrication can alleviate this, besides reducing waste and construction time. Being a programmed process it is more reliable and accurate. 4D printing is being developed, which enables a 3D structure to be transformed by heat, water, sound or vibration.

Robotics

Robotics can be used in construction and in operation of buildings. They can relieve heavy work on site but can also carry out diagnostic maintenance like filter changing or using micro- or even nano-robots in fluid networks to keep them clean, as they are often inaccessible. Researchers at MIT Computer Science and Artificial Intelligence Laboratory (CSAIL) and elsewhere are working to develop methods that will allow robots to respond to situations they have not been programmed for[8].

Building Information Modelling

Building Information Modelling (BIM) creates, visualizes and manages digital information throughout the planning, design, construction and operation processes. This makes it easier to involve all stakeholders, including clients, so that each can contribute into the whole process. This helps to deal with difficult spatial interactions between services; it enables the aesthetics and effects of lighting for example to be foreseen; it helps a systems approach to be taken up on projects.

Blockchain

The premise of Blockchain is to make the handling of lots of data easier and more efficient. Put simply it is a ledger of all transactions carried out on a project. Once a record is created it cannot be changed without leaving evidence of the change, thus making fraud virtually impossible. This is a transformative technology which can streamline the process of carrying out transactions making it fault-free, reliable, secure and guaranteed. It could make design, construction and project management processes in building more reliable and efficient. According to news in *The Buzz Business* (May 2018) it is reckoned that Dubai will have the world's first Blockchain-powered government by 2020. This will enable effective connectivity between government, the private sector and the international community and that principle could make the interactions between consultants, contractors, manufacturers and facilities managers smoother with effective connectivity.

Wearable technology

Wireless sensor networks can take us further down the road of discovery by embedding sensors into structures, systems, equipment and even the clothing of the occupant. This will bring the linkage between occupant and building even closer, so allowing more personal control of microclimates near the person. In this way buildings, as well as people, can be considered as organisms because they become more responsive, continually adjusting to changes in climate, work needs and ultradian rhythms. People will learn about how their mind and bodies are reacting, giving real meaning to subjective responses by interpreting the sensor data measured.

Various wearables are available and some companies offer them to their employees. There are examples of wearables woven into clothing and beyond that being embedded into the body. Their speed of development is rapid. Looking to the future, Wade (2018) describes innovations in wearable technology for making health digital (with acknowledgements to the Takao Someya Research Group) including:

- Woven data storage – data storage in clothing
- Fabric photovoltaics – stretchable and ultra-thin
- Cell monitors – attaching sensors to skin
- Bionic eyes – interactions between implants and tissues
- Artificial muscles – using organic polymers[9] for throat sensors that stick on to monitor muscle and vocal cord movements
- Skin interfaces – flexible and deformable skin displays, e.g. DuoSkin from MIT
- Epilepsy treatments using EEG brain monitoring

New materials

> Biotech and nanotech are two technologies that we have talked about for decades but maybe their time has come to develop appropriate synthesized materials from plants.
>
> Tristram Carfrae, Deputy Chairman of Arup (2019)

Materials form structures which are the frameworks of buildings, and they moderate heat, sound, moisture. Their surfaces offer a variety of textures. However, they use energy and water in production and emit volatile organic compounds. In on-site construction there is much waste; 50 per cent of all material resources and 16 per cent of water consumption go into construction.

But materials are the very essence of buildings[10]. They affect the sound and thermal characteristics of a space. Natural materials like wood[11] positively affect our health and wellbeing, as the work of Cooper and Browning (2015) shows (described in Chapter 3).

Can we use materials that reduce consumption, embodied energy, pollution, waste and toxicity? We often see guidance which recommends the use of locally sourced materials, a focus towards off-site construction which can reduce waste and on-site pollution, and the use of recycled materials/waste composites.

At the same time there are exciting technological developments utilizing traditional materials including timber, straw, hemp, rammed earth, cardboard and even lotus leaf. Cellulose from trees or grasses can be made into effective construction materials, offering affordable housing in some parts of the world. Straw bale construction, as described by Barbara Jones in her guide *Building with Straw Bales* (2015), and the Hemcrete House developed by the Building Research Establishment (BRE) are some UK examples. The Renewable House at BRE Innovation Park has a Hemcrete-timber structure fitted with sheep's wool insulation and a bio-renewable carpet made from corn and sugar.

Wood has roughly the same strength as concrete or steel and is becoming used particularly in 3D printing prefabrication applications and this could extend, if recent research is proven, to the possibility of high-rise buildings. Bamboo skyscrapers are anticipated in the Far East over the next decades. As of 2019 there is a 49m-high fourteen-storey wooden residential tower in Bergen, Norway and a 53m-high eighteen-storey timber tower with concrete core in Vancouver, Canada. An 80m-high wooden tower is under construction in 2019 near Oslo ('Change makers' by K. Smale in *New Civil Engineer*, March 2019).

So simple natural materials should not be forgotten. And even traditional building materials like bricks, stone and concrete are not untouched by technology, as self-cleaning and self-healing materials are now available[12]. We are learning a lot from the way nature optimizes the use of materials as well as energy[13].

Concrete, bricks and steel have relatively high levels of embodied energy compared with timber for example. But developments are being made by studying the basic chemical processes and using innovative approaches to reduce these levels. Advancements in modifying traditional materials as well as developing new ones are described in the book *Nanotechnology in Eco-Efficient Construction* (Pacheco-Torgal et al., 2019). It describes how nano-technology is making cement, concrete, asphalt, steel, thermal insulation, windows and paints more sustainable in use. Materials are evolving for example with embedded graphene, which will give control over thermal and electrical properties besides adding strength to materials.

Our bodies are constantly self-repairing. Could the development of smart materials help urban infrastructure to do the same? Mark Miodownik (*FT magazine* March 31, 2018) believes this may be possible. The next paragraph is based on his comments.

Lime mortar used to cement bricks and stone together has been around for thousands of years. Cracks can open up between the mortar and the masonry but there is an autonomous repair that can take place as a result of a crystallization process inside the material. This happens when a crack lets in damp air which reacts with lime inside the mortar. Today the aerospace industry has been developing self-healing composites as a way to deal with cracks that can grow in the fuselage of aircraft. These technologies work by incorporating microcapsules of liquid resin inside the material and by coating the reinforcing fibres inside the composite with a catalyst. If a crack occurs the microcapsules burst open and liquid resin flows into contact with the fibres. The catalyst causes the residue to solidify rapidly and so heal the crack. This is comparable to the clot-

Fig. 5.2 Microbial fuel cell.

ting mechanism that our body employs to heal a wound.

Miodownik describes how self-healing materials take inspiration from biological organisms. A bacterium called *bacillus pasteurii* can withstand high alkaline environments such as those found in concrete. It excretes a mineral called calcite, which is a constituent of concrete. Together these have made the production of self-healing concrete viable. If a crack appears the bacteria are then exposed to humid air, which activates them and they start looking for food and find it in the form of starch capsules left in the concrete. When they eat they excrete calcite, leaving pristine material behind them.

Repairs and maintenance of infrastructure or buildings are costly operations and take time. They also cause disruption to users. By using robots or drones to monitor and deal with problems, services can run continuously without interruption. In the UK, railways have problems with leaves or ice on the rails but such measures could prevent the disruption associated with these weather events. 3D tar could be produced to repair roads, thus reducing disruption as well as repair and maintenance costs.

Professor Jiaxing Huang leads research at Northwestern University in China developing a self-healing oil-based coating that can patch up imperfections in materials in a matter of seconds. Lightweight graphene capsules thicken the oil and help it stick to the metal. This will make self-healing even more effective.

New phase change materials (PCMs) are promising fillers in the form of microcapsules which can offer multi-functional concretes, combining good mechanical properties with enhanced thermal storage capabilities within building envelopes. These materials are currently receiving a growing interest in the scientific literature. PCMs embedded as soft or stiff microcapsules are particularly suitable for applications in concrete. Overall, new multi-functional concretes with PCM inclusions appear promising for achieving sustainable and lightweight concrete structures (D'Alessandro et al., 2018).

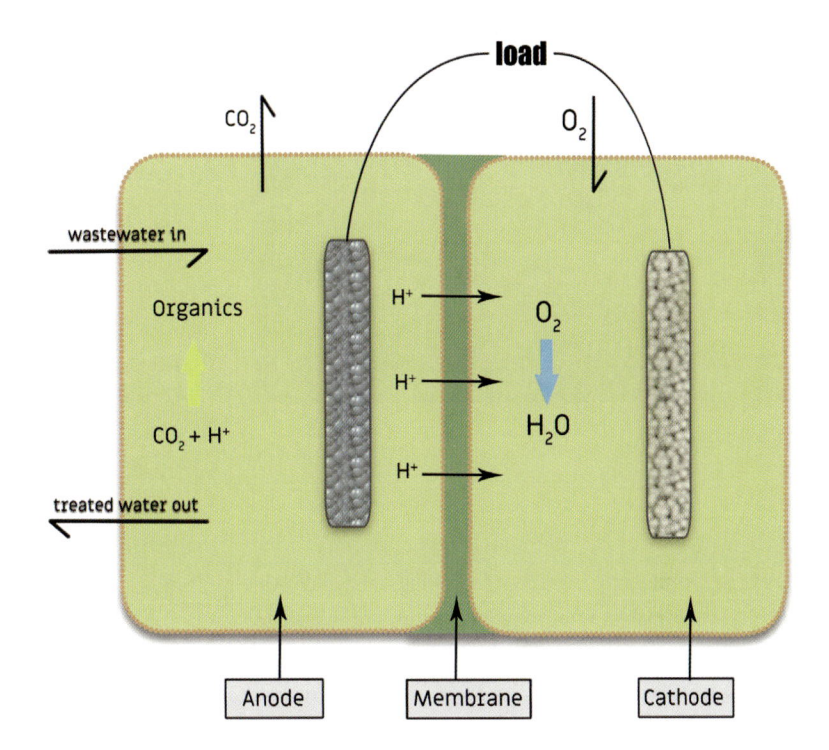

Here is just one example of how the humble brick can become smart:

Microbial fuel cells are energy transducers that exploit the metabolic activity of the constituent microbes to break down organic waste and generate electricity. This is a novel application for microbial fuel cells (MFC) modules to be made into actuating building blocks as part of wall structures. MFCs embedded into the bricks give them their 'smart' capabilities; they can be used to generate electricity from human urine, dead flies or just plain old mud.

Ioannis Ieropoulos, Professor at UWE Bristol's Robotics Laboratory

Fig. 5.3   Bee brick.

In contrast to this, the Bee Brick is simply constructed from waste used as a composite. The brick is pierced with holes, which provide egg-laying homes for solitary bees – a sort of 'bee hotel'. There are about 250 species of bee in the UK and 90 per cent are solitary bees that do not go to hives. They are good pollinators, especially of fruit trees. This is an example of using a sustainable solution with respect for nature in a very simple way but no less innovative for being that. Our creative imagination can be evident in many kinds of ways and we need to capture those.

Wood has a cellular structure and this makes it strong. Scientists at the US Universities of Pennsylvania and Illinois, and at Cambridge University (UK), have developed a layer of nickel with a cellular structure, which makes it as strong as titanium but lighter. The wood-like cellular feature has led to the nickel being referred to as metallic wood.

Acting as passive 'air scrubbers', the application of nano-structured titanium dioxide (TiO_2) coatings can save façade maintenance costs, conserve water, eliminate contaminants and provide an improved air environment, as attested by Chew, Conejos and Law (2017).

Effects of materials on people

Materials, including the substances that coat or join them to other parts, have emissions, the so-called volatile organic compounds (VOCs) that affect the

Fig. 5.4 Mushroom Tower. (Photo: Amy Barkow, courtesy of David Benjamin at The Living Architects)

respiratory system. They also affect the distribution of sound and heat via their texture, mass and insulating properties. Metal-organic frameworks (MOFs) are a class of crystalline materials whose structure is characterized by an open framework making them porous so they can be used for gas storage, purification and separation, as well as catalysis and sensing applications. It is possible that MOFs can be developed to clean the air and reduce sulphur dioxide and nitrogen oxide gases which are harmful. They also impact us psychologically because of their look and feel, which stir our senses.

Stone can speak to us; it speaks to us by means of the wall. This wall is my daily friend.

Le Corbusier

Graphene

Graphene and other 2D materials do have a big potential for many applications. The electric charge carriers in graphene move at speeds 10 to 100 times faster than in silicon chips. Graphene is a better conductor of electricity than copper, it is impermeable to

Fig. 5.5 Examples of cybertecture. (a) Central Monetary Authority Financial Academy, Riyadh; (b) Mumbai Convention Centre, Mumbai; (c) The Crescent, Dubai. (Images: James Law, Cybertecture)

Technology as an enabler 97

gases and is stronger than diamond. A team at MIT have produced 3D graphene.

Graphene has many evolving applications and possibilities, for example by enhancing advanced composite materials or by being combined with metallic nano-structures to advance high-speed internet. Besides graphene, other materials offering great potential are phospherine, boron nitride, molybdenum disulphidem, tungsten disulphide, and no doubt others in the future.

Bio design

Bio design involves using living organisms as design elements to bring us products that adapt, grow, sense and repair themselves. Industrial and mechanical systems are replaced with biological processes. Bio design overtakes imitation and biomimicry, completely dissolving the boundaries between organisms and objects. Chapter 3 gives examples of how biomimetics and biophilic design can enable a more economic use of resources as well as improving people's wellbeing. This includes the use of artificial leaf façades to generate hydrogen.

Bioreactive façades using algae tanks as part of the façade, like for example the BIQ offices in Hamburg (*see* page 44), are evolving (Jan Wurm in *Cities Alive*, 2016). Artificial leaves, as developed by Daniel Nocero at Harvard University, could form a façade that generates hydrogen (*see* articles by Tom Whipple in *The Times*, 2016 and 2017).

Hydrogen

Hydrogen buses are beginning to make their mark in London and now this is being considered for trains. Hydrogen trains have already replaced more polluting diesel trains on a line in Germany, and these could be running in the UK by 2022. They are an important step towards reducing the carbon footprint of transport systems by eliminating diesel and overtaking the more expensive electric transport as well as reducing pollution (Scott-Quinn in *The Conversation*, Reading University, February 2019 and *The Week*, 19 January 2019). Hydrogen could also present possibilities for

Fig. 5.6 Hydrogen bus in London in 2019.

architecture and we can learn about handling hydrogen from the experiences in transport.

One way to incorporate hydrogen is to use fuel cells that combine hydrogen gas with oxygen from the air to produce electricity and water. Hydrogen can carry more energy than the same weight of batteries, meaning fuel cell systems could be lighter. The hydrogen gas would need to be compressed into tanks that would usually be stored on the train's roof (like you see already on buses or at the fronts and rears of the trains). Adding a regenerative braking system to charge an additional small battery would reduce the amount of hydrogen needed to power the train.

The other problem with hydrogen fuel cells is that the fuel is currently manufactured from methane (natural gas) using a process called steam method reforming, which also produces a large output of highly toxic carbon monoxide. This can be converted to carbon dioxide but unfortunately the use of hydrogen fuel cells still contributes to greenhouse gas emissions.

A pollution-free way of producing hydrogen is through electrolysis, by passing an electric current through water. A second alternative is to use a 'thermochemical' production method that involves water reacting with sulphur and iodine in the presence of heat.

Despite the current limits of hydrogen as a transport fuel, as more and more countries (in particular Japan) undertake further research on the hydrogen economy Scott-Quinn believes that costs will fall substantially, just as they have done for solar and wind power. Hydrogen could even eventually replace natural gas and this would help bring down not only the costs of transport but open up the chance to develop hydrogen-driven homes and buildings.

Conclusions

We need to put building occupiers at the heart of any digital strategy. The technology needs to be user-friendly and reliable. It can be used to streamline processes from the initial planning and design stages through construction and commissioning to the building in use. Embrace change and innovation but only with technology that enables an agile approach to the management of the building operations, the health and wellbeing and sustainability objectives of the organization.

Monitoring and user-interactive facilities management help to ensure a better behaviour culture in respect of sustainability and environmental quality. There is concern about privacy but here personal choice is important; there also needs to be a trust between the parties involved. Monitoring can help to raise our awareness about issues and also, on matters like air pollution, help us to work together by giving feedback to local authorities, for example.

Plan and design for the long term and concentrate on the realizable value by investing in integrated technology solutions. Cheap solutions often result in being more expensive in the long term.

The occupier experience underlies the success of any company because companies that care for their staff have a high staff retention rate besides attracting new staff. Their productivity is likely to be higher than companies that do not provide their staff with a stimulating and healthy place to work. Happy staff are a productive staff.

Will the technology mean that we do not need offices or shops any more? It is convenient to shop online when you know what you want and can order it directly, but moving between home and shop or office involves physical activity, which is healthy at all ages. Laura Barnett (*The Guardian*, 2007) asked the world-famous violinist Sarah Chang, 'What's the greatest threat to music today?' She replied, 'The internet. It puts everything at your fingertips, so people want instantaneous entertainment. It's much better to dress up and go out for the whole live, sensory experience.' She still believes this. I can download and listen to the sumptuous playing of music by the Berlin Philharmonic here in my study in the UK, which is wonderful, but when I went to Berlin and heard them in the Berliner Philharmonie concert hall it was even more wonderful.

The use of sensor technology means that you are building up a personal preference portfolio which can be used in various ways to satisfy user needs. Internet platforms can update you on things relevant to your portfolio, which some welcome; for others this is an invasion of privacy.

Providing workers with the relevant and reliable technologies will create a more positive working environment, boost productivity and recover the investment over a short period of time but if they are not user friendly or have unreliable IT issues which waste time then productivity will fall. A healthy human brain has seamless connectivity, and buildings with their systems and occupiers should operate in this way too.

Technology is evolving rapidly so we need to remain open to new ideas but have a critical but objective way of reviewing them. We are becoming aware of the contradictions and counterpoints technology brings in its use[14]. The connectivity can be wonderful but if used irresponsibly can bring social distress. Endless streams of emails can be tiring so the need there needs to be a balance between all the choices we have and accommodate new technologies within a whole landscape setting. Ironically, as we celebrate the ease of communication it has given rise to a number of privacy and security problems so more restrictions on communication are becoming necessary.

Artificial intelligence is making its mark in the healthcare delivery field and it can not only save costs but also improve quality. However as Reddy *et al.* (2019) point out there needs to be a certain amount of caution and careful planning in matters of fair and open access, legal aspects, and equitable distribution. Self-monitoring with analysis tools, for example, is useful but still there needs to be human interpretation. Dressed with more and more sensory clothing and body implants, will humans and machines converge to become cyborgs? We have to wait and see but current trends indicate this is a possibility.

Schwab (2017) believes that in dealing with the disrupting technologies human beings are developing we need to apply four types of intelligence which relate to understanding, emotions and feelings, and the physical health of the mind and body. But our spirit and soul too need inspiration, not just for oneself but the good of humankind. In his words:

> The Fourth Industrial Revolution can compromise humanity's traditional sources of meaning – work, community, family, and identity – or it can lift humanity into a new collective and moral consciousness based on a sense of shared destiny. The choice is ours.
>
> Klaus Schwab

END NOTES

[1] The digital world should serve humankind, not master it.

BSRIA, *At a Glance – 3D Printing,* August, TG14/2017

[2] Dr Sophie Armanini, research associate at the aerial robotics laboratory of Imperial College London, has made an Aqua Micro Aerial Vehicle (AquaMAV) based on a cross between a gannet and a squid.

Her department specializes in bio-inspired robotics, using nature as a basis for creating robotic solutions. For example, the gannet-squid idea came as a result of needing a robot that could provide aerial–aquatics locomotion – basically the ability to transition between air and water with equal power in both elements. The research combined the way a gannet folds its wings underwater, allowing it to hit the water and then continue its downward momentum at speed, with the way a squid propels itself along using a water jet, to give the robot enough energy to rocket out of the water again. The result was the AquaMAV.

[3] Bill Gates in the *MIT Technology Review,* March/April 2019, suggests the following breakaway technologies:

- Robot dexterity
- New wave of nuclear power
- Blood tests with DNA/RNA diagnostics
- Gut probe pill
- Custom cancer vaccines
- Cow-free burger
- CO_2 catcher
- Wrist ECG heart monitor
- Sanitation without sewers
- Virtual and Reality AI assistants

Some of these exist already in primitive forms. Not surprisingly half of these developments are directly concerned with health and the impact of technology on medicine which we know is immense already. This is a good reason we in architecture and construction need to look across sectors as developments in those outside our own give us clues and knowledge as to what we can apply in our field which will be durable.

[4]Sensors can transform buildings into living laboratories.

> We're reaching the point where people can customise their environment and also buildings will learn with them and will be able to predict the settings and environments that people like to work in.
> It will be a lot less about creating detail and more about being a conductor of information in the future.
>
> Nicola Gillen, 2019.

[5]I have suggested there could be a convergence between humans and robots with the increasing use of embedded sensors in clothing and the body. James Lovelock (2019) advances this idea with very much more certainty and describes an AI-dominated future in Novacene, in contrast to the human-dominated or Anthrocene world. Cyborgs will think faster and handle masses of data easily, but organic humans will still be needed to regulate temperature levels.

[6]Professor Zdenka Kuncic at the University of Sydney carries out research on synthetic intelligence. Artificial intelligence uses masses of data and analyses this using programmed algorithms, referred to as machine learning or deep learning. The big advantages humans have is that they react to circumstances not programmed; they are creative and can use common sense; can interpret the data and give meaning in various contexts. Another fact that is of interest is that computer systems consume significant power, but the brain only uses mW of power.

Synthetic intelligence replicates the brain by a process of using low power nanowire networks, which more closely resemble the brain's neural circuitry and enable synaptic plasticity, allowing non-programmed events to be reacted to. Professor Kuncic (2019) talks of neuromorphic devices that more closely emulate the brain.

We still need the human insight coloured with emotion, and also AI, but synthetic intelligence, Kuncic feels, can offer cognitive machines, which could for example be used in high-risk situations or to help people with neurological disorders. However, synthetic intelligence is still in its infancy.

[7]What is a digital twin? The business and technology consultant Bernard Marr suggests:

> Think of a Digital Twin as a bridge between the physical and digital world. Quite simply, a digital twin is a virtual model of a process, product or service. This pairing of the virtual and physical worlds allows analysis of data and monitoring of systems to head off problems before they even occur, prevent downtime, develop new opportunities and even plan for the future by using simulations.

A digital twin is an exact virtual representation of a physical object by connecting large amounts of data to a 3D virtual model replica. Digital twins can be applied in many decision-making situations and can aid design and planning for example.

[8]Latest advances in bionic limbs and prosthetics include mind-controlled limbs and sensory hands, in which prosthetic limbs are wired to the nervous system. Some body parts are beginning to be reproduced using 3D printing. (See 'Future of Prosthetics and Rehabilitation', 27 June 2019, Raconteur.net)

[9]Research at the University of Tokyo by Professor Kozo Ito is developing a new family of lighter polymers called 'polyrotaxanes' (poly – many; rota – wheel; axis – axle), so-called slide-ring materials, that lead us towards molecular machines. The industry will use many more robots in the future and currently it takes 10kg of robot to move 1kg of weight. These polymers are light and tough and so using them for car chassis, self-healing screens and artificial muscles are possible, but in time they will be part of the materials inventory for buildings. (See 'Kozo Ito's Revolutionary Polymers' by Robin Harding, *FT*, 9 August 2019.0)

[10]Research that is measuring the environmental impact of nanomaterials is described in *Physics World Focus on Nanotechnology and Nanomaterials* (2019).

> Transforming to new technologies presents several difficulties. Changing cultures and outlooks is not easy to bring about. Some of the difficulties include: recruiting and continual upskilling and training staff to deal with new methods; budget constraints; selecting the most appropriate technologies which give value; disruption to a company during change; negative perceptions and concern over technology eliminating jobs. These factors cause concern and can impede innovation.

[11]Wood contains lignin, which absorbs solar radiation. By removing it, this leaves cellulose nanofibres which, when stretched, emit infrared light at all angles. The result is that more heat is emitted than absorbed, thus giving passive cooling. The vibration and stretching treatment of the fibres increases the strength and the toughness of the wood too. This research is by Liangbing Hu at the University of Maryland, and a spin-off company, Inventwood, is commercializing the technology. (Hu's research is outlined in *Physics World*, August 2019, page 5.)

[12]The basis for self-healing concrete is the reaction between a crack and water, which activates bacteria to produce limestone, which in turn repairs the crack. This is the basis of the research being carried out by Professor H.M. Jonkers at Delft University of Technology, in conjunction with the firm Basilisk.

Concrene™ is a new type of concrete, which is reinforced with graphene on the nanoscale level. It has been developed at Exeter University by Professor Monica Craciun and Dr Dimitar Dimov. This innovative technology improves the mechanical properties of the structural material, allowing a reduction in the volume of concrete, thus saving costs and reducing carbon emissions. Dr Dimov is founder and now CEO for Concrene Ltd.

[13]It is interesting how words in nature are used to describe developments in technology. These include tweet, cloud, stream, web, tree, virus, surf, bug, swarm….

[14]Constellation Research in 2018 (in *Raconteur Business Transformation*, April 9 2019) took a survey among decision-makers on the top factors keeping digital transformation leaders awake at night. The findings are listed below:

Changing the culture of the organization
Staffing, recruitment and training
Limited budget
Selecting the technology which gives value
Disruption
Negative perceptions about technology
Workforce displacement

To these we can add a continual need to update technology.

Chapter Six

Sustainable architecture

THE BRUNDTLAND REPORT OF 1987 – *Our Common Future* – recognizes the necessity of having various political, economic and social systems in place if the aims of sustainability are to be achieved. Broadly we need to envision how we can in an increasing world population:

- make social progress which recognizes the needs of everyone;
- give protection of the environment;
- achieve a prudent use of natural resources;
- maintain high and stable levels of economic growth and employment.

Water, air, food and shelter are basic necessities for people everywhere, but environment and health are interrelated. For example, poor air quality means that the ingredients in the air that we breathe are quickly ingested into the human body and these can very quickly affect our capacity to think clearly and if severe can make people ill or even die. Changes in climate as a result of greenhouse gas pollution may increase heat-related stress and cardiovascular problems. Being too cold or too hot can cause illness and even death.

The Commission of the European Communities (1992) proposed some principles for the EU action on the environment and these were embodied in the Fifth Action Framework Programme: *Towards Sustainability*. These included the precautionary principle, the principle of prevention, and the polluter-pays principle.

The world population is now 7.7 billion and expected to be at least 9 billion by 2050 and 11 billion in 2100, with most of the growth being in developing countries. About 50 per cent of the world population now live in cities and this is expected to rise to 75 per cent by 2050.

According to Levin (2002), the impact of climate change will be 3.5 times present levels by 2050. In 2016 there were 336 cities with a population of more than 1 million. In 2018 there were thirty-three mega-cities with populations exceeding 10 million (UN data, The World's Cities in 2018). Meta-cities have populations over 20 million – places like Shanghai and Chongqing, for example. The creation of a sustainable infrastructure requires considerable skills in planning and a long-term visionary investment. Population growth can easily outstrip even fairly modern transport systems. Congestion, waste management and air pollution are all problems created by dense populations. If we are going to design sustainable ecosystems that integrate human society within its natural environment for the benefit of both, then we have to question the basis of our social and economic systems. For example, can a nation prosper by increasing its material wealth but halving its resource use? This is the so-called actor Four inspiration referred to by the Club of Rome during the late 1990s (von Weizsäcker *et al.*, 1997).

Schumacher (1973) discusses how communities can establish fulfilling work roles for everyone without aspiring to traditional markers of economic success. Humankind has been using the natural capital of the Earth at an increasingly alarming rate, seemingly unaware of the consequences until recently. With such large increases in populations envisaged in this century, societies have to question, for example, the problem of production and begin to discover new lifestyles which are less consumptive and have much less impact on the natural environment if a viable balance between people and the Earth is going to endure. We also need to learn lessons from how nature optimizes material and energy usage.

> The attempt to conceive the world as a whole has developed from the union and conflict of two very different human impulses: one urging man towards mysticism, the other towards science.
>
> Giuliani (2000)

'One Planet Living' is a view of the world where people can live happily and healthily within the natural resources of the Earth, leaving space for wildlife and wilderness. The framework devised by social enterprise charity Bioregional brings together a number of goals:

- Health and happiness
- Equity and local economy
- Culture and community
- Land and nature
- Sustainable water
- Local and sustainable food
- Materials and products
- Travel and transport
- Zero waste
- Zero carbon

The United Nations issued seventeen Sustainable Development Global Goals, which I have adapted here to include fresh air as a separate, eighteenth goal (this is only implied in the UN listing):

- No poverty
- Zero hunger
- *Good health and wellbeing*
- *Quality education*

Fig. 6.1   The Global Goals for Sustainable Development (adapted from the UN Global Goals by Derek Clements-Croome and Viorel Mihailuc, David Miller Architects).

- *Gender equality*
- *Clean water and sanitation*
- *Affordable and clean energy*
- *Decent work and economic growth*
- *Industry, innovation and infrastructure*
- Reduced inequalities
- *Sustainable cities and communities*
- *Responsible consumption and production*
- *Climate action*
- Life below water
- Life on land
- Peace, justice and strong institutions
- *Partnerships for the goals*
- *Clean fresh air*

The goals in italics are directly pertinent to this book but all are relevant to the construction industry.

The Brundtland Report makes it clear that there are three cardinal dimensions to sustainable development – environmental, economic and social ones – but these underpin the basic premise that we need to improve the quality of life for all.

> Sustainable development is development that meets the needs of the present without compromising the ability of future generations to meet their own needs.
> Brundtland Report (1987)

Some definitions of sustainable design

Creating space which is energy efficient, healthy, comfortable, flexible in use and designed for long life.

Doing the most with the least means. 'Less is more' is, in ecological terms, exactly the same as the proverbial injunction 'Waste not, want not'.

It is about ideally using passive architectural means to save energy – rather than relying on wasteful mechanical services, which use up dwindling supplies of non-renewable fuel and produce pollution that contributes to global warming. But in the final analysis, sustainability is about good architecture. The better the quality of the architecture – and that includes the quality of thinking and ideas as much as the quality of the materials used – the longer the building will have a role, and in sustainability terms, longevity is a good thing. Obviously, if a building can be long-lasting and energy efficient, that is even better.

Norman Foster, in Edwards (2001)

Sustainable design aims to meet present needs without compromising the stock of natural resources remaining for future generations. It must include a concern for the principles of social and economic sustainability as well as the specific concerns of the energy use and environmental impact of buildings and cities. The key issues are: low energy; loose fit; resource efficiency.

Richard Rogers, in Edwards (2001)

The major aspects of sustainable design are choice of materials and the performance of a building once it is built. Buildings have to be self-sufficient in energy – 80 per cent or more. It is even now possible to be selling energy back into the electricity grid overnight. Long-term performance, however, is very difficult to quantify. There is as yet no real unit of measurement. Energy also has to be considered in the construction of a building: how much will be consumed during construction and before that in the production of the materials. This also means that the quantity and weight of materials have to be given serious consideration for the first time. The fewer materials a building uses the greener it is – less resources and energy are used to produce it.

Jan Kaplicky, Edwards (2001)

Sustainable design can be defined as ecological design – design that integrates seamlessly with the ecological systems in the biosphere over the entire life cycle of the built system. The building's materials and energy are integrated, with minimal impact on the environment from source to sink.

Ken Yeang, in Edwards (2001)

> The creation and management of healthy buildings based upon resource efficient and ecological principles.
>
> Guy and Moore (2005)

Sustainable development is a process that allows achievement of individual human and social potential but one that protects, and where necessary regenerates, the natural environment rather than destroying it. The world's resources can be categorized as those that are natural, such as the oceans, the air, the land, the forests, the waterways, the energy resources and the atmosphere that envelops the Earth.

There is the human capital, which covers knowledge, skills, intuition, health, morals and ethics. The natural and human capital is put to use by people to design and construct buildings and machines which all require forms of infrastructure. Social capital includes the structure of our organizations ranging from families, communities and governments to businesses, schools, trade unions and voluntary groups. Buildings are part of the manufactured capital, which includes all of the human-fabricated infrastructure. Parkin *et al.* (2003) argue that financial capital should be included as it reflects the productive power of other types of capital and enables them to be owned or traded.

We speak of a triple bottom line comprising the pillars of environment, economy and society as the basis for understanding sustainability in a systemic way. This is proving to be challenging.

> The social pillar has been largely neglected and remains poorly defined as a wider debate has prioritized environmental concerns (energy and climate change) and economic considerations (cost savings, speed of construction).
>
> Terri Peters (2016)

Human and social issues are often seen as less easy to quantify and evaluate but this is changing as social value[1] is becoming an important part of planning and design processes (Gehl, 2010).

In general, as the population of the world increases the impacts of human (anthropogenic) endeavours become more and more evident and urgent, although one could argue that as there is more human capital these problems can be solved by imaginative and creative thought. Sadly, increased populations can overwhelm this idea by increased demands for energy and fossil fuel resources, and increased water consumption and waste generation, all of which can exhaust the Earth's natural resources. Over the last half-century or so there have been many meetings of minds where politicians together with scientists have tried to map ways forward; some of these were described at the Paris climate conference in 2015.

The Paris Agreement is an agreement within the United Nations Framework Convention on Climate Change (UNFCCC), dealing with greenhouse-gas-emissions mitigation, adaptation and finance, starting in the year 2020. The Agreement was negotiated by representatives of 196 state parties at the 21st Conference of the Parties (COP21) of the UNFCCC held in Le Bourget, near Paris and adopted by consensus on 12 December 2015. As of March 2019, 195 UNFCCC members have signed the agreement, and 187 have become party to it.

The Paris Agreement's long-term goal is to keep the increase in global average temperature to well below 2°C above pre-industrial levels; and to limit the increase to 1.5°C, since this would substantially reduce the risks and effects of climate change.

The Katowice agreement announced in December 2018 known as COP24 aims to deliver the Paris goals of limiting global temperature rises to well below 2°C by each country abiding to a set of agreed rules from 2020 onwards to ensure that countries keep their promises to cut carbon.

In order to comply with COP21 there is a need to decrease the use of fossil fuels, increase the use of renewable ones, decrease energy consumption when designing buildings by using more passive means, and improve energy efficiency. The International Renewable Energy Agency (IRENA) (2018) sets out the following recommendations if we are to comply with COP21:

- Emissions worldwide must be reduced a further 470GT by 2050 compared to current plans, aiming towards the range 0 to 9.7GT/year.
- Renewable energy share of the total primary energy supply was about 20 per cent in 2018 and needs to rise towards 66 per cent by 2050.
- The electric power sector needs renewable growth from 25 per cent in 2017 to 85 per cent in 2050, mainly through solar and wind generation.
- For industry, transport and buildings renewables are becoming very significant. The energy provision could be biomass 66 per cent; solar thermal 25 per cent and the remainder from other sources depending on their availability. (However, technological developments could alter these predictions, for example in solar photovoltaics.)

Note: Figures on energy use are constantly being updated.

Energy efficiency in the building sector requires novel solutions and lifecycle thinking. It has been estimated that as many buildings will be designed and constructed globally over the next fifty years as have been over the last 5,000 years, so the need for a sustainable approach to architecture is urgent and has to be robust. For example, burning fossil fuels not only increases CO_2 emissions, but also increases air pollution and this has a significant impact on the health and wellbeing of a nation. Planning to be sustainable needs long-term thinking, innovation and investment.

During the twentieth century, the global average energy needs of a person increased by a factor of four. As life expectancies, populations, and material wealth increase, a very high demand is made upon the ecosystem of the Earth. Most people live and work in buildings and these already use about half of the world's energy. Edwards (2002) and others point out (*see*, for example, Willmott Dixon 2010) the following factors:

- Materials: 50–60 per cent of all resources (sand, gravel, clay, iron ore, wood) globally go into the construction of buildings and roads.
- Energy: 45 per cent of energy is used to heat, light and ventilate buildings and 5 per cent to construct them.
- Water: 40–50 per cent of water used globally is for sanitation and other uses in buildings; 16 per cent of water is consumed in construction.
- Land: 60–80 per cent of prime agricultural land is used for building purposes not farming.
- Timber: 60–70 per cent of timber products end up in building construction.

Willmott Dixon (2010) estimates that the global pollution attributable to buildings covering climate change gases, drinking water, landfill waste, and ozone depletion is 40–50 per cent in each case. In addition there is air quality at 23 per cent. Sustainable intelligent buildings and cities – whether existing or new – have a key role to play.

The World Economic Forum and the Boston Consulting Group steered a report *Shaping the Future of Construction* (Gerbert *et al.*, 2017) in which they advocated innovative developments that they believe are revolutionizing the construction industry:

- Project delivery – creating certainty of timely delivery and to budget, and generally improving the productivity of the construction sector.
- Life-cycle performance – reducing the life-cycle costs of assets and designing for reuse.
- Sustainability – achieving carbon-neutral assets and reducing waste in the course of construction; reducing water consumption; developing buildings which generate energy.
- Affordability – creating high-quality, affordable infrastructure and housing, giving good value.

- Disaster resilience – making infrastructure and buildings resilient to climate change and natural disasters such as flooding, earthquakes and forest fires.
- Flexibility, liveability and wellbeing – creating infrastructure and buildings that improve the wellbeing of end-users.

The greenhouse effect

Solar radiation passes directly to the surface of the Earth but some is indirectly transmitted via clouds. The Earth is surrounded by a blanket of gases called the troposphere and is situated up to about 15km above the surface of the Earth. Global warming is a natural process by which the gases in the troposphere absorb the longwave radiation from the Earth and this is needed to keep the Earth at an equitable temperature; without it, the Earth would be some 30°C colder than it is at present.

Nitrogen, oxygen and argon make up over 99 per cent of the troposphere. Carbon dioxide (CO_2), methane (CH_4), nitrous oxide (N_2O), hydrofluorocarbons, perfluorocarbons, sulphur hexafluoride, ozone and water vapour comprise the greenhouse gases and these make up less than 0.05 per cent of the total atmosphere but they are important because they absorb some of the long-wave radiation from the Earth and keep it warm. If their proportions change this alters the long-wave radiation transmission characteristics. Industry, agriculture, buildings, transport, electricity and heat production are responsible for the emission of greenhouse gases.

Water vapour is the most prolific greenhouse gas, but human activities do not affect it directly. Carbon dioxide (CO_2) is by far the most important gas in the sense that it accounts for over 80 per cent of the total greenhouse gases. Besides the industrialized processes mentioned above, the natural sources of CO_2 are the oceans, plant and animal respiration, soil respiration and decomposition, and volcanic eruptions. The atmospheric content of CO_2 is currently about 410ppm. The lifetime of carbon dioxide is difficult to predict but it is longer than most of the other gases, but it is its role as the main constituent that makes it the gas of main concern.

It is the build-up of greenhouse gases and CO_2 in particular which is producing notable climate changes, which are of concern. These changes are evidenced by temperature rise, sea-level rises, changes in precipitation patterns, melting of mountain glaciers and decreasing snow cover. Patterns of climate change over the past 400,000 years are described in IPCC (1994, 2001).

Table 6.1 Greenhouse gases (DETR, 2000a; Fawcett *et al.*, 2002).

Gas	Greenhouse gas emissions (%)	Key sources
Carbon dioxide (CO_2)	84	Fossil fuel energy use (households, commerce, industry, transport, power stations), land use change
Methane (CH_4)	8	Agriculture, waste, coal mining, natural gas distribution
Nitrous oxide (N_2O)	7	Agriculture, industrial processes, fuel combustion
Hydrofluorocarbons (HFCs)	1	Refrigerants, general aerosols, solvent cleaning, firefighting
Perfluorocarbons (PFCs)	0.1	Electronics, refrigeration/air-conditioning
Sulphur hexafluoride (SF_6)	0.2	Electrical insulation, magnesium smelting, electronics, training shoes

Colls (2002) gives UK emissions for CO_2, CH_4 and N_2O. The greenhouse gases in order of importance as related to their impact on the greenhouse effect are shown in Table 6.1.

The Intergovernmental Panel on Climate Change (IPCC, 2001) states that human influences (anthropogenic effects) will continue to change atmospheric conditions throughout the twenty-first century. Increases in global mean temperatures are expected in the range 1.4–5.8°C by 2100. Water levels are anticipated to rise by a further 0.09–0.88m by 2100; half of this is due to thermal expansion and the remainder to melting of glaciers and the Greenland ice sheet. There are a number of other impacts such as increases in heat waves, flooding, coastal erosion and malarial disease; increases in agricultural outputs will be affected in some countries.

Sustainability highlights the problem between the developed and the developing world. Countries with high gross domestic products (GDPs) consume many more resources than those countries with low values of this traditional but limited economic indicator. Large growths in population are occurring in the developing countries and it is only to be hoped that they will not follow the trend of the developed countries but rather learn the lessons from the lack of thought and attention that has been paid over many years, until more recently when nature herself has spelt out via climate change the problems that are arising.

Environmental design and management

Buildings account for about 50 per cent of energy consumption in the UK and about half of the national CO_2 emissions. Production of building materials consumes some 29 per cent of UK industrial energy. Commercial buildings alone account for 119 million tonnes of CO_2 emissions[2]. The main benefits of 'green' buildings are the reduction of environmental impacts, costs, and health and safety risks; they also improve lettability and increase marketing advantage, give a better social and aesthetic image, and improve health, wellbeing and productivity in the workplace.

Capital characteristics of green buildings are low-energy consumption achieved by passive environmental design such as natural ventilation combined with the use of suitable materials; building mass and careful orientation; the use of greywater recycling systems for toilets inside buildings and for landscaping irrigation; maximum use of natural light; individual environmental control for the building occupants; observation of site ecology combined with internal as well as external landscaping; and smart waste management systems. Great attention is being given to refurbishing existing buildings and introducing these features in addition to their being directly applicable at the design stage to new buildings.

There is a growing interest from company investors and operators about the environmental impact of their businesses. Corporate environmental management is defined as the identification, control and continual improvement of environmental impacts arising from business activities (McAllister, 2003). The main areas of concern are the use of energy and materials, generation of waste, pollution control, health effects outside and inside the buildings and application of transport policies within the company. BS 7750:1994 (the predecessor to ISO 14001) defined an environmental management system as the organizational structure, responsibilities, practices, procedures, processes and resources for implementing environmental management. ISO 14001:2015 is the UK industry standard for environmental management and specifies a means of setting up a system to organize this. Eco-Management and Audit System (EMAS) complements ISO 14001. Briefly, companies need to identify and evaluate significant impacts, set targets for reducing them and implement procedures to achieve the set targets.

Assessing sustainable design

How can green buildings be assessed? There are a number of systems being developed in various countries. The real difficulty is data availability; there are also not enough benchmarks against which to judge whether a particular building is successful in achieving a good green building rating. Life-cycle assessment (LCA) methods attempt to assess the environmental performance of systems and constructions and also the elements of which they comprise. The difficulty here is that the performance of an element in its own right often changes when it is linked to a system as a whole. Understanding system behaviour is paramount. The basic methodology for LCA involves defining the goal and scope, inventory analysis, impact assessment and interpretation as set out in BS EN ISO 14040:1997 and ISO 14044:2006. Another difficulty is tracking all the flows in and out of a particular system, but in general the objective function is to minimize life-cycle flows from and to nature (Trusty and Horst, 2003). An example of this is shown in Table 6.2.

The results given are for the complete building life-cycle including maintenance and replacement of materials, demolition, and transport to landfill of materials not likely to be reused or recycled. Operating energy is excluded. This analysis could be carried out for alternative designs and a selection made of the one that provides the best performance. Considerably more experience is needed before we can confidently score and compare buildings. The various phases of LCA depend on defining the goal and scope of any particular study followed by an inventory analysis and then an assessment of the environmental impact. There then has to be some interpretation of meaning in relation to the applications being analysed. The ultimate objective is to have systems which are highly durable and reusable. Other relevant standards are BS ISO 15686-1:2011 Buildings and Constructed Assets – Service Life Planning and ISO 15686-5:2008/2017 Buildings and Constructed Assets – Service Life Planning – Part 5: Life Cycle Costing; Parts 2, 3 and 4 deal with Service Life Prediction, Performance Audits and Data Requirements, respectively.

Sustainable design considers the long-term effects on the building, its users and its environment and the preservation of our natural resources for future generations. A number of measures have been developed to try to evaluate how successful any development is with regard to balancing energy, environment and

Table 6.2 Summary of total life-cycle embodied effects by major building components for an eighteen-storey office building using the LCA method of ATHENA (Trusty and Horst, 2003).

Building components	Embodied energy (GJ)	Solid wastes (tonnes)	Air pollution (index)	Water pollution (index)	Global warming potential (equivalent CO_2 (tonnes)	Weighted resource use (tonnes)
Structure	52,432	3,273	859	147.0	13,701	34,098
Cladding	17,187	281	649.8	24.7	5,727	2,195
Roofing	3,435	145	64.8	5.8	701	1,408
Total	73,054	3,699	1,573.6	177.5	20,129	37,701
Per m$_2$	2.36	0.11	0.05	0.006	0.65	1.21

ecology, taking into account both the social and the technological aspects of projects. In the USA there is the Leadership in Energy and Environmental Design (LEED), which is a certification process developed to create an industrial standard. It covers five environmental qualities: sustainable siting; water efficiency; energy and atmosphere; materials and resources; and indoor environmental quality. There are also points awarded for process and innovation. Australia has a National Australian Building Environmental Rating System (NABERS), which takes a similar approach to LEED, and in the UK, BREEAM is constituted in terms of rating design strategies aimed at maintaining or improving biodiversity. Comparisons are described in a report prepared for CoreNet Global by Ove Arup & Partners Ltd: *International Sustainability Systems Comparison: Key International Sustainability Systems: Energy and Water Conservation Requirements* (2014).

In the UK and abroad the Building Research Establishment Environment Assessment Method (BREEAM) is widely used and has versions covering communities, new construction, in-use and refurbishment. BREEAM has a system of credits covering:

- Management
- Health and wellbeing
- Energy
- Transport
- Water
- Materials
- Waste
- Land use and ecology
- Pollution
- Innovation

In the case of building design one can, for example, aim for a certain amount of energy or water to be used and this can be converted into CO_2 emissions. The health risk and the impact of buildings on their local environment in terms of waste and pollution are other indicators. These techniques require a holistic view of design and construction to be taken, embracing the concept of design, alternative designs, installation and construction, commissioning, post-occupancy evaluation together with monitoring and auditing of the building in use, recycling or disposal.

The Housing Quality Indicator published by the UK Building Research Establishment in 2015 is a measurement and assessment tool for new or old housing schemes to evaluate quality. Location, design and performance are key features and these are associated with quality indicators covering:

- Location
- Site – visual input, open space, access routes
- Unit – size, layout, noise, light and services, access, energy, internet connectivity
- Performance in use

Rating schemes are evolving and continually being updated as our knowledge and experience database deepens. For example, as I write this in 2019 there is a draft document on BREEAM New Construction SD 5078 2018 available on which people may comment.

The Through Life Environmental Business Model (TLEBM) is a representation of sustainable issues and whole life performance of a building (Clements-Croome *et al.*, 2003; John *et al.*, 2002). The TLEBM is the process whereby the technological issues and economic issues of whole life performance about a building are considered. TLEBM goes further in addressing the sustainable issues arising out of the development, construction, operation and maintenance of the building in a pragmatic way. Within this framework, the sustainable issues of environment, social and economic are addressed. The TLEBM framework addresses the processes and sustainable issues using an integrated logistic analysis approach. There are three layers to this model. The first is the connectivity of the supply chain processes and the interrelated working conditions of the practitioners of the industry; the second addresses the sustainable aspect that embraces the economic, social and environmental concerns within each phase of the building life cycle; and the third is the value associated with the project on the minimization of the impact or risk assessment to these strands.

Edwards (2002) summarizes the aspirations of sustainable development by emphasizing the three Es (energy, environment and ecology) and the four Rs (reduce, reuse, recycle and recover). These should feature in any green policy for companies and building developers, and must embrace operational and embodied energy, waste, water, transport energy, and a respect for biodiversity. They represent principles for society as a whole as reflected in the circles of sustainability shown in Fig. 6.2.

Renewable energy

The International Energy Agency (IEA) Report (2015) *World Energy Outlook Scenario*, paints a picture of possibilities showing primary energy demand could trend upwards from about 14,000Mtoe in 2015 to 20,000Mtoe in 2030. Accompanying CO_2 emissions could rise from about 16GT per year to 48GT per year (1Mtoe = 11.63TWh).

As mentioned previously, in 2018 the International Renewable Energy Agency (IRENA) published a roadmap on global energy transformations. It states

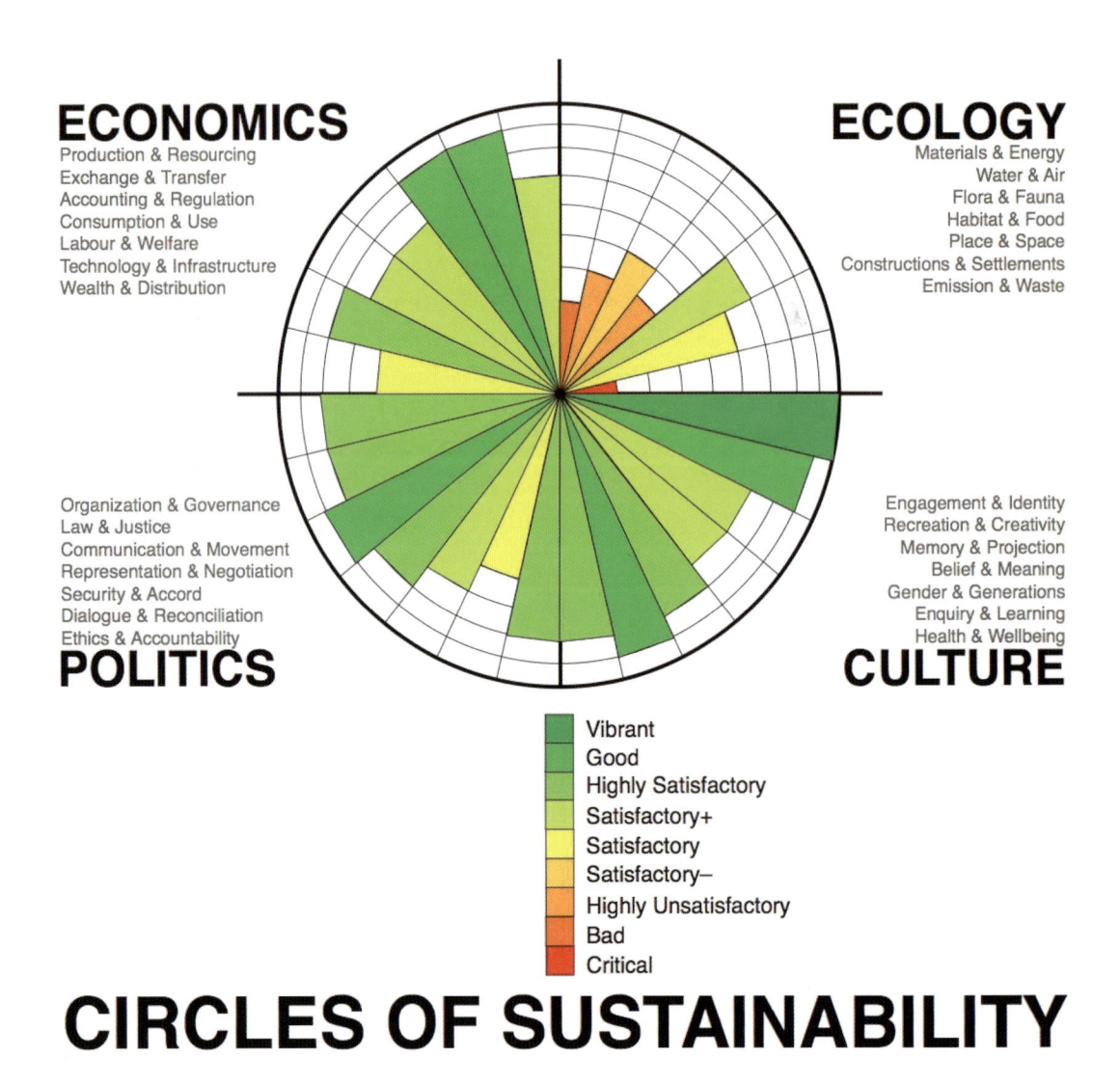

Fig. 6.2 Circles of sustainability (Edwards, 2002).

112 Sustainable architecture

Table 6.3 The change in global electricity mix from 2016 to 2050 as percentages.

	2016	2050
Coal	37	5 (CCS*)
Oil	4	–
Natural gas	23	5+5 (CCS*)
Nuclear	11	17
Solar PV	2	13
Concentrate solar power	–	4
Biofuels/waste	2	8
Hydro	16	18
Wind	4	19
Other	–	4

*Note: CCS refers to carbon capture sequestration.

that the renewable share in energy use in buildings will rise from 36 per cent to 77 per cent. The electrical share of these figures will be 31 per cent rising to 56 per cent. In transport electric vehicles are emerging but beyond 2040 hydrogen may become the major fuel.

The section specifically on buildings made the following conclusions in comparing the years 2015 and 2050:

- Biomass will increase from 4 to 7.6 EJ/year
- Solar will increase from 622 to 6,299 million m² collector area
- Geothermal will increase from 0.30 to 1.76 EJ/year
- Heat pumps expected to rise from 20 to 253 million units
- Energy related emissions expected to decrease from 2.8 to 0.8GT CO_2/year

This assumes that the worldwide building stock will rise from 144 to 269 million m_2. Windpower and hydro power are not referred to directly in this report.

It is a combination of using more renewables and increasing the efficiency of designing and operating energy, water and waste systems that can make the difference. Passive design is a fundamental step to ensure that the active services systems have low energy needs.

The sun provides 173,000TW of solar power every year; at present we use 12.6TW compared with 2.5TW for other renewables. The energy needed worldwide is predicted to be 27.6TW by 2050. Today all types of solar sources provide about 10 per cent of the energy worldwide but this will likely increase with advancements in technology. There are over fifty solar thermal plants providing over 50MW worldwide. The most recent ones are at Ouazazate in Morocco (360MW), Kathu Solar Park in Northern Cape South Africa (100 MW) and Delingha in China (50MW). In addition there are a growing number of solar photovoltaic power stations over 200MW, with some more recent ones being the Tengger Desert Solar Park in China (1,547MW), Rewa Ultra Mega Solar in India (750MW), Villenueva in Mexico (310MW), and Panoche Valley in US (240MW).

In *Nearly Zero Energy Building Refurbishment*,

Zhao and Zhang (2013) predict that solar photovoltaic energy will deliver about 5 per cent of global power in 2030 and 11 per cent by 2050. Sivaram (2018) predicts the global electricity mix from 2016 to 2050 as shown in Table 6.3.

We can see from this projection that renewables used worldwide grow from 24 per cent in 2016 to 66 per cent in 2050. Yet in spite of the enormous potential offered by renewables, progress has been slow. Low combustion efficiency and some political issues remain problems. There is a range of technologies available, from landfill gas to municipal waste combustion, sewage gas, agricultural residues and from specially grown willow and miscanthus grass which can be gasified into liquid biofuels.

Energy-efficient buildings

Passive environmental design is the essential ingredient of bioclimatic architecture: building form, mass of structure, orientation and insulation are important to minimize energy requirements and hence reduce the capacity of any active systems of ventilation, heating or air-conditioning. Here is a basic list of guidelines:

- Design the façade, including windows, to give suitable internal thermal, sound and daylighting conditions in all seasons[3].
- High levels of thermal insulation for the fabric; use values lower than those recommended in national building regulations.
- Natural ventilation should be used whenever possible. Connected spaces can help to promote air movement. Avoid excessive infiltration but remember a lack of fresh air can give rise to sick building syndrome. In houses natural infiltration needs to be a minimum of about 0.4 air changes per hour.
- Utilize daylight design to ensure there is plenty of natural light but to exclude excessive solar gain and glare.
- Use individual control measures which are effective. Central control will be necessary for emergency situations such as fire and security incidences.
- Use high-efficiency lighting and check latest developments in LED, circadian lighting and other possibilities.
- Use systems, equipment and appliances which are both effective and efficient and employ fault-finding diagnostic techniques[4, 5].
- Employ effective facilities management procedures, which includes helping building owners to save resources and save operating costs but also ensures the good health and wellbeing of the occupants.

Consider the use of the wide range of heat and cooling sources available, such as ground source heat pumps, microbial fuel cells, biomass boilers, condensing boilers and combined heat and power (CHP) systems. Waste can be fed to energy plants operating CHP systems with a potential to generate electricity and provide community heating. CHP is flexible in terms of size and fuel source.

Day and artificial lighting

Daylight is very important for people inside buildings from both physiological and psychological points of view. An overview of recent developments including daylight-guiding venetian blinds, mirror louvres, optical mirror elements, holographic optical elements, prismatic systems, transparent insulation, movable glass louvres and 'light sculptor' systems is given by Laar and Grimme (2002).

However, artificial lighting will be necessary. Lighting consumes 20 per cent of the electrical supply but recent technological advances in light-emitting diodes (LEDs) could reduce this to 5 per cent by 2030. There are many benefits of using LED lighting systems, especially as they have lower running costs than incandescent bulbs and they last around

100,000 hours with luminous efficiencies of about 160 lumens/W (Moram, 2011). LEDs can be tailored to boost vitamin D levels and reduce seasonal affective disorder. They can also boost serotonin levels.

Intelligent lighting systems can offer more control to the occupant in respect of settings to suit mood. Circadian lighting 'mimics' sunlight and its colour variations through the day to match with the serotonin and melatonin circadian rhythm of the body.

Solar energy and photovoltaics

Rawlings (1999) proposed the following rules of thumb shown in Table 6.4 for solar design:

As insulation levels of buildings have increased and energy needs lowered, the use of solar energy has become more attractive. There are three main types of photovoltaic (PV) systems, as shown in Table 6.5.

Gallium arsenide is sometimes used instead of silicon and is more efficient but more expensive. Emerging types of solar cells for photovoltaics include perovskite types made from organic compounds but they have a short life span; organic cells have low efficiencies; dye-sensitized ones have modest efficiencies. There is some research being carried out on kesterite photovoltaics. Solar cells using quantum dot technology are being developed which have high efficiencies; if successfully applied they could possibly lead to significant reductions in costs.

World floating solar panel systems grew a hundred-fold from 2014 to 2018, especially in the Far East. As well as freeing up scarce land, floating solar panels also stop the growth of algae, which can harm

Table 6.4 Rawlings (1999) rules for solar design.

Form	Create sun spaces, light ducts, light shelves
Orientation	Main glazing to face 30° either side of due south
	Reduce north glazing
	Minimize tree overshadowing
	Design atriums/roof lighting in accordance with the position of the sun in both summer and winter
Fabric	Fabric transmission losses may be reduced by improving insulation or by lower mean inside temperature

Table 6.5 Properties of common photovoltaic cell types (CIBSE 2000; Donev et al., 2018). (a) For amorphous silicon, lower values are for single junction (stabilized efficiencies) and higher values are for multiple junction types. (b) The usual colour is blue-black, but a range of other colours including bronze, magenta and light blue are available.

Property	Monocrystalline silicon	Polycrystalline silicon	Thin-film amorphous silicon
Cell efficiency (%)	13–17	12–15	5–10
Module efficiency (%)	12–15	11–14	4–7.5
Appearance	Blue-black, homogeneous	Blue, multi-faceted	Grey, brown or black, matt

fish stocks and slow the rate of evaporation from reservoirs. Critics worry they may harm marine ecosystems by blocking sunlight; another concern is their vulnerability to bad weather.

Solar hot water systems

These systems consist of a solar array of flat plate or vacuum tube collectors, which generate heat that is then drawn or pumped through to a conventional hot water boiler or coupled with a heat exchanger to give hot water whenever there is sunlight present.

Hot water generation varies throughout the year but with as little as 4m$_2$ of collector, sufficient hot water can be gained to sustain about 60 per cent of hot water service (HWS) requirements for the needs of a two-person household in the UK. It must also be noted that hot water use for hand washing, showers and baths stays at a steady rate throughout the year and does not peak in cold weather as had been originally thought.

A useful detailed practical design guide issued in the US is *Solar Water Heating* by Andy Walker (2016), part of the US Department of Energy Federal Energy Management Programme.

Fuel cells

Fuel cells work using an electrochemical process whereby hydrogen combines with oxygen from the air to generate DC electricity, water and heat. It is expected that eventually their production and consequent use will increase and will reduce the price to a more competitive level. Fuel cells can be used as a reliable form of on-site generation to replace the more conventional diesel generator or CHP unit. There is a body of opinion that believes fuel cells systems have the potential to revolutionize the way in which power is generated, and for building applications they also offer modularity, high efficiency across a wide range of low conditions, minimal environmental impact and opportunities for integration into co-generation systems.

They have key advantages in that they do not emit pollutants or noise and generally have low maintenance needs.

Proton exchange membrane fuel cells are most commonly described and are mainly used in transport but have been used for residential homes. Alkaline fuel cells require pure hydrogen and oxygen and are unlikely to be commercialized for buildings. Phosphoric acid fuel cells have some potential for small power generation systems; solid oxide fuel cells are best suited for large-scale power generators that could provide electricity for buildings, factories or towns; molten carbonate fuel cells are again more suitable for large generators but can be used for building applications. There are other types of fuel cells too such as direct methanol, solid polymer fuel cells and reversible fuel cells. A microbial fuel cell (MFC), or biological fuel cell, is a bio electrochemical system that drives an electric current by using bacteria and mimicking bacterial interactions found in nature and mainly used in waste water applications where their low power is suitable (*see* page 95).

A useful summary of the characteristics of fuel cells is given to help designers by Galliers (2003); Mott *et al.* (2003) together with Davis Langdon and Everest; CIBSE, CHP Group Data sheet 4 (2017).

Rainwater and greywater use

The average UK semi-detached house has a roof area of about 42m^2, which given the average UK rainfall of 2.3mm per day results in a potential recovery of 96 litres of rainwater per day (35m^3 per year).

Rainwater is used in non-potable applications and there always needs to be a backup. Dirt on roofs can be washed into a rainwater collection system by the first rain after a drought, so it is advisable to direct the first flush to drain to avoid normally high levels of contamination. Potable and rainwater must not be mixed and therefore piping systems need to be clearly identified.

Water consumption from hand basins, baths and showers makes up 28 per cent of the waste water used in the average dwelling and 35 per cent for WC flushing. Use of greywater can reduce mains water consumption by up to 35 per cent. Storage should be sized to meet peak demands in the mornings and evenings (250 litres for a typical house). Rainwater does require treatment using biocides, otherwise it begins to smell.

The order of preference for ease of reuse of water is first for shower and bath water use, followed by hand basins; washing machines; sinks and dishwashers.

Greywater cycling

It is estimated that such systems can reduce water consumption by up to 30 per cent. There are a number of biological systems on the market which collect greywater from the showers, baths, hand basins, washing machines and dishwashers. The water is filtered to remove particulate solids and delivered to a storage tank where it is sterilized. This cleaned greywater is then used to flush toilets, from where the waste then goes directly to the sewage system. If there is insufficient greywater available, then the greywater storage tank is topped up from the water supply or alternatively from rainwater collection tanks. Any excess greywater will drain directly into the sewer system or be used to water gardens (but not food or fruit areas), or to serve wetlands. The greywater system must be kept separate from the potable water supply.

Waste and recycling

In the UK, domestic waste amounts to about 31 million tonnes per year but construction site and demolition waste amounts to nearly 120 million tonnes per year; a similar amount of waste is generated by commerce and industry.

In waste management, the priorities should be given to reducing the amount of waste, then reusing it, followed by recovery and finally disposal. It is reckoned that about 65 per cent of domestic refuse is possible to be recycled. Composting schemes can remove recyclates and organic composts that have commercial value from the waste stream (Rawlings, 1999).

Municipal waste in Europe varies from about 250kg per head per year in Romania to nearly 800kg per head in Denmark according to Eurostat figures in 2016, which give an average of 483kg per person, 29 per cent of which is recycled. There is a trend to less landfill. The EU is looking to recycle 65 per cent by 2030.

In 2014 UK households generated about 482kg per head of municipal solid waste and recycled 45 per cent, but construction waste was over four times that of domestic waste. Recycling rates in Europe vary from 66 per cent in Germany to 42 per cent in France but is only 37 per cent in Hong Kong and 34 per cent in the US. These figures are adjusted in some cases for waste that is not strictly defined as municipal (World Economic Forum, Gray, 2017; Eurostat for European Commission, *see* ec.europa.eu).

Waste incineration plants emit fewer dioxins than coal- or gas-powered electricity generation plants but recycling and composting systems are preferred. However, they provide an alternative energy source to fossil fuels and their greenhouse emissions are less than for coal- or gas-fired power stations.

Overall recycling and energy from waste schemes are increasing and landfill is decreasing but there still are considerable variations over Europe and the wider world.

Pongrácz (2003), and Teo and Loosemore (2001) describe approaches to waste management and believe that more research is needed to guide decisions about the selection of the most appropriate systems in given situations.

The circular economy

> The essence of the circular economy lies in designing goods to facilitate disassembly and re-use, and structuring business models so manufacturers can reap rewards from collecting and refurbishing, remanufacturing, or redistributing products they make.
>
> Ellen MacArthur Foundation (2012)

Reuse and recycling keeps materials and resources in use, so retaining their value. Cheshire (2016) describes the principles involved and shows how we can design for adaptability, disassembly and reuse.

There are barriers to overcome. The industry is often not sure how recycling for example is affected by regulations. There are tendencies sometimes to 'over-engineer' and hence use more materials than we really need. The construction industry is conservative and risk-averse, and uses methods they know work in practice. Perceptions about cost are often found to be without any real basis[6].

Examples abound which show the circular economy can work well. The Empire State Building in New York was refurbished and had a short payback time of three to five years according to an article by Leslie Guevarra in *GreenBiz* (2011). A UN17 eco-village is being built in Copenhagen with recycled concrete, wood and glass for completion in 2023 (United Nations Environment: www.unenvironment.org).

Landscape

Cities are full of buildings which heat up in hot weather and this heat is released when it is cooler so making cities warmer; this is referred to as the heat island effect. Greenery can reduce the heat island effect in cities significantly. But consider also creating networks of interlinked open green spaces which integrate public, semi-public and private open space and so enhance recreation, wildlife, flora and education opportunities. Human beings have an innate sense of nature and it can have a very calming effect on people's lives. Buildings without landscaping are arid, barren and naked. It is a good idea to consider planting on surfaces like walls and roofs for insulation, amenity and wildlife value, with appropriate hardy species.

Plants in buildings can absorb carbon dioxide during daytime; some can absorb particular pollutants; they have a small effect on decreasing temperature and increasing humidity. People like plants because they are aesthetically pleasing visually and some are fragrant, but care needs to be given to their maintenance. Even more important, plant species have to be chosen carefully besides ensuring sufficient density of planting. Landscaping whether outside or inside a building is an art and a science.

The way ahead

> We are in unprecedented territory when it comes to climate change. How young people choose to tackle this problem will be a major factor that sets the world on its future path.
>
> Maria Ojala (2019)

Greta Thunberg, aged sixteen, addressed the COP24 meeting in Poland in December 2018 and spoke of the burden we are leaving to younger generations. If sustainability is to mean anything in practice, it has to be taught to children from an early age, preferably within a sustainable environment, hence schools and homes need to be refurbished or new ones built with all of the sustainability indicators in mind. The school and home buildings can be part of a sustainability learning experience.

If sustainability is to have any real deep meaning, it is essential that industrial and commercial organizations make it part of the ethos of a company with real commitment from the highest levels within the company. This belief has to percolate through various layers of the organization and on a global front, through nations, communities and then to and from the individual. Clearly, communication will be a very important aspect of this. Too often details are spoken about without any context or vice versa, so it is essential to achieve a balance between detail and context.

We need to understand the barriers to sustainable design. Traditionally location, quality, function and aesthetics are identified as the cardinal factors which constitute value. Cole (2000) describes a wider range of issues that are highlighted by various authors in a special issue of *Building Research and Information* entitled 'Cost and value in building green', pointing out that different stakeholders have different perceptions. For example, many developers are looking for a return on investment whereas quantity surveyors see sustainable buildings as being significantly more expensive from the outset without considering the added values they bring. It is important that the added value gained by being sustainable is properly accounted for and that mistaken perceptions are not allowed to ruin the design.

It is important to consider developing more effective feedback systems which can provide useful evidence for future designs and help to allay some of these perceptions. The design, construction and management teams need to reform to ensure that creative integration is allowed to take place and that there is a shared view and belief in the project from the outset, in addition to setting performance targets. This will mean, for example, that there will be a balanced view of the technical and social inputs necessary to make the project truly sustainable; this will necessitate much more systems thinking and analysis than has been customary.

Traditional terminology such as building services will take on a wider meaning as passive design becomes more common and efforts are made to use resources in a more efficient and effective manner, thus deriving buildings which are durable, flexible, adaptable and simple to operate. Cole (2000) makes the point that this will require redefining the fee structure for professionals. It is obvious to say that all of this requires industries to ensure that they have coordinated and reliable data sets by which we can increase our understanding and continually improve the processes of design and construction, as well as our building operation. Of course, communication is vital. This means having mutual respect between fellow professionals and an open mind to include expertise from backgrounds different to those with which the building industry is familiar. For the long term, it is important that these issues are reflected in education and training courses.

Governments have to think long-term. The research and development budgets across countries varies a lot. We do however need to ensure research is carried out on all the many aspects of sustainability covering the wide spectrum of environmental, social and economic issues. As just one example of some very innovative thinking, I recently read about research at the Salk Institute, which was aiming to design plants to store more CO_2 in their roots (Hook, 2019). Such nature-based solutions together with various technologies can make a very significant impact on ensuring sustainable futures. Some of these ideas are referred to in Chapters 3 and 5.

But governments also need to realize there is a skills gap which widens as more new technologies emerge. A project may have well-intended sustainable design content but putting this into practice with contractors who only know traditional approaches can prove difficult. Training programmes need to respond to change and be freely available to practitioners so they can continually update their skills.

Global social science, biophysical science and socioeconomic science indicators are listed by Hoornweg *et al.* (2018), which help planners to define sustainability design targets. Sustainability cost curves for infrastructure planning are described, showing how these can be derived from measuring and prioritizing targets such as the United Nations sustainable development goals.

Poverty eradication, changing and sustainable patterns of production and consumption and protecting and managing the natural resource base of economic and social development are overarching objectives of, and essential requirements for, sustainable development.

Commission for Sustainable Development (2002)

We have a collective responsibility to make this happen.

CASE STUDY: STONE-SHAPED 3D-PRINTED HOMES IN THE NETHERLANDS BY HOUBEN/VAN MIERLO ARCHITECTS (PROJECT MILESTONE)

Fig. 6.3 Stone-shaped 3D-printed homes in the Netherlands. Project Milestone will consist of five 3D-printed houses designed to look like large stones. (Image: Desislava Veleva; adapted from photo: Houben/Van Mierlo Architects)

CASE STUDIES: DESIGN WITH NATURE FOR PEOPLE BY NINA MARITZ ARCHITECTS

Fig. 6.4 A twenty-bed luxury lodge has emerged in an extremely harsh and desolately beautiful landscape. In addition to achieving almost zero environmental impact and a high level of guest comfort, potential full removal of the infrastructure at the end of the twenty-five-year concession period has been factored into the design. Shipwreck Lodge, Skeleton Coast National Park, Namibia. (Photo: Denzel Bezuidenhoudt)

Fig. 6.5 a and b   Habitat resource and development centre, Windhoek, Namibia.

Fig. 6.6 a–e   Regional study and resource centres for indigenous tribes – Gababis, Helao Nafidi and Oshakati, Namibia. (Photo: Christine Skowski)

Sustainable architecture   121

CASE STUDY: 30 ST MARY AXE, LONDON: THE GHERKIN

Fig. 6.7 The iconic Gherkin building at 30 St Mary Axe, London. There is a debate about how sustainable the Gherkin actually is, but since its opening in 2004 there have been many advancements in sustainable design thinking. Iconic buildings are not necessarily sustainable.
(Photo: Alejandro Carvajal)

122 Sustainable architecture

A holistic approach by Clare Bowman

> Regional government legislation is vital for both meeting the targets and generating changes in the construction industry worldwide to deliver viable sustainable development which contributes to protecting and enhancing the environment.
>
> Clare Bowman (2015)

Globally every country and continent follows different guidelines and therefore it is essential to provide holistic guidance which covers all aspects of sustainable design that we consider in our work.

The built environment has a direct impact on the natural environment, the economy and human health. We can actively improve the built environment by achieving comfort through passive design strategies and promoting a holistic approach to development with the aim of contributing to the three pillars of sustainability and the intended impact outcomes for:

- Social: quality of life, accessibility, community benefits, wellbeing and connectivity.
- Environmental: passive design, CO_2 reduction and protection of natural resources.
- Economic: viability, whole life value and benefit to local communities.

Methodology for sustainable architecture

To support a consistent approach to sustainable design, through applied research projects throughout the world over the last decade, 'The Green Plan' methodology has been developed to ensure that sustainability is considered throughout the design process. It is based on the RIBA *Green Overlay* by Bill Gething (2011), and *The RIBA Guide to Sustainability in Practice* developed in 2012 by Lynne O'Sullivan OBE (LSA Studio). Sustainability maps are available too from various sources such as the International Trade Centre which help businesses to map out their pathways for sustainable trade. These various guidance approaches aim to identify project-specific sustainable development targets.

Sustainability targets

The Green Plan diagram includes all aspects that we consider in the design and construction process. To measure the requirements there are three rings:

1. Outer ring: mandatory requirements in national and local planning policy.

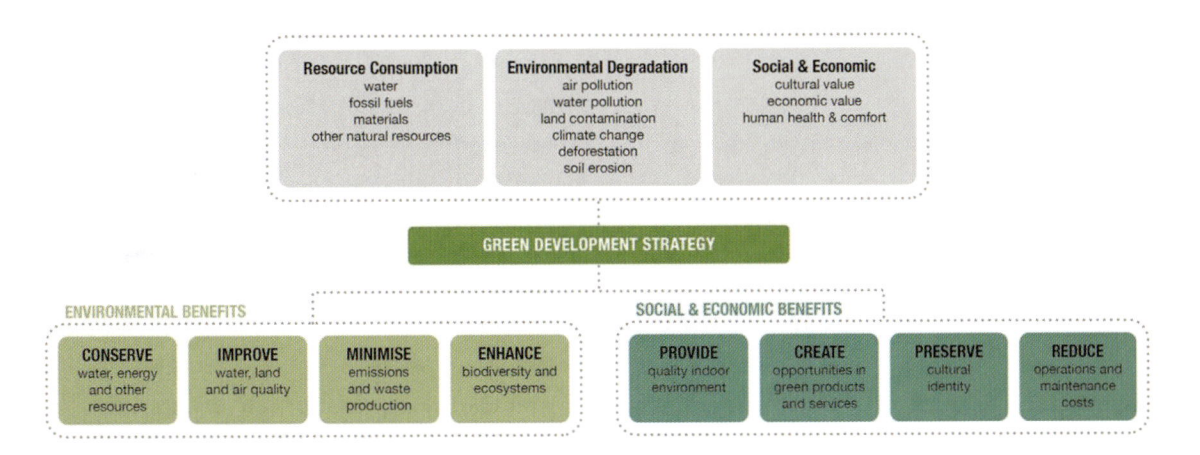

Fig. 6.8 Green Development Strategy 2015. (Clare Bowman, RCZM Sustainable Design + Research/Julia Francis, Graphic Design Broadway Malyan)

2. Middle ring: UK Building Regulation or International Code requirements.

3. Inner ring: all requirements to achieve BREEAM/LEED and WELL Accreditation.

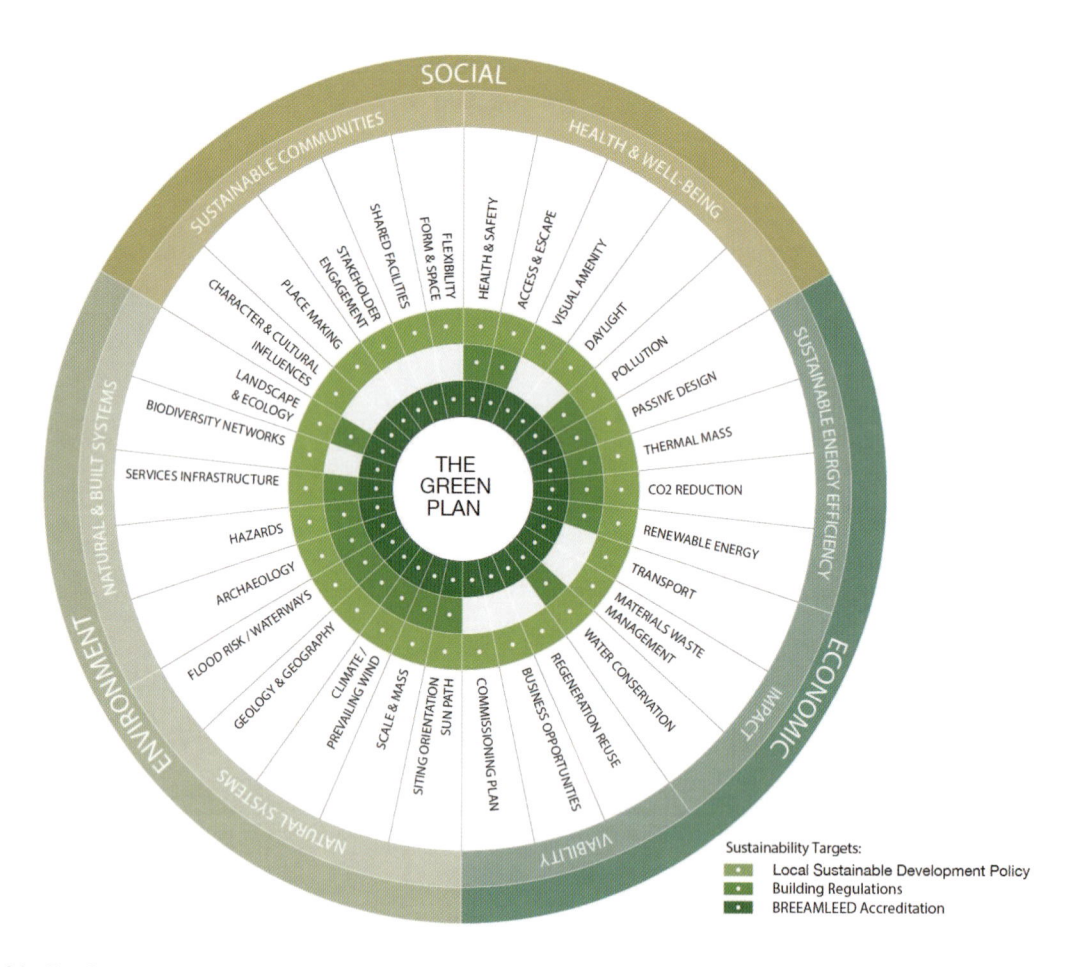

Fig. 6.9 The Green Plan 2015. (Clare Bowman, RCZM Sustainable Design + Research/Julia Francis, Graphic Design Broadway Malyan)

END NOTES

[1] Better engagement with the social side of sustainability offers a chance to integrate architectural perspectives and reconnect people, places, community, experiences and spatial quality into the concept and practice of sustainability.

Terri Peters (2016)

[2] Embodied energy is high for highly processed materials such as concrete and steel. There are ways of reducing this as developments like Novacem concrete have shown. The use of waste composites is another way being now commonly practised. The use of wood for timber constructions including high buildings is being developed.

Façades are emerging that can finely tune energy pathways through building envelopes. One way is to make building surfaces cooler. Photonics gives an opportunity to finely tune the reflection of solar radiation. Ultra-thin (1.8-micron) coatings of substances like sulphur dioxide with hafnium oxide on a silver sheet act like a mirror and reflect 97 per cent of solar radiation (*see* research of A. Raman at Stanford University). Bio-façades are also cooler.

124 Sustainable architecture

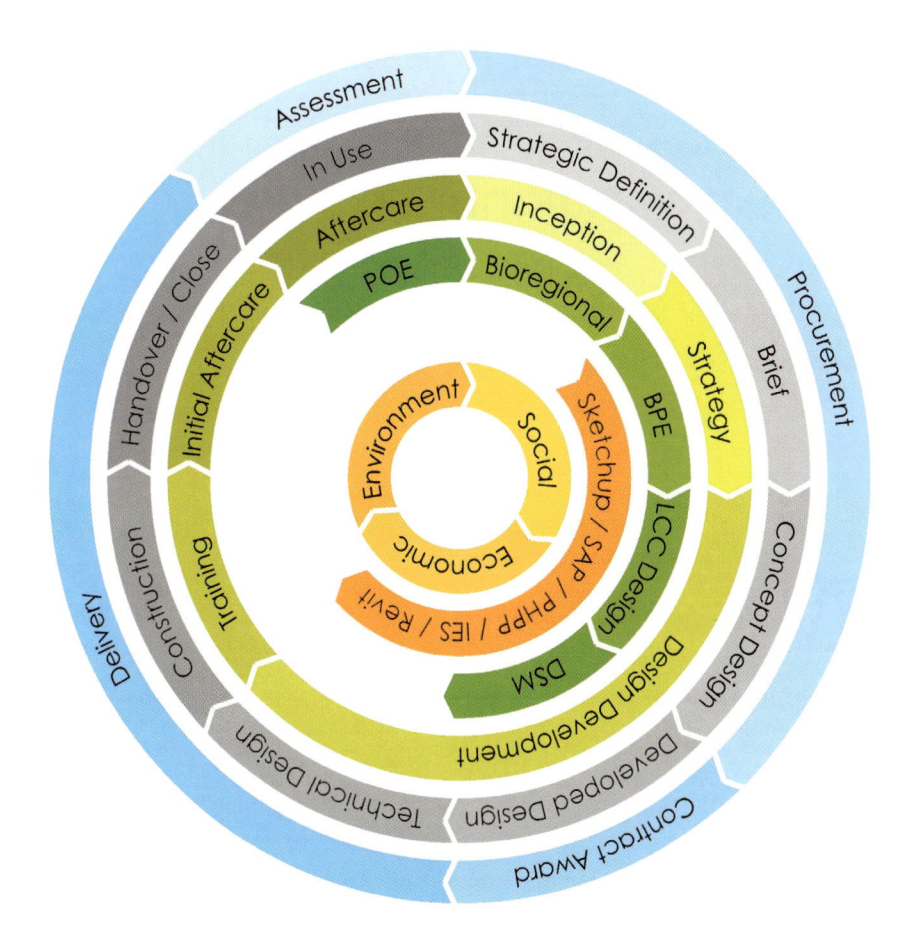

Fig. 6.10 Environmental Design and Management 2015. (Richard Bowman, RCZM Sustainable Design + Research)

[3] James Law talks of intangible materials or materials embedded with digital devices so the envelope can be not only an energy channel, but also one for communications (*see* page 146). The multi-functional façade is emerging. This also means we can monitor heat and moisture transmissions and take corrective actions.

[4] AI will make its impact at design, construction, commissioning and POE stages of buildings. Already we see glimpses in monitoring, data analysis for assessing building performance, predictive maintenance, off-site construction and POE. AI links with virtual reality, 3D printing and wearable sensors – all are making building performance and its connection with the occupants a more realistic possibility and materials as a host for devices will advance this process. Materials with 'extras' are happening.

[5] According to the UN, 50 per cent of world population will face water scarcity by 2030, by which time the global demand will have increased by about 50 per cent. About a third of the water supplied is lost through leakage. AI can monitor energy and water use, and detect losses and maintenance needs. This data can help to forecast future consumption patterns and trends besides curbing waste. (*See* 'The future of water' in Raconteur.com, 31 July 2019.)

[6] The cost of electricity from renewable resources is decreasing. *See* Appendix, Tables 5–8.

Sustainable architecture 125

Chapter Seven

Decision-making

> We cannot solve our problems with the same thinking we used when we created them.
>
> Einstein

> Simplicity is the ultimate sophistication.
>
> Leonardo da Vinci

WE ALL THINK BUT DO WE REALLY understand how we think? Consciousness has been and remains a much-debated issue. Treatises by the likes of David Chalmers, Steven Pinker, Susan Greenfield and Francis Crick are only some of a distinguished gallery of writers who have researched the true meaning of what is happening when we think. How do we come to decisions? It is an intricate interplay of intuition, experience and intellectual knowledge which leads us to make decisions.

The philosopher Sir Isaiah Berlin in 1953 quoted a line among the fragments of writings by the Greek poet Archilochus which says: 'The fox knows many things, but the hedgehog knows one big thing.' Scholars have offered differing opinions about the correct interpretation of these dark words, which may mean no more than that the fox, for all his cunning, is defeated by the hedgehog's one defence. This reminded me of a vivid experience I had in South Africa in 2013 when I witnessed a porcupine being chased by five lionesses, but its quills like the spines of the hedgehog kept them at bay so this one form of defence was lifesaving.

Since then there has been much debate on how this applies to different ways of thinking. The fox is a holist and the hedgehog is a detailer with tunnel vision. Of course we need both patterns of thinking and some people can think in breadth and in depth.

Goethe, Aristotle, Erasmus and Balzac are examples of foxes and Plato, Dante and Proust hedgehogs. The engineers Brunel, Telford, Missenard and the architect Frank Lloyd Wright would be fox-type thinkers. The distinguished heat transfer analysts like Fourier, Kollmar and Liese were hedgehog-type thinkers, all of whom worked in great detail. I was spurred on to consider this Greek thought by an article entitled 'My proposition? Infrastructure planning needs more foxes, fewer hedgehogs' by Neil Bennett (in the April 2014 issue of the *New Civil Engineer*) in which it was argued that we may need more foxes to deal with infrastructure planning. Certainly this is an important aspect to consider, as we do need to balance fox- and hedgehog-type thinkers in team building, whether in planning, design or management, and also in education courses at all levels. Foxes ensure we consider the interconnections between things but the hedgehog-type thinkers carry out the detailed analysis.

Ideas about how we think were also explored in the 25 January 2014 issue of the *Financial Times*. Here Antonia Macaro (psychotherapist) and Julian Baggini (philosopher) argued the case for interdisciplinary knowledge. Specialized disciplines and analysts rule the day but sustainability, for example, calls for holistic vision and synthesists to be an intrinsic part of the story too. Even universities with their specialized subject structures are not immune from the lopsided view that in-depth analysis is the main thing, but what use is this if the interconnections with other sectors are ignored? In the words of Macaro and Baggini:

> ... glad that some people have a narrow focus and so spot the detail generalists miss. But there

should be more space for those who attempt to join the dots. We need both close-ups and landscapes.

Macaro and Baggini (2014)

Perhaps in design and management we should give more thought to how we think things out rather than assume it just happens. This is related to the gender debate as recent research concludes that the brains of women and men are wired differently but some deny this. However, research by Ragini Verma and his team at the University of Pennsylvania found that men's brains appear to be configured to co-ordinate perception and action whereas women's are more towards integrating heart and mind thought processes, thus linking analytical and intuitive reasoning. Both of these virtues are vitally important. Let us work towards understanding these differences and deploy them to advantage in professional situations so overcome the gender gap and use the human potential of all effectively rather than argue defensively about gender differentiations.

Isaiah Berlin (*Times Higher Education*, 2014) comments on the virtues that a leader should have. He believed that the qualities that leaders or heads of organizations should have are justice, kindness, imagination and intellectual power. This reminded me of the popular book *The Fifth Dimension* by Peter Senge, published in 1990, in which the author proposes that we have to learn to master our discipline and rid ourselves of rigid, closed perceptions of the world. We can do these things individually but then we have to share our visions and learn with others. Our knowledge develops individually by reflection on experiences, organized learning and is punctuated by short periods of refreshing the brain by meditation, for example. This has been common practice in the Far East but is gradually being extended into Western professional business as companies realize that the mental health and wellbeing of their staff is vital in driving forward their values, mission and vision.

We are now beginning to see mindfulness enter into the personnel development strategies within business organizations as a way of refreshing the mind and increasing the creative mind flow by concentration, clarity of thought and flexibility of mind to go with the flow. Mindfulness originates from the meditative practices in Buddhism but in practice it is more like increased awareness. Unlocking creative flow brings more individual fulfilment and of course this benefits organizations.

The Nobel Prize Laureate Daniel Kahneman describes two modes of thinking in his 2011 book *Thinking, Fast and Slow*. He discusses Systems 1, which is the quick intuitive decision-making, and Systems 2, the rational, cognitive long process of coming to decisions. The problem is then, how do we come to judgements? Many of our problems in the construction industry involve multifarious skills distributed among individuals in multidisciplinary teams. Decisions have to be taken which take into account practical issues concerning function, reliability, safety, convenience and various other performance measures without ignoring the human and socio-economic consequences.

The term 'wicked problems' was coined by Rittel in 1973 and refers to problems that resist solution – hence the use of the word 'wicked' – because of incomplete, contradictory and changing evidence. They are characterized by complexity because they contain uncertainties and conflicting conditions. Often technical quantitative issues are surrounded by what may seem fuzzy social qualitative issues. Solutions are often reached as in the construction industry by collaboration involving all the stakeholders and this has to involve looking at complementary points of view. Sometimes the team is reduced to sub-groups so each can give an authoritative opinion on particular facets of the problem. In the UK the fast train network HS2 or the planning for a third London airport runway are just two examples of more recent wicked problems. The work of Professor Valerie Brown and her team from Australian universities is summarized in her book *Tackling Wicked Problems* (2010).

Too often you hear a response to any sum of money as being expensive before any real value assessment has been made. For example, does being sustainable really cost more? The real question should surely be, can we afford not to be sustainable? Often quantities of money are stated by politicians and the media without any context, so are meaningless to the public in a population with an average salary in the UK of about £26,000 per year. A billion pounds may be large or small, depending on the context, but to most of us these sums are always enormous and beyond our imagination.

In London in 2017 the UK experienced a devastating fire that engulfed an apartment block called Grenfell Tower in which seventy-two people lost their lives. Since then there has been another fire at the Glasgow School of Art (June 2018), only four years after a previous fire there, and this was followed by a major fire at Notre-Dame in Paris in April 2019. Whatever codes and regulations there may be, they are not far-reaching enough.

The pain of the Grenfell tragedy lives on. How could this happen in this century? We have to question the way we do things. It is likely that there were fault lines at every stage of the decision-making chain. In her book *The Silo Effect* (2015), Gillian Tett discusses the causes of the 2011 fire in the Bronx area of New York in which three people died. A principal cause was found to be the 'silo effect', which happens when different departments and agencies do not communicate with each other. This paralyses the connectivity and flow of communication and information. Cost-cutting too will no doubt be evident as the causes of the Grenfell fire emerge. It is endemic in many cultures and acts like a tumour in our heads that paralyses any hint of long-term value assessment. Cost-cutting is often a vacuous exercise devoid of human needs and any sense of long-term value.

The effective measurement and dissemination of the impact of design on building users requires an evaluative shift away from measuring building performance towards measuring the outcomes experienced by people. Watson and Whitley (2017) propose using the social return on investment (SROI) method that measures and recognizes social value. The benefits of this are that organizations feel and function better simply because people are valued.

This comment made by Sir David Dalton (Chief Executive of Salford Royal NHS Foundation Trust) in 2018 strikes a chord:

> You maintain services which are responsive to local needs but you do it within an operating framework where people do cede their sovereignty into the group to determine what's in the best interest of all.
>
> Sir David Dalton, in Neville (2018)

This seems to recognize that there are constraints but acknowledges the need to share what you have with others for the social benefit of all – a message that applies to urban development, building design and even international matters. 'Give and take' is a principle that applies in all situations; generosity and kindness subjugate selfishness and greed. The importance of social value is at last being realized in practice.

Sorrows and joys in decision-making

Designing, constructing and managing buildings is a messy business and presents many challenges, but there are rewards too. It involves so many stakeholders who have been educated in different disciplines. The architect-engineer Vitruvius (c. 80–1 BC) believed one should be educated in the arts and humanities as well as architecture and engineering. Since that time specialization has taken place in our universities and also in the professional institutions that emerged during the nineteenth century in some countries. How different it is for an author, composer, artist or sculptor working alone: their outputs are from individual minds and not blighted by having to negotiate with lots of others with all kinds of attitudes to reconcile, although they have other problems to face in what are capricious market places.

How can people work together on buildings that can take years to build and are expected to last for several generations? The dangers include fragmentation due to different mindsets and cultures. The silo effect and short-termism have already been mentioned. Then there is the enormous amount of data needed from many sources to erect the knowledge base for each project. How do we ensure the data is reliable and up to date? As we have seen in Chapter 5, Building Information Modelling (BIM) and Blockchain are ways to ensure that objectives are realized whilst minimizing risks due to errors in information handling. Keeping abreast of rapid change in knowledge and innovation is another challenge.

Building Information Modelling (BIM) is a process involving the generation and management of digital representations of physical and functional characteristics of places. It supports stakeholders throughout the design build processes by creating, visualizing and managing digital information at all stages of design and construction. Building information models are files that can be extracted, exchanged or networked to support decision-making regarding a building or other built asset.

As mentioned in Chapter 5, Blockchain is a digital ledger technology used to store, authenticate, and audit information. It is the infrastructure behind a new way of managing information with the potential to improve human agency in economic markets significantly.

In order to set missions and visions we need an integrated team from the outset which involves designers, contractors and facilities managers. In addition there will be interventions by specialists, such as health and wellbeing professionals, manufacturers and others. Collaboration and cooperation[1] are vital but this is easier said than done. How do we ensure there is a good integrated team with effective leadership? Can selection be enriched by more innovative approaches to enrich face-to-face interviews?

On selecting personnel, Vivienne Ming (Foroohar, 2018) argues that deep neural networks can overcome corporate diversity issues. Her goal is to use AI and neuroscience to enrich skill sets with sets of values known to be appropriate as well as to discover new ones. We need to define the criteria for selection relevant to the job specification. These criteria can cover strategic and tactical issues. Leaders need to be good communicators and be able to see the big picture in the short and long terms as well as the qualities attributed by Isaiah Berlin already referred to: justice, kindness, imagination and intellectual power. Another job may be more specific and require detailed knowledge in a particular area. It is also useful to know if a person is introvert, extrovert or ambivert. In general successful people are resilient and have a growth mindset, social skills, emotional intelligence, creativity, and so on which can be indicators for selection. Ming creates algorithms that can search the web to find people with these characteristics for selection. But this approach has drawbacks, because beyond intellectual ability so often it is those indefinable traits that are part of one's personality which mark out those people who are successful from those who are not[2].

Of course well-proven methods of team building will continue to be used. Reputation and proven track records are hard to beat but as architecture and building changes a new range of professionals enter the field; issues like sustainability, new technologies, health and wellbeing become more prominent.

One of the disadvantages of the current age is that in spite of the digital technologies seemingly speeding things up there is increasing bureaucracy. David Graeber in his book *The Utopia of Rules* (2015) questions why we seem to enjoy devising endless rules and regulations, which can so often restrict creative thinking. Graeber writes persuasively about the dead zones of imagination. The mind and brain have finite energy so if we saturate them with piles of administrative tasks this will sap any energy left for creative thinking. Digitization enables people to communicate with family, friends and colleagues all over the world, which is marvellous, but the same method is used with the colleague in the next office space. Then the simplest of tasks, which used to take a decision between two or three people at most, now has to pass through several more layers, so lengthening the process and leading to what I call the 'digital slowdown'. This is happening in many different types of organizations. Virtual digital assistants are emerging (like Alexa, for example) and these may save the day.

Can we imagine different structures for organizations that ensure better, cleaner decision-making and enduring motivation for workers? Laloux in his book *Reinventing Organizations* (2014) describes the virtues of self-managing teams, quoting the Dutch *Buurtzog* (neighbourhood care) as an example reminiscent of the ideas proposed by Schumacher in his classic book *Small is Beautiful* in 1973. This is the opposite of centralization, with control from a centre with rules and administration channelled down to all sectors of the organization. Encouraging and maintaining human motivation is so important at all levels of an organization and people work better when they have some degree of ownership of their daily working lives.

Transdisciplinarity

> The relationships which form a complex system are more influential than any particular content of the system.
>
> Norbert Wiener (1954)

'Multidisciplinary' refers to different disciplines contributing knowledge separately to a project whereas 'interdisciplinary' extends this to a deeper collaboration with joint team-working. 'Transdisciplinary' goes beyond this and includes working across sectors. So in construction for example, ergonomists, health and wellbeing specialists, innovative technologists, occupational psychologists, social scientists or others working in different sectors can contribute their experience from their different fields of expertise by making interventions and so enrich the knowledge base, besides offering the latest reliable evidence in their speciality (Boger *et al.*, 2017). Across-sector brainstorming can spark ideas besides learning from real experience and this is best done with a group with a broad discipline base.

The transdisciplinary approach offers a way of dealing with wicked problems by collective thought (Rittel and Webber, 1973). A collective mind is one that harnesses multiple ways of understanding in thinking about the whole (Brown *et al.*, 2010, 2014). Seven aspects of understanding which the individual can make as a basis for collective thinking are suggested by Brown and Harris (2014) and Hocking *et al.*, (2016). These are:

- Internal questions:
  - Personal experience (introspective)
  - Meaning (reflective)
- External preconceived ideas and assumptions:
  - Measurements
  - Social
  - Ethical
  - Aesthetics (patterns)
  - Feeling

In a paper by Valerie Brown ('Utopian thinking and the collective mind: Beyond transdisciplinarity', 2015) she wrote:

> The future is frequently presented as a forced choice between human sustainability and human extinction, utopia or dystopia. ...[There is a] different option: to develop the full capacity of the human mind to remain open to all possibilities, guided by utopian thinking. An inquiry into the creative potential of the human mind finds that collective thinking from a collective mind goes beyond transdisciplinarity as currently constructed. In collective thinking, knowledge boundaries are reframed as dynamic inter-relationships, and due weight is given to each of personal, physical, social, ethical, aesthetic, sympathetic and reflec-

tive ways of knowing. In applying the collective mind in these times of transformational change, there is hope for innovative solutions to seemingly intractable, aptly labelled wicked problems.

Collective thought is a way that decision-making can be effective and influence transformational change without losing the detail of individual inputs, whilst respecting that the behaviour of the whole is greater than the sum of the parts[3].

Engagement

Many people are not engaged in their work. Elliott and Corey (2018) describe evidence showing that the percentage of staff who are highly engaged may be as low as 24 per cent. They propose the Engagement Bridge, which is a ten-part model (see Fig. 7.2). Many elements of it echo the Maslow hierarchy of needs expressed in various ways via connecting elements like purpose, communication, recognition, leadership (see Fig. 7.1), and management, but the elements underpinning these which provide stability are wellbeing, workspace, benefits and pay. This demonstrates the significance of the work on workplace described in Chapter 4 as a bedrock for organizations.

Emerging scenarios

So what are the things that can make the construction industry more resilient and less risk-averse? Changes in society and developments in technology will determine the future. We must learn from the past but companies need to keep abreast of the continual developments that are occurring, not just in terms of new innovations, but with people's expectations as well.

The Fourth Industrial Revolution is with us and the technologies described in Chapter 5 are worth repeating but adapted to include health and wellbeing here. Some of them are already having an impact on our industry and hence our decision-making. They include:

- Robotics
- Artificial intelligence
- Internet of Things
- Big data collection and analysis
- 3D and 4D printing
- Smart materials and nano-technology
- Biomimetic architecture
- Big data management and analysis via BIM and Blockchain
- Prioritization of climate change and health and wellbeing issues in the workplace

Technology does not solve everything but it can enable some factors to be handled more easily. We will need to adapt to the new technologies and let them enable more efficient and effective design, construction and management to occur. Some examples include prefabrication using 3D printing, robotic maintenance and wearable technology. Predicting the future cannot be done with certainty, as futurologists like Ray Kurzweil (2006) and Michio Kaku (2011, 2014) acknowledge; but possibilities include:

- The invisible will become visible as we will see how effectively our mind is working in terms of focus and concentration. The sensory environment (sounds or smell, for example) will be visualized.
- Our connection with nature will continue to be prioritized. Biomimetics and biophilia are emerging areas which show how nature can teach us lessons about optimizing resources as well as simply calming and inspiring our minds by its presence.
- Thought control computing will become normal, together with voice control.

Some of the endemic problems which require more open and creative thinking to overcome them are:

- The silo thinking culture

Ten things great leaders do

1. Own + live the company values
2. Communicate openly + early
3. Inspire people to reach higher
4. Own their mistakes
5. Recognise big wins, small wins + hard work
6. Trust people
7. Make the right decision not the popular decision
8. Add value to their teams, helping them to succeed
9. Have the courage to be naked and visible
10. Take care of people

Fig. 7.1   Ten things great leaders do. (Credit: Debra Corey)

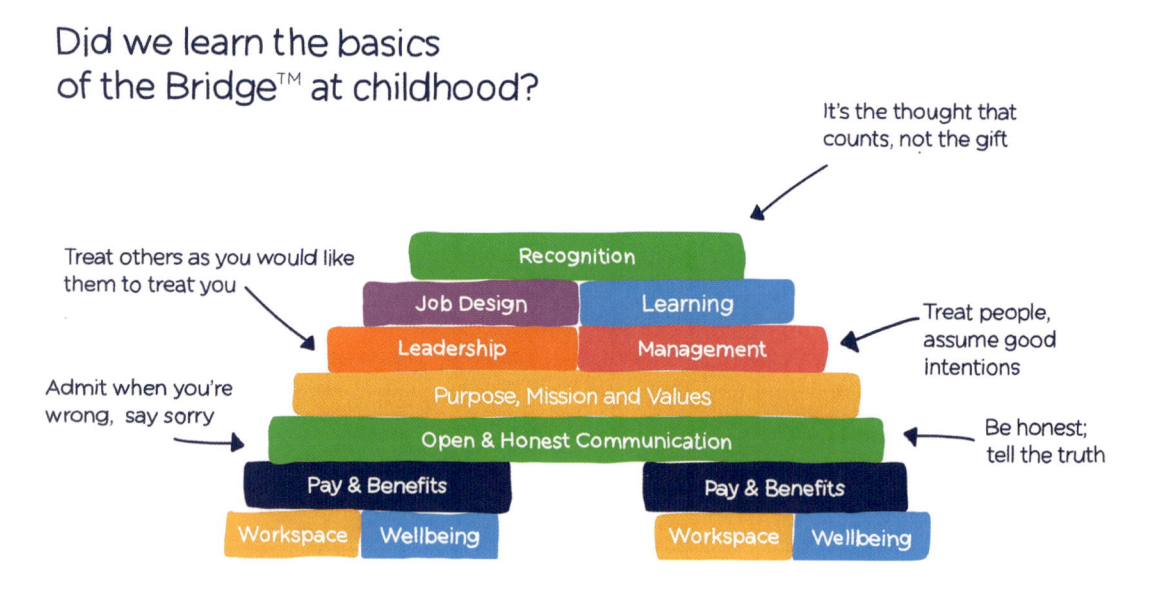

Did we learn the basics of the Bridge™ at childhood?

- It's the thought that counts, not the gift → Recognition
- Treat others as you would like them to treat you → Job Design / Leadership
- Treat people, assume good intentions → Learning / Management
- Admit when you're wrong, say sorry → Purpose, Mission and Values
- Be honest; tell the truth → Open & Honest Communication

Pay & Benefits | Workspace | Wellbeing   Pay & Benefits | Workspace | Wellbeing

Fig. 7.2   The Learning Bridge. (Credit: Debra Corey)

132   Decision-making

- Increasing bureaucracy
- Poor connectivity in the supply chain
- Short-termism
- Emphasis on low-cost solutions rather than value
- Gender imbalance
- Fragmented education system

A more humane architecture is emerging, which will balance function, human and social needs and the need for a more sustainable world. Can we imagine the design team taking a Hippocratic oath (like medics do) to put people's health and wellbeing first in parallel with envisioning and achieving sustainable solutions?

Above all we need a change of mindset and an integrated decision-making chain where transdisciplinary working overcomes the silo thinking rampant in our industry, together with developing a value approach rather than a capital cost one[4]. The construction industry is currently too short-term minded. Sustainability, health and wellbeing are long-term not short-term aims. Mariana Mazzucato in her book *The Value of Everything* (2018) argues strongly for a value-based economy and that equally applies to procuring, planning, designing and managing our built assets.

Machines can deal with collecting and analysing big data but the human mind has imagination, creativity influenced by emotions, and experiences as well as the intellect. Will the mind become more creative as routine jobs are taken over by machines? Will sensors embedded in our bodies become common? Will we become cyborgs or remain as we are but complemented by digital robotic assistants? Reverse-engineering the brain may be the most important project in the universe, according to Ray Kurzweil (*How to Create a Mind*, 2012), and the neuroscientists may be discovering the answers as to how our minds may change and transform our future (Michio Kaku, *The Future of the Mind*, 2014).

> We need to create things that have a good purpose and serve humanity. In that way the aim for being productive takes a more humanized view of the world and becomes something that speaks a language to all.
> Michio Kaku (quoted in Sinchenko, 2018).

For now we have the means to simplify complex problems by using technology like the Internet of Things, BIM and Blockchain to manage big data in a reliable way and deal with the intersection points in laying out the complex geography of all the services that a building contains. We can measure more and learn from the feedback we obtain from the building, its atmosphere and the people. This helps to improve design and construction. However, we still have to think more creatively using a transdisciplinary approach in which the value of the building over the long term benefits all stakeholders – particularly the users. Such an approach also eliminates the silo effect and streamlines connectivity. As a result decision-making can become more reliable and consistent.

But beyond technology there are other issues that are essential for company success and should feature in the background of decision-making. Deloitte advocate five primary elements that drive work engagement; these five are expanded below ('What we have learned: Five elements drive engagement', *Deloitte Review* 16, 2015):

- Mission and purpose
- Meaningful work
- Hands-on management
- A positive, humanistic, diverse and flexible work environment (*see* Chapter 4)
- Growth opportunity
- Trust in leadership
- Training and support on the job
- Autonomy; clear and transparent goals

These considerations empower people and encourage them to do their best with pride for an organization. The reputation of a company grows and attracts talented people. People have aspirations and company culture can help them to achieve these.

Fig. 7.3 Innovators' skills. (Credit: Tanmay Vora)

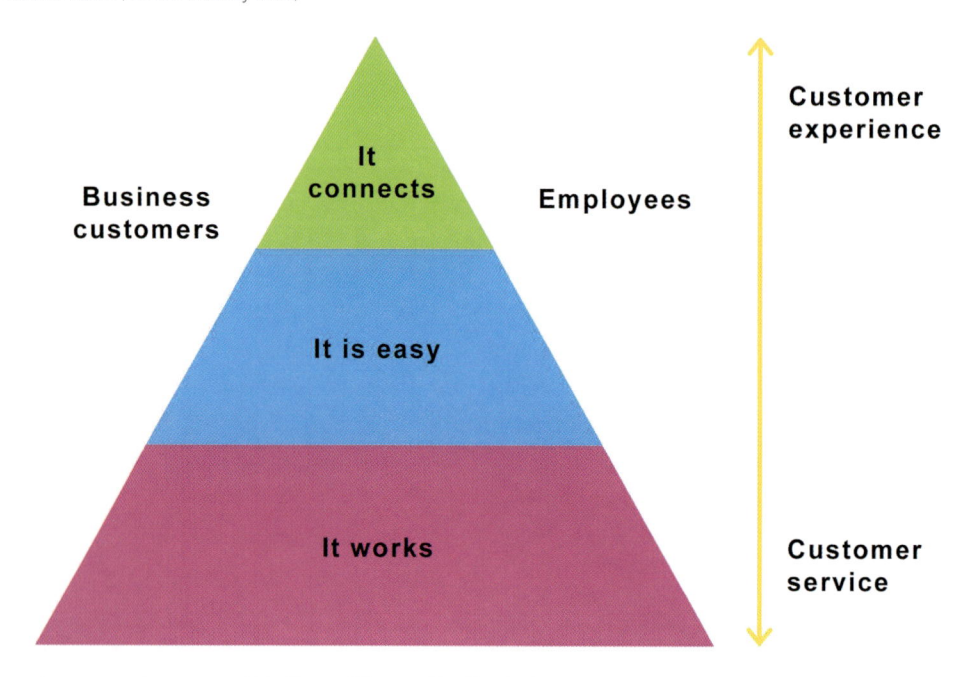

Fig. 7.4 The customer experience pyramid by Howard Morgan (RealService).

Fig. 7.5 The new customer hierarchy (adapted from Howard Morgan, RealService).

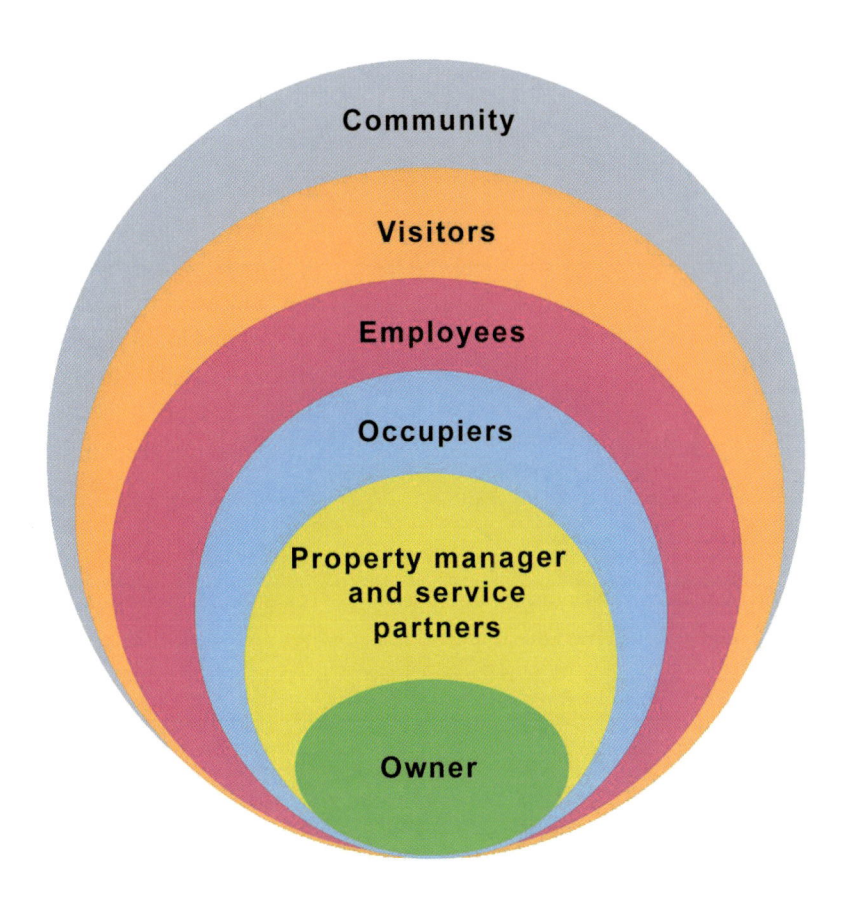

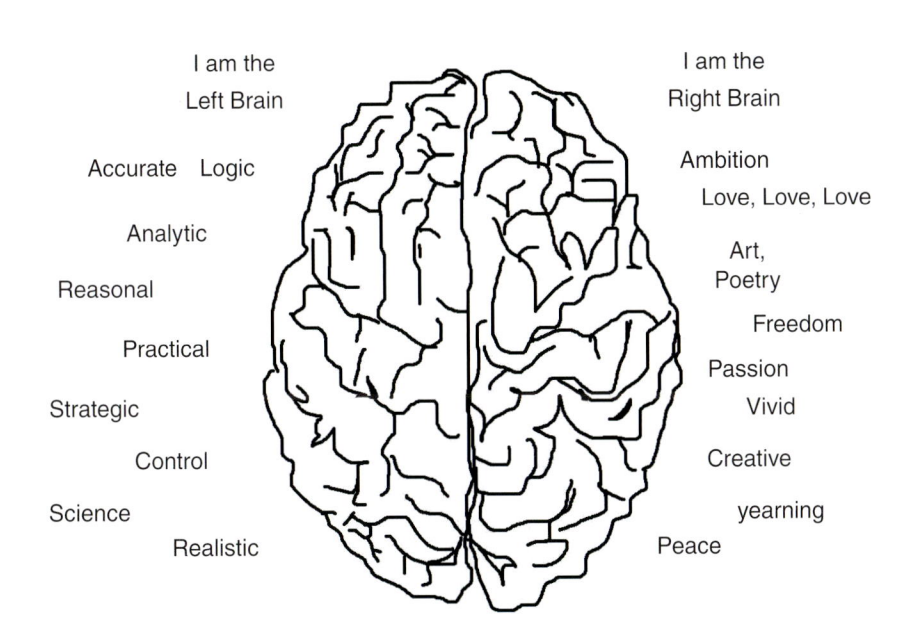

- Community
- Visitors
- Employees
- Occupiers
- Property manager and service partners
- Owner

I am the Left Brain

Accurate Logic
Analytic
Reasonal
Practical
Strategic
Control
Science
Realistic

I am the Right Brain

Ambition
Love, Love, Love
Art, Poetry
Freedom
Passion
Vivid
Creative
yearning
Peace

Fig. 7.6 Emotions Matter (credit: Howard Morgan Real Service, adapted by Desislava Veleva). 95 per cent of our purchase decision-making takes place in the subconscious mind (Professor Gerald Zaltman at Harvard Business School).

Decision-making 135

Figs. 7.3–7.6 highlight the importance of innovator skills, customer service and understanding the brain as part of decision-making.

END NOTES

[1] The important 5 Cs for collaboration and innovation:

- Creativity
- Critical thinking
- Communication with clarity
- Cooperation
- Collaboration

[2] Decision-making is hardly ever taught because we assume it just happens, but various search methodologies and algorithms that filter data can help to produce the most desirable solution for the most challenging problems. Alessio Ishizaka, Professor of Decision Analysis at Portsmouth University, has developed software which can aid decision-making (*Business Talk* 2019/20 (1), Faculty of Business and Law at University of Portsmouth).

The datasets collected are not just about measuring quantitative factors (like consumptions of energy and water, or levels of temperature, air quality or noise, for exxample); they also help us to gain deeper insights into and understanding of patterns of human behaviour. Data analytics make sense of high volumes of data by demonstrating trends and patterns: so-called 'deep learning'. New and evolving sense technologies, such as eye tracking and brain scans, delve deeper into our subconscious minds and let us explore human behaviour, but it is the human mind, not AI, that interprets and applies the insight which leads to foresight. (*See* 'Insight economy' in Raconteur, *The Times*, July 29, 2019)

[3] For good decision-making we need a diversity of cognitive minds to deal with problems. This allows for conflicting mindsets to converge with confidence towards a preferred solution. This is the essence of Matthew Syed's thinking described in his 2019 book *Rebel Ideas: the Power of Diverse Thinking*.

[4] Return on investment (ROI) + Value of investment (VOI) = Return on value (ROV) (lower absenteeism, higher staff retention rates). For more on value and engagement, *see* Elliott and Corey (2018).

Chapter Eight

Gallery of case studies

ARUP

The King Abdullah Petroleum Studies and Research Center (Kapsarc), Riyadh, Saudi Arabia

Arup worked side by side with Zaha Hadid Architects to develop the buildings' form. The buildings have been designed to 'turn their back to the sun' to minimize solar gain, and are shaped to enclose shaded courtyards cooled by the prevailing desert winds. We also envisaged a self-supporting cellular structure, providing flexible spaces that can be adapted to the multi-functional uses within the buildings. The buildings are connected by an elegant 10,000m² canopy, which unifies the campus and provides shading to the people moving through the external spaces.

White Collar Factory, London

The White Collar Factory embraces industrial spaces that provide generous naturally-lit volumes enhanced with innovations in technology. The ambition was to anticipate as-yet unexpressed needs from tenants, rather than simply respond to established office design trends. This exploration led to five principles: high ceilings; a thermal-mass structure; simple passive façade; flexible floorplates and 'smart' servicing.

The striking façade, now synonymous with the White Collar Factory, incorporates a unitized curtain walling system, which is broken down into three key elements: opaque, fully glazed and glazed two metre-high inward-opening windows that are partially shaded by large perforated panels. The core cooling system contains chilled water pipes embedded in the concrete slab. This enhances the natural effect of the thermal mass to regulate internal temperatures and provide radiant cooling.

Fig. 8.1a–b   The King Abdullah Petroleum Studies and Research Center, Riyadh. (Photos: Hufton and Crow)

Fig. 8.2a–c   White Collar Factory, London. (Photos: Tim Soar)

Sagrade Familia, Barcelona

In 2014, with the basilica 70 per cent complete, the Sagrada Familia Foundation approached Arup to help with the structural design, particularly how to construct the remaining six towers, dedicated to the Four Evangelists, the Virgin Mary and Jesus Christ. The client was aware of the challenge that the 136m tower, dedicated to the Virgin Mary, would pose, as this would bear the weight of the crypt below. We suggested that the stone itself could act as the structure, producing a beautiful finish, whilst reducing the weight of the tower by a factor of two. This solution also reduced build cost and accelerated the construction programme. The resulting design used pre-stressed stone masonry panels as the primary structural element.

Through our work on the Sagrada Familia we have embraced a new generation of digital software to produce workable and elegant designs. This approach combines deep human knowledge of the structural variables in the Jesus Tower's 'nucleus' form and position with powerful algorithmic tools that can model hundreds of subtle variations of geometries for the design.

Design Museum, Kensington, London

Retaining and converting the 1960s Grade II listed building demanded a creative approach to a number of engineering challenges. One of these was to develop a solution to create a new two-storey basement beneath the building's distinctive copper-covered

Fig. 8.3a–b   Sagrada Familia, Barcelona, Spain. (© Construction Board of La Sagrada Familia)

hyperbolic paraboloid roof. The approach involved suspending the 1,500 tonne roof 20 metres above ground level by temporary works to enable the removal of the foundations, the internal structural frame to let the new basement to be excavated. Movements of the key supports had to be controlled to within 5mm to avoid damage to this historic roof.

The central hyperbolic paraboloid shell resembles a giant manta ray in full flight. The radiating rafters of the outer warped roof introduce a new dimension with the building appearing to come to life as people move around the upper exhibition space. Its elegant construction was realized using post-tensioned concrete. This same technology was used extensively in the modern interventions.

This astonishing roof showcases great engineering design from the past and forms an ideal backdrop for the Design Museum's exhibition space that will inspire and delight all those who visit.

Fig. 8.4a–b   The new Design Museum, London.(a) Exterior.. (Photo: Luke Hayes); (b) interior. (Photo: © Arup)

Gallery of case studies   139

Jaguar Land Rover Advanced Engine Facility, Wolverhampton, UK

Innovation, collaboration and the wellness of people at the facility is at the heart of its success. Blurring the boundaries between production and offices through visual transparency, clear movement and social spaces, breaks down the barriers of communication between people. North skylights provide daylit spaces throughout the complex. Unusually, glazing strips at ground level provide views to adjacent landscaped surroundings. These vistas provide the visual respite to support personal health, wellbeing and productivity.

As part of JLR's ambition for low-carbon manufacturing, the facility is one of the largest to achieve BREEAM Excellent. Sustainable features include natural ventilation, daylit office and production spaces, extensive grey water recycling and the largest rooftop photovoltaic array in the UK. 21,000 photovoltaic panels provide energy to power 30 per cent of the facility, equivalent to 1,600 homes.

Flexibility and resilient adaptability continue to be key drivers for manufacturing facilities. The large span steel roof, based on classic industrial forms, is spaced at 30m intervals and is arranged in a clear hierarchy to provide space for high level modularized services. This design incorporated within the sawtooth roof forms breaks down the massive scale to humanize the production space.

The Circular Building (Prototype)

We explored some of the challenges the industry faces when incorporating circular economy thinking, including the impact on design, procurement, construction, operation and deconstruction of the building. This prompted conversations between the designers, contractors and the wider supply chain around the ownership of assets and new business models. Taking a life cycle approach is critical to achieving true circularity.

In building this prototype, the multi-disciplinary team has learnt that there needs to be a significant step change in the design process, how components are assembled and the inherent value that we create over the life of the building if we are going to put the circular economy (discussed in Chapter 6) into practice.

Fig. 8.5a–b   Jaguar Land Rover Advanced Engine Facility, Wolverhampton. (Photo: Simon Kennedy)

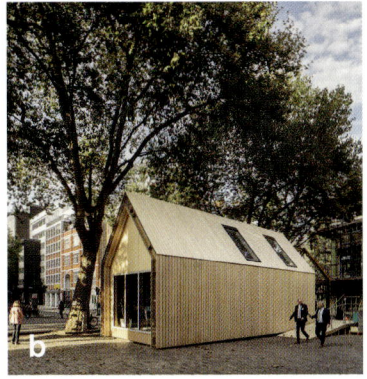

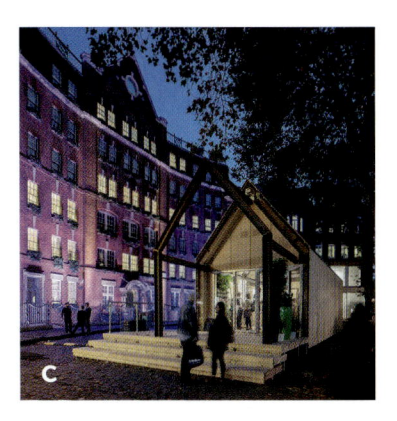

Fig. 8.6a–c   The Circular Building. (Photo: Simon Kennedy)

Believe in Better, London

This timber building has captured the imagination for a number of reasons, the main one being the client's leap of faith. As architect and engineer, Arup persuaded the client that Believe in Better would be super-fast to build, bringing efficiencies if designed and built in timber. More importantly, the brief focused on the people who would occupy and visit the building. The layout of Believe in Better has been designed to be intuitive to visitors, with all spaces visible from the stunning main stair.

The second floor houses collaborative office space which allows people to work in a freeform, flexible and social approach. The open plan design can be converted into a multifunctional events space. The top floor has a restaurant and roof terrace, which affords views across the Sky Campus and towards central London.

Fig. 8.7   Believe in Better Building, London. (Photo: Simon Kennedy)

Gallery of case studies

Television Centre, London

Arup, in collaboration with Allford Hall Monaghan Morris and Duggan Morris Architects, show their design for Television Centre is a showcase of integrated engineering on a herculean scale. Their work produces a design which sensitively unwraps the former broadcasting HQ, converting and expanding it to create a new neighbourhood for West London.

A truly mixed-use development, each building is distinctive. New buildings are designed for office space while others, such as the famous 'doughnut building', are being redeveloped to create residential accommodation. The design seeks to maintain the charm of the original building, namely the brick façade hosting the BBC Television Centre sign, while

Fig. 8.8a–b   Television Centre, London. (Photos: © Arup)

sympathetically integrating the new modern aesthetic. Complementing the mix of uses, on offer are a cinema, hotel and vibrant retail area.

Victoria & Albert Museum, Europe Galleries, 1600–1815, London

The objects on open display in these galleries include wooden furniture and large historical interiors, which are particularly sensitive to fluctuations in relative humidity. We agreed with the museum conservators the need to ensure an absolute limit on low relative humidity to prevent deterioration of the furniture in particular. This meant providing limited humidification to maintain humidity levels, even during week-long, exceptionally cold spells that occur occasionally during winter. This system limits the impact on energy use. This has also resulted in subtle changes to the way the systems are controlled, demonstrating the adaptability of this approach to environmental conditioning.

Achieving gallery spaces with stable conditions suitable for displaying artefacts that are sensitive to light, and fluctuations in humidity and temperature, was further complicated. Many of the galleries are south-facing. Control of direct light and solar gains was imperative in ensuring conditions are maintained and operational savings from this passive approach were also part of the overall

Fig. 8.9   Victoria and Albert Museum, Europe Galleries 1600–1815. (Photo: © ZMMA)

ambition. This sophisticated approach to controls is based upon a revisionist view of setting environmental design criteria, which has been championed by the museum's past and present directorate. The project, as an evolution of previous work at the V&A, is an important next step for both the museum, and the wider industry's movement towards reduced energy use and greater sustainability.

Broadgate Circle, London

Precision retrofitting to create a new functional layout into the existing structure was essential. To

Fig. 8.10a–b   Broadgate Circle. (Photo: Simon Kennedy)

Gallery of case studies   143

dence for the coordination of existing structure and services.

Facilitating a digital design process enabled the client and collaborators to engage and deliver this ambitious vision with increased confidence.

Beirut Terraces

The city of Beirut is often perceived as a focal point within the region, as a cultural and geographical link between Europe and the Middle East. The moderate climate of Beirut is undoubtedly one of the city's greatest assets; making outdoor living an integral part of its urban culture. For this residential tower, indoor and outdoor merge into each other in order for the generous terraces to become true living spaces.

achieve the necessary accuracy, Broadgate Circle was fully laser scanned creating a highly accurate digital 3D representation of the as-built condition. This was used as the basis of the digital models for design work for all disciplines. The pioneering adoption of this technology provided accuracy and confi-

The slabs of each floor protrude around the entire circumference by a minimum of 60cm, easing construction and maintenance of the extensive double-glazed façades. The density of floor plates balance the daily temperature cycles by virtue of their thermal mass, storing cold through the night and releasing this during the day.

Waste heat generated by the building will be reused. This innovation will reduce running costs and energy consumption. Rainwater and waste water from basins, sinks, baths and showers will be captured, treated and recycled for the flushing of toilets, thus preserving this precious resource. Achieving LEED TM Silver, such passive strategies make the building a truly sustainable place to live.

A 119m tall tower, with twenty-seven storeys, Beirut Terraces opened in 2017 and was the first building to be affected by a tightening of the local seismic regulations. Our specialists helped formulate the strategies to adhere to these requirements. The use of voided slab technology, which utilizes long cantilevers and spans, is also a first. This has minimized the weight, and therefore reduces seismic loads.

Fig. 8.11   Beirut Terraces. (Photo: © Arup)

Herzog and de Meuron used five principles to define the structure and appearance of the project:

Layers and terraces, inside, outside, vegetation
Views
Privacy
Light
Identity

The variation in projecting or setting back the slabs generates terraces and overhangs, light and shadow, and places of shelter and exposure. Considered environmental engineering and imaginative use of vegetation enhance the quality of life within this magnificent building.

Algae Bio Active Façade, Hamburg – The Bio-Intelligent Quotient House (BIQ) opened 2013

The BIQ residential building is the first algae-powered building in the world. The sides of the building that face the sun have a second outer shell that is set into the façade itself. Within this shell there are 129 photobioreactive tanks, which are filled with water in which microalgae are cultivated. As a nutrient, CO_2 is added to the culture which converts the growing algae to biomass, enabling the building to supply its own energy. Microalgae use sunlight for photosynthesis and this involves the conversion of CO_2 to organic matter, hence this means CO_2 emissions are reduced via the building façades. This bioreactive façade has been referred to by Jan Wurm in the book *Cities Alive* by Arup as a solar leaf system. Another type of solar leaf system is described in Chapter 3.

Bosco Verticale, Milan

Luca Buzzoni, Arup
Services by Arup included:

Landscape architecture
Structural engineering
Sustainable buildings design
Tunnel design
Acoustic consulting
Advanced technology and research
Geotechnics
Seismic design
Vibration engineering
Wind engineering

Bosco Verticale are two residential towers within Milan's Porta Nuova area, one of the biggest urban redevelopment projects in Europe. The building is placed in Porta Nuova Isola, an area which was historically dedicated to light industrial and craft activities.

The project was set to create a new standard for sustainable housing to counteract Milan's increasing pollution threat. As a new model for urban regeneration, the design creates a biological habitat within a total area of 40,000m² and includes a total of 900 trees between 3m and 6m in height planted on the terraces up to the twenty-seventh floor, along with 5,000 shrubs and 11,000 floral plants. The vast amount of greenery on the building encourages the production of energy. The plants produce oxygen and

Fig. 8.12 Algae Façade, Hamburg, Germany. (Credit: Fondazione Eni Enrico Mattei, FEEM [www.feem.it]; Arup [www.arup.com/projects/solarleaf.aspx])

Fig. 8.13   Bosco Verticale, Milan, Italy. (Photo: © iStock/35007)

humidity and absorb CO_2 and dust particles, thus improving the surrounding environment.

Arup engineers delivered the structural and geotechnical design and provided consultancy services on acoustics, vibrations, ground-borne noise and tunneling. As the site lies above the M2 line of the Milan Metro system, Arup designed Bosco Verticale's structures incorporating advanced solutions that helped to mitigate the effects of the existing underground tunnels.

During the construction of the buildings the tunnels were monitored to control any possible unexpected effects and to verify that the real behaviour matched the numerical predictions.

Arup also provided advanced design solutions to counteract the effects of the two existing railway tunnels by means of a vibration base-isolation system for the main buildings. This solution also provides additional seismic protection.

JAMES LAW CYBERTECTURE

The Cybertecture Egg Office Building in Mumbai blends natural shape with innovative technology

Set in the Mumbai central business district, the Egg is a green commercial building designed as a sustainable green office with iconic architecture, parametrically designed shape to minimize solar gain and high efficiency floor plates with innovative column-less steel diagrid shell structure.

James Law writes in *Inhabitat* that cybertecture integrates technology, multimedia, intelligent sys-

Fig. 8.14a–c   Egg-shaped office building in Mumbai blends natural shape with innovative technology. (Credit: James Law Cybertecture)

146   Gallery of case studies

tems and user interactivity to create customizable living and working spaces that focus on experience. The Cybertecture Egg takes this principal working theme a step further with 'cybertecture health' – interactive features that monitor occupants' vital health statistics, like blood pressure and weight. In keeping with the focus on health and wellness, users can customize their views with real time virtual scenery.

The oblong office building incorporates passive solar design to decrease heat gain and lower energy loads. An elevated garden also moderates temperatures by using natural vegetation to assist with cooling the building envelope. The Cybertecture Egg will use solar photovoltaic panels and rooftop wind turbines to generate onsite electricity. Water conservation will be managed with a greywater recycling system that will harvest water for irrigation and landscaping.

Other examples of cybertecture are shown in Chapter 5, Fig. 5.5.

FOSTERS INTELLIGENT BUILDINGS

Masdar City – Nigel Young and Fosters and Partners

Masdar City in Abu Dhabi combines state-of-the-art technologies with the planning principles of traditional Arab settlements to create a desert community that aims to be carbon neutral and zero waste. The 640-hectare project is a key component of the Masdar Initiative, established by the government of Abu Dhabi to advance the development of renewable energy and clean-technology solutions for a life beyond oil. The city will become a centre for the advancement of new ideas for energy production, with the ambition of attracting the highest levels of expertise. Knowledge gained here has already aided the development of Abu Dhabi's 'Estidama' rating system for sustainable building.

A mixed-use, low-rise, high-density development, Masdar City includes the headquarters for the International Renewable Energy Agency and the recently completed Masdar Institute. Strategically located for Abu Dhabi's transport infrastructure, Masdar is linked to neighbouring communities and the international airport by existing road and rail routes. The city itself will be the first modern community in the world to operate without fossil-fuelled vehicles at street level. With a maximum distance of 200 metres to the nearest rapid transport links and amenities, the city is designed to encourage walking, while its shaded streets and courtyards offer an attractive pedestrian environment, sheltered from climatic extremes. The land surrounding the city will contain wind and photovoltaic farms, research fields and plantations, allowing the community to be entirely energy self-sufficient.

Fig. 8.15 Masdar City – Nigel Young and Fosters +Partners. (Credit: (a)-(p) Nigel Young Foster + Partners; (q) Roland Halbe)

The development is divided into two sectors, bridged by a linear park, and is being constructed in phases, beginning with the larger sector. The masterplan is designed to be highly flexible, to allow it to benefit from emergent technologies and to respond to lessons learnt during the implementation of the initial phases. Expansion has been anticipated from the outset, allowing for growth while avoiding the sprawl that besets so many cities. While Masdar's design represents a specific response to its location and climate, the underlying principles are applicable anywhere in the world. In that sense it offers a blueprint for the sustainable city of the future.

148 Gallery of case studies

Gallery of case studies 149

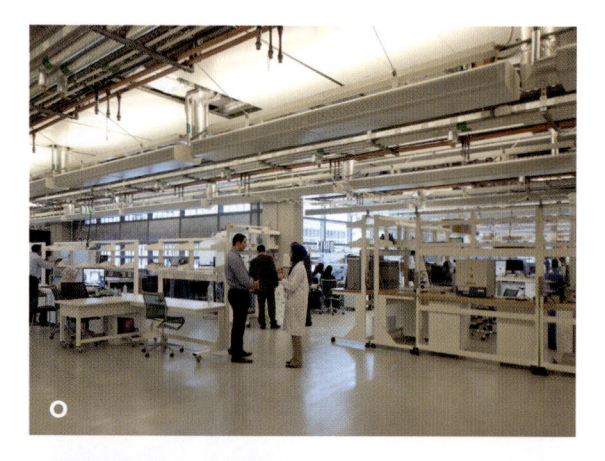

SKIDMORE, OWINGS AND MERRILL

Mina Hasman, SOM

Pearl River Tower in Guangzhou, China

With a focus on minimizing environmental impact and harvesting energy from the natural forces surrounding the building, the LEED Platinum, 309m-tall, Pearl River Tower embodies the idea of humankind existing in harmony with the environment.

The tower's sleek, aerodynamic form was developed through a careful understanding of solar and wind patterns around the site, minimizing energy consumption and optimizing renewable energy harvesting. Wind is drawn into openings at the mechanical floors, where turbines generate energy for the building, and a high-performance, double-skin envelope includes automated shading with integrated photovoltaic systems. Together these features support a 58 per cent energy usage reduction compared to similar buildings.

Pearl River Tower also uses daylight harvesting, a radiant ceiling system, and underfloor ventilation in combination with direct outdoor air systems (DOAS) to improve environmental comfort and promote the health of its occupants, who benefit from high walkability, transit connectivity, and direct park access in a dense urban district.

While many of these sustainable attributes were being incorporated individually into skyscrapers being built in the early 2000s, the Pearl River Tower was one of the first to use them collectively, setting a sustainability standard for the City of Guangzhou in China, and for tall buildings around the world.

Los Angeles Courthouse

The new United States Courthouse in Los Angeles is located on a prominent block in the city's downtown civic centre neighbourhood. The ten-storey, 633,000 sq ft building contains twenty-four courtrooms

Fig. 8.16a–c Pearl River Tower, Guangzhou. (Photos: (a) Tim Griffith; (b) Si-ye Zhang; (c) Tim Griffith)

and thirty-two judicial chambers. It houses the US District Court of the Central District of California, accommodates the US Marshals Service, and provides trial preparation space for the US Attorney's Office and Federal Public Defender.

From the beginning, sustainability was a driving factor in the courthouse design. The building achieved LEED Platinum certification and meets the General Services Administration's 2020 energy objective. Sustainability features include a distinct glass façade that mitigates heat gain, while taking advantage of natural light and views; abundant daylighting; rooftop photovoltaic array; water capture and recycle system; native, drought-tolerant landscaping; and high indoor air quality, including low-VOC finishes.

The well-being of building occupants and visitors was also an important part of the courthouse design. Court proceedings are often stressful, so the project includes features intended to provide a sense of calm and respite, such as reflective pools at the entrance, major artworks in public areas, and a courtyard that offers a contemplative space. Daylighting is used throughout the facility to both conserve energy and provide a high level of user comfort.

Gallery of case studies   151

Fig. 8.17a–c   Los Angeles Courthouse.
(Photos: (a) © Bruce Damonte; (b) © Benny Chan; (c) © David Lena)

The Kathleen Grimm School, New York

In September 2015, New York City's most sustainable school opened its doors. Designed to generate as much energy each year as it consumes, the Kathleen Grimm School for Leadership and Sustainability at Sandy Ground is the city's first net-zero-energy school, and one of the first of its kind in the United States. SOM worked with the NYC School Construction Authority to design the school as the city's first 'sustainability lab' – a place to test strategies that could be implemented throughout the city.

Mounted on the façade and roof are more than 2,000 photovoltaic panels that generate the energy required to power the school. The building design features dozens of energy reduction strategies, including solar thermal, geothermal, a high-performance enclosure, and demand control ventilation and lighting. Passive strategies, such as the building's shape and orientation on the site, reduce dependence on electric lighting. Skylights and clerestory windows fill the classrooms and corridors with daylight – an approach that not only saves energy, but also creates an uplifting learning environment for more than 400 elementary students and faculty.

SOM also created learning tools to help faculty and students participate in meeting the net-zero energy goal. Interactive dashboards that are tied to the building management system help students understand their impact – placing sustainability at the centre of the curriculum.

Fig. 8.18a–c The Kathleen Grimm Scool, Los Angeles. (Photo: James Ewing_OTTO)

TOBY BENZECRY, WORKPLACE FUTURES GROUP AND MODUS: DESIGN, CULTURE AND HAPPINESS IN THE WORKPLACE

The SLG Project: Studio 19, Cheltenham

The vision for Studio 19 was bold, ambitious and multi-faceted. With an unshakeable commitment to championing the location and supporting the prosperity of where SLG began, SLG invested in a 30,000 sq ft 'blank canvas' – a concrete shell in Cheltenham's Brewery Quarter. The design focused on delivering something bold, beautiful, adventurous and functional as well as aesthetically empowering, with a view to not only reflect SLG's brand and values but enhance them. Aimed at blending the creative with the cohesive, and the functional with the inspiring, engaging and unexpected features were incorporated, forming the backbone of the entire workspace. Some of the key features included an orange box meeting room, red shipping container staff shop, the lab, bleacher retractable seating, teapoint and social bar, hammock avenue and the freeway, which acts as a central spine for the building, connecting all of the design zones, with SLG branded skateboards that employees use daily.

Fig. 8.19a–f The SLG Project, Cheltenham: (a) bleacher seating and informal meeting space, (b) feature lighting and staircase, (c) soft seating breakout space, (d) Chilli Bean room and hammock avenue, (e) Orange Box meeting room, (f) reception and soft seating area. (Photos: Design and Build by Modus)

Gallery of case studies 153

The SLG project is notable for creating a varied space with strong brand reinforcement. There was a lot of coordinated social media activity around the opening to create a buzz with the staff and wider audience.

The Mitie Project

In 2018 Mitie moved into their new offices in the iconic Shard building in London. With this move, Mitie wanted to reposition the brand and create an energetic, agile environment that would showcase their 'Connected Workspace' Facilities Management offering. The key to success was the creation of a range of settings for focus, socializing, collaboration, inspiration and rest. Mitie regularly undertakes satisfaction surveys to capture the feedback of their diverse workforce and previous surveys were used to inform the design. In addition to 176 sit/stand desks and a range of bookable meeting rooms, the new office offers a wide range of settings, including townhall and demonstrations spaces, individual focus booths, productivity lab, team huddle and brainstorming areas, formal meeting spaces, communal

Fig. 8.20 The Mitie Project in the Shard, London: (a) breakout area, (b) communal breakout area, (c) high- and low-level touchdown, (d) individual focus booths, (e) informal meeting and teapoint, (f) regeneration pods. (Photos: Design and Build by Modus)

154 Gallery of case studies

breakout areas, soft breakout spaces, regeneration zones including meditation pods, informal meeting spaces, and touchdown points and teapoints.

The Mitie project implemented activity-based design with a very wide range of assets as the photos demonstrate, including things like relaxation pods referred to in Chapter 4, and the Work Lab, which studies people's self-assessed productivity against varying lighting and temperature conditions.

PLP ARCHITECTURE

The Edge Deloitte

Ron Bakker

When The Edge in Amsterdam was opened in 2015, it was the world's most sustainable office building, and 'possibly the smartest', according to Bloomberg. It was an ambitious and very innovative pilot project, designed in close collaboration between PLP Architecture, developer OVG and main tenant Deloitte, where smart building design and innovative technologies were combined to improve sustainability, workforce interaction, productivity and end-user experience. Most machines, devices and systems in the building are connected (often through IoT) and controlled within a single network. 28,000 sensors measure various aspects of the environmental conditions within the workspace and this data is fed back into the building management system. The workers

Fig 8.21a–c   The Edge Deloitte, Amsterdam.
(Photos: Ronald Tilleman)

are communicating with the building through an application on their smartphones, about their workspace requirements and their preferred space temperature and lighting conditions.

The results speak for themselves. Space is used optimally – over 3,000 workers share 1,000 workspaces. Facility management cost and energy use are much lower than in comparable contemporary office buildings and the project is carbon neutral. User satisfaction is high and absenteeism is down substantially. Somehow the excitement about the project has not waned. Besides anecdotal learnings about the benefits of combining smart technologies with environmental thinking and attention to the wellbeing of the inhabitants of the building, the process of analysis of the pool of data generated by the project is starting to provide deeper understanding.

HOK

Ng Teng Fong General Hospital, Jurong Health Services, Singapore

Joyce Chan Schoof, Sustainability Lead, UK Parliament

The 1.85 million sq ft Ng Teng Fong General Hospital is Singapore's first medical campus to combine continuing care from outpatient to post-acute care. The human-centric design is based on passive principles. Sustainable design strategies create a facility that functions like a vertical healing garden. Oriented to reduce solar gain and capture prevailing breezes, the unique floor arrangement allows for double the amount of natural ventilation. The project also includes solar thermal hot water heating and a large photovoltaic array. It has been rated Platinum under Singapore's Green Mark programme.

Fig. 8.22 Ng Teng Fong General Hospital. Biophilic design strategies provide a view out and fresh air for every patient. (Credit: Jurong Health Services, Singapore)

Based on the design team's client mandate to give 'every patient a window', the design brings plants, gardens and daylight into each patient's view. Controlled access to vegetation on terraces provides a therapeutic environment for healing.

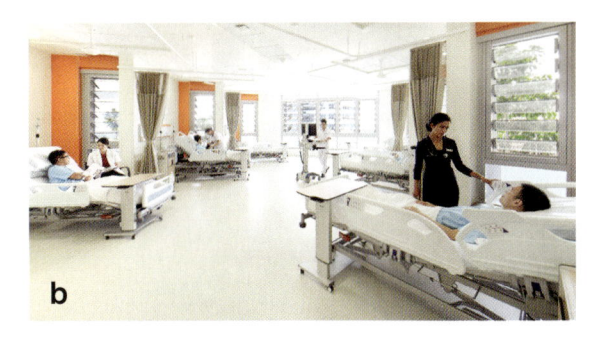

The International School of Kuala Lumpur, Malaysia (HOK London)

Working closely with ISKL's faculty, students and parents, HOK's team designed a campus that promotes sustainable living. From the clean air the students breathe to the natural light that illuminates their classrooms and the shaded outdoor spaces that connect them to nature, this new campus blends the indoors and outdoors to embody sustainable living.

Fig. 8.24 ISKL environmental diagram. (Credit: HOK London)

Gallery of case studies 157

Fig. 8 24   Tao Zhu Yin Yuan a sustainable residential double-helix twenty-one-storey tower in Taipei designed by Vincent Callebaut and his collaborators completed in 2017 referred to as the Agora project. (Photo: Tô Chông-ióng)

for its solar panels, recycled rainwater system and on-site composting. The anti-seismic structure and its landscaping are being built to absorb 130 tons of CO_2 a year.

The complex will be covered vertically as well as at ground level with 23,000 trees and shrubs. Natural lighting and ventilation, plus rooftop solar panels and rainwater harvesting, make it a low-energy building. The double helix was inspired by the DNA structure, the source of life and the symbol of harmony. Callebaut refers to himself as an archibiotect – combining architecture, biotechnologies and digital technologies. This is an example of a transdisciplinary approach, which is featured in Chapter 7.

FCB STUDIOS (FEILDEN CLEGG BRADLEY)

The Hive – Worcester University and Public Library

The name 'The Hive' was chosen to represent the purposeful activity, and sense of community which the development will help to create. It is also a reflection of the building's appearance, with its bold, distinctive golden 'honeycomb' cladding, which will mark it out as a physical as well as a cultural landmark for Worcester.

On a riverside site in Worcester city centre, this is a highly sustainable building and the first joint-use library in the UK, serving both the University of Worcester and the general public.

The project team developed an innovative way of utilizing parametric modelling to explore design ideas, enabling the manipulation of form within the boundaries of the structural and environmental constraints, resulting in a design that takes out 250 tonnes of steel from the roof and replaces it with laminated timber, thus saving an estimated two months of design work. This research won first prize at the International Bentley Awards for 'Innovation in Generative Design'.

ISKL is also the first school to register and achieve Malaysia's Green Building Index Platinum rating for sustainable design.

VINCENT CALLEBAUT ARCHITECTURES

Tao Zhu Yin Yuan (DNA Twisted Taipei Tower)

Vincent Callebaut[1] is the architect of this 93.2m-high tower. The project broke ground in 2013. The Paris-based firm, known for oddly-shaped, eco-friendly superstructures, is also designing a resort in the Philippines, with space-capsule-like rooms jutting into the ocean, and circular wooden residential towers surrounded by food-producing farms in New Delhi. Tao Zhu Yin Yuan has already earned a US Green Building Council LEED Gold accreditation

The building provides an integrated academic and public library, a county archive accommodating 2,600 historic documents, a local history centre and a local authority multi-agency service centre providing frontline services for local residents. The development also provides retail space and a high-quality public realm connecting key levels in the city centre.

The gold shingled form draws inspiration from both the historic kilns of the Royal Worcester works and the undulating ridgeline of the Malvern Hills. The structure incorporates solid laminated timber roof cones, which optimize daylighting and natural ventilation throughout the building. Water from the nearby River Severn is used to provide cooling.

The library reached its millionth issue shortly before its first birthday, a huge increase on the old library, and in the first five years of the library, 62,780 new members joined, 40,800 of whom were children or young people. The project has been awarded a BREEAM Outstanding rating.

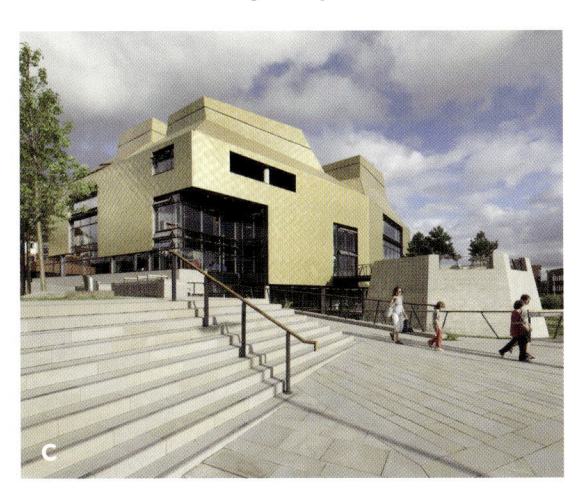

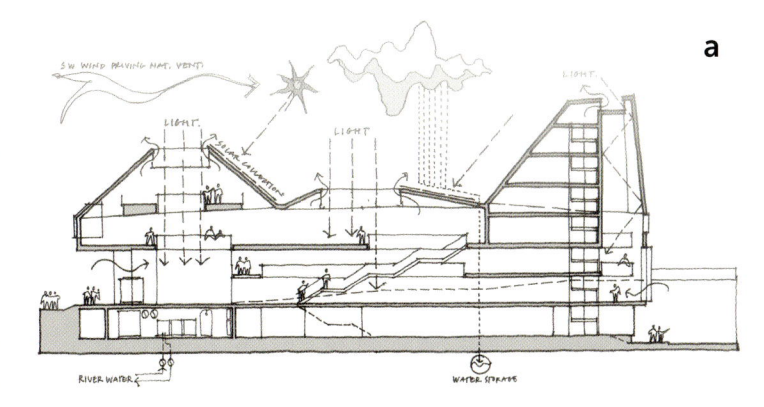

Fig. 8.25a–d   The Hive, Worcester, UK. (FCB Studios; photos: Hufton and Crow)

Gallery of case studies   159

PLP ARCHITECTURE

Bishopsgate, London

Karen Cook

The City of London is changing, placing more focus on public realm and making the City a cultural destination. 22 Bishopsgate, designed by PLP Architecture for AXA IM - Real Assets and Lipton Rogers Developments, the tallest tower at the heart of the City of London's financial district, advances the workplace and contributes to the City public realm.

On the skyline, its twenty-three glass facets make a calm foil to the surrounding articulated towers and to the historic fabric of the Bank of England Conservation Area. Its bright silvery white glass is the world's tallest closed cavity façade, or CCF, and in combination with clear floor heights greater than BCO standard it transmits approximately sixty per cent more daylight in comparison to a conventional double-glazed façade. The glass character responds to changing light conditions appearing alternately transparent, white or shimmery.

22 Bishopsgate has office space for 12,000 workers and visitors, a critical mass to support a wide spectrum of conveniences outside the office to support the individual. A Vertical Village of approximately 100,000 sq ft is dedicated to amenities and restaurants, from London's largest Bike Park to its highest free-to-access public Viewing Gallery. The Incubation Hub offers reduced rents to qualifying start-ups, the Fitness Hub makes a vertiginous workout with a glass climbing wall, and the Zen Zone a refuge of quiet restoration.

A new open-air passage at ground level unlocks pedestrian permeability, connecting Bank Interchange to St Mary Axe. A consolidated delivery strategy, whereby all parcels are delivered to a remote warehouse and reloaded onto hybrid electric vehicles, improves security, reduces air pollution, and reduces the number of vehicle trips to the building, increasing pedestrian and cycle safety. Wind mitigation for pedestrian comfort informed the design of architectural elements. An iterative process in collaboration with wind tunnel engineers and Formula 1 engineers resulted in cornices, canopies and vanes. Art and craft, incorporated into the external architectural design in the tradition of centuries-old City guilds, enrich the pedestrian experience.

Fig. 8.26a–b 22 Bishopsgate, London. (PLP Architecture Karen Cook, *et al.* Photo: Miller Hare)

CARLO RATTI ASSOCIATI (CRA) AND BJARKE INGELS GROUP (BIG)

New Tower for CapitaLand, Singapore

Adapted from Carlo Ratti Associati Newsletter, February 2018

The 280m-tall high-rise on 88 Market Street, jointly designed by CRA-Carlo Ratti Associati and BIG-Bjarke Ingels Group, is an oasis in the bustling Central Business District (CBD) of Singapore. The tower,

Fig. 8.27   Singapore, Church Street. (Image: BIG-Bjarke Ingels Group+VMW)

one of tallest in the city, blends urban life with tropical nature, redefining workplace and living standards for its users while adding a new landmark to the Singapore skyline.

The new 93,000m$_2$ green skyscraper is tech-integrated and includes the 'office of the future' as well as serviced residences and retail units. CRA and BIG were selected to design the fifty-one-storey highrise, which transforms the site of a former car park complex built in the 1980s following an international architectural competition hosted by Asia's leading real estate company CapitaLand.

The tower is set to make a distinctive mark on the Singapore skyline. Its exterior façade consists of vertical elements that are pulled apart to allow glimpses into the green oases blooming from the base, core and rooftop. The building shows an interplay of orthogonal lines interweaved with tropical vegetation.

The indoor space is characterized by an array of hi-tech solutions, shaping a series of fully responsive spaces for work or leisure. Sensors, Internet-of-Things (IoT) and artificial intelligence capabilities are scattered throughout the tower, which will enable the tenants to customize their experience of the

Fig. 8.28   Singapore, Green Spring Level 17. (Image: BIG-Bjarke Ingels Group)

Fig. 8.29   Singapore pedestrianization. (Image: BIG-Bjarke Ingels Group)

Gallery of case studies   161

building. The focus on achieving a truly responsive architecture advances CRA's decade-long research in this field, following up projects such as the award-winning renovation of the Agnelli Foundation headquarters in Italy.

The development is expected to be completed in 2021.

LANDSECURITIES

80–100 Victoria Street

Neal Pennell and Paneet Hoonjan

In December 2016, Landsec, the largest commercial property company in the UK, moved their office headquarters to 80–100 Victoria Street, London.

Relocation provided Landsec with the opportunity to adopt a new workplace strategy aimed at increasing communication and collaboration. All employees, approximately 470 people, could be accommodated upon a single floor plate, designed to promote activity-based working and improve staff health and wellbeing.

The project reduces negative impacts on the environment through responsible sourcing, minimizing embodied carbon intensity and reducing waste to record low levels. It demonstrates how an existing building could be adapted to meet the highest standards in health and wellbeing. The project was the first dual-certified workplace in the world to reach the level of BREEAM Outstanding and WELL Silver, setting a global benchmark for sustainable office space.

The drive to provide healthy office space was part of a wider health, wellbeing and productivity aspiration at Landsec, with BREEAM providing the framework to ensure positive levels of thermal, acoustic and environmental comfort.

Health and wellbeing

- Employee wellbeing: a juice bar and free healthy snacks; shower rooms to encourage cycling; first aid and multi-faith prayer rooms.

Fig. 8.30a–g LandSecurities (Landsec) building, 80 Victoria Street, London. (Photo: Paneet Hoonjan)

- Providing the right conditions for productivity: white-noise generators strategically placed throughout open-plan areas reduce background distractions and increase privacy levels without the need for physical walls; there are also quiet rooms and soundproof booths.
- Ensuring comfort: maximized access to natural light; artificial lighting is programmed to be neither too bright nor too dull; circadian lighting systems match the behaviour of natural light, changing to mimic the time of day.

Energy

Energy efficiency is a core component of the company sustainability framework – Landsec uses 100 per cent renewable electricity.

LED lighting and efficient building services were carefully selected to enhance performance and reduce energy demands.

Materials

Landsec set high standards for the sustainability of the materials used, and designers worked closely with the BREEAM team to adapt and innovate accredited products. The construction team also worked closely with the client to co-ordinate the works to reduce construction waste:

- 99.91 per cent of materials achieved BREEAM requirements. FSC (Forest Stewardship Council) Project Certification was also achieved with furniture also assessed, achieving 99 per cent FSC certified.
- The team persuaded suppliers to deliver materi-

als in reusable plastic crates and surplus materials were returned to their manufacturers, which reduced total construction waste to just 50 cubic metres.

Our workplace strategy was the key driver in the relocation project for our new HQ. From office culture and changing the way we work to providing an environment to promote collaboration and improve productivity. At the heart of this, our main focus was health and wellbeing and the happiness of the staff in the space - and for this to be achieved in the most sustainable way.
Neil Pennell – Head of Design, Innovation and Property Solutions

SAVILLS UK

Kings Place, London

Sylvain Thouzeau

Kings Place is located next to Regent's Canal and is a multi-tenanted building of exceptional quality and design, combining a seminal office building and blue chip occupiers with a restaurant, music performing spaces, theatre and various art facilities.

The building is therefore unique and means that its tenants do not just have a corporate identity. There is also a main central atrium with seating areas set over three floors which are normally open to the public. Savills UK have been managing Kings Place since 2012. Kings Place respects the urban context with its unique external characters: a triple wavy glass façade running parallel to York Way, a Jura limestone façade on the canal side, an elegant limestone rotunda forming the hinge between Regent's Canal and the Battlebridge Basin, and a waterside colonnade providing a spectacular space for external dining and relaxation. The building draws on a simple palette of quality materials: toughened glass, limestone, stainless steel and oak. The Sculpture Gallery provides a variety of viewing areas including a large shop-fronted area and various small viewing windows facing York Way, their ever-changing quality artworks enriching the public space in the building.

A seating area and long table are available on the ground floor for visitors, staff and the public. Offices for the two resident orchestras are just next to this public area on the north side. The Atrium Coffee Bar offers coffee and light snacks that can be eaten in or taken away. A double escalator give access to the heart of the arts, events and music within the building and notably to the entrance of the impressive sound-proofed auditorium and rehearsal halls.

The Rotunda Bar and Restaurant offers indoor and outdoor services all day and evening with views over

Fig. 8.31a–d Kings Place achieved the BREEAM outstanding award 2017 for property management. (Photo: Savills)

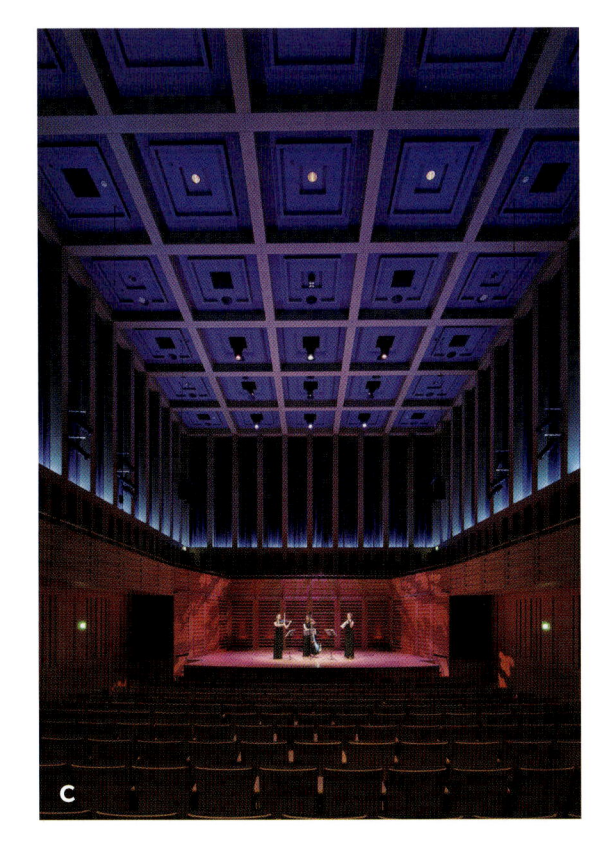

the canal and basin. The transition from the public space to the office space is through the calm, secure glass-walled main reception and pleasant waiting area. There are security barriers and the assistance of a security officer if required.

The upper floors provide large flexible office space with plenty of natural light and provide all-round views which are a benefit of this unique island site.

CETEC

The Rose Bowl Building, Leeds Beckett University

The Rose Bowl building at Leeds Beckett University (LBU) is an iconic working and teaching centre which has been designed as a building that is concerned with sustainability and the wellbeing of peo-

Fig. 8.32 The Rose Bowl building – main entrance.(Photo: Leeds Beckett; David Hemming; CETEC)

Table 8.1 IEQ parameters measured at the Rose Bowl.

Room	Air speed	Temp	RH	CO_2	CO	O_3 (2.5)	PM	PM (10)	TVOC	Forma	dB	lux
Classroom 513	pass	pass	pass	pass	pass	pass	pass	pass	pass	pass	pass	fail
Classroom 525	pass	pass	pass	fail	pass	pass	pass	pass	n/m	n/m	fail	fail
Office 404	pass	pass	pass	pass	pass	pass	pass	pass	n/m	n/m	pass	pass
Office 421	pass	fail	pass	pass	pass	pass	pass	pass	n/m	n/m	pass	pass
Classroom 320	pass	fail	pass	pass	pass	pass	pass	pass	n/m	n/m	pass	pass
Classroom 307	pass	fail	pass	pass	pass	pass	pass	pass	n/m	n/m	pass	fail
Lecture 241	pass	pass	pass	pass	pass	pass	pass	pass	fail	fail	pass	pass
Classroom 208	pass	fail	pass	pass	pass	pass	pass	pass	n/m	n/m	pass	pass
Office 148	pass	pass	pass	pass	pass	pass	pass	pass	fail	n/m	pass	pass
Canteen	pass	fail	pass	pass	pass	pass	fail	pass	n/m	n/m	pass	pass

Key: pass / fail / not measured

ple. Accordingly design themes focused on sustainability in relation to BREEAM, a UK certification tool. The Rose Bowl building achieved a BREEAM Excellent score, which is considered highly successful.

Building performance, indoor environment quality and occupant satisfaction & wellness

Mr Paul Ajiboye, Dr Vyt Garnys, Mr David Hemming

Following complaints from staff and students within the building the head of facilities management sought to quantify the indoor environmental experience. Discussions with CETEC identified a relevant approach to measuring indoor environment quality (IEQ). The tool used is the National Australian Built Environment Rating Scheme for the Indoor Environment (NABERS IE), which is an independent Australian Government-owned scheme.

The range of indoor environment quality parameters examined in the Rose Bowl is shown in Table 8.1. Detailed measurements in the building indicated that a number of IEQ parameters were failing. This could be linked to the low energy ventilation strategy implemented in the building.

Surveys of staff and pupils using The Rose Bowl showed that there was evidence to support the IEQ measurement findings. Thermal comfort and perceived ventilation problems existed. The overall results from the survey are shown below, which indicate that the Rose Bowl performed less well against the benchmark for all building.

As a result of the measurements and survey data the approach to ventilating some of the locations within the Rose Bowl was updated. This meant providing more ventilation and thus rowing back a little on energy savings. The re-aligned ventilation strategy was found to improve air quality in the places it had failed.

AECOM

Aldgate Tower, London

AECOM[2] seeks measurable connections between behaviour, space and business performance in a real working environment at their offices in the Aldgate Tower. It is essential to have a transdisciplinary team to include a range of occupational psychologists, human relations managers, business people, and building designers such as architects to achieve a value output which benefits the individual, the company and also deepens our understanding of how the building's environment affects its occupants.

The results showed that agile, flexible environments are good for work performance in terms of concentration and multi-tasking. Creativity and collaboration across disciplines increased and staff turnover rates dropped.

Fig. 8.33a–g   AECOM Offices in the Aldgate Tower, London. (Photo: Hufton and Crow)

168 Gallery of case studies

RAIN LIGHT STUDIO, LONDON

Joe and Rika Mansueto Library, University of Chicago, Interior by Yorgo Lykouria

This project demonstrates our integrated approach to architecture where the inside and outside correspond to fulfil the architectural intention. The traditional cloistered experience of the library is transformed by contemporary sensibilities of connectedness to the world. The elliptical glass dome envelops the reading space and crowns the underground book vault, which contains 3.5 million volumes of rare books in preservation-optimized conditions, accessed via a robotic retrieval system. The elliptical floor plate is perceived as a floating platform that folds into a continuous curving bench at the perimeter, before falling away to meet the dome. This edge condition forms the boundary to the acceptable head height limits without interrupting the feeling of spatial expanse.

The library tables are arranged in a boat-like fashion, reflecting the idea of moored objects grounding the experience within the sea of information. The substance and mass of the solid oak tables bring a feeling of permanence into this ethereal space surrounded by the temporality of the surroundings. The chairs consist of a simple 3D veneer shell and a laser-cut stainless steel base. The fixed lamps at the perimeter tables are also designed by Lykouria; slender stainless steel arcs housing LED lighting.

The opposite end of the ellipse contains the preservation and restoration facility. It is a combination of real world craft with digital archiving to preserve and protect knowledge for the future.

Fig. 8.34a–b The Joe and Rika Mansueto Library, University of Chicago. (Photos: Helmut Jahn and Yorgo Lykouria)

SUSTAINABLE COMMUNITY DEVELOPMENT, FINC ARCHITECTS

Limebrook Park Garden Suburb, Maldon, Essex

The Limebrook Park Garden Suburb comprises 1,000 new homes, a primary school, two nurseries, elderly person accommodation, retail space, a local centre, commercial buildings, allotments, sports pitches and extensive public open spaces. The proposal pro-

Fig. 8.35 Limebrook Park garden suburb development, aerial view. (Image: FINC Architects)

vides sustainable growth to South Maldon by natural extension of the settlement boundary, within walking distance of public transport and local facilities/amenities. Maldon suffers from a lack of public green spaces, and the proposal provides this in abundance, helping connect the site to the wider area. The proposals provide additional infrastructure, enabling future sustainable growth to take place.

It is based on UN sustainable development goals (*see* Chapter 6) to promote a healthier and happier lifestyle by encouraging the occupiers to walk or cycle when travelling locally. The intention is for the timber to be as locally sourced as possible to suit the programme. The existing brook is to be retained as a water feature, to provide a natural environment and habitat for ecology, and sustainable drainage has been introduced around the site, along with provisions for rainwater harvesting at design stage.

Homeless Pods – Architectural Design Addressing Social Sustainability

Current segregation and separation within communities requires the need for inclusive environments, iterated through inclusive design. Inclusive design is the design of an environment that can be accessed and used by all people, regardless of age, gender, social class and disability, creating a socially sustainable environment. Throughout the years it is apparent that the design of social space has been motivated by a series of rules, regulations and theories.

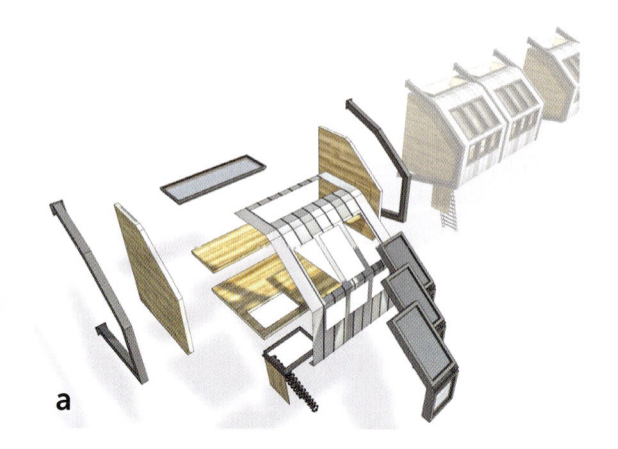

The homeless shelters are a response to these theories and rules and aim to provide a place of security for those sleeping rough. The beach hut shelter uses the familiar, and accepted, forms of the beach hut, constructed using prefabricated timber, A-frames and beautifully illuminated polycarbonate panels. These shelters can be collated as entire communities or small manageable clusters. Constructed for minimal cost, they are easily erected, relocated and maintained. Using a self-policing system, the shelters can be used to create a sense of worth and ownership. They can also be used as part of a reintegration process.

Each shelter is born and developed from its predecessor. The final beach hut scheme has derived from a series of design iterations that have

Fig. 8.36a–g Homeless pods. (Images and photos: James Furzer)

been led by the reaction of the public. The original parasitic pod, which can be attached to the side of any existing building or structure, was designed to test the boundaries of what is the norm. Gaining support from celebrities such as Ellie Goulding, and broadcast on national television channels such as the BBC, ITV, London Live and CNN, the concept gained an enormous, international, public following reaching hundreds of thousands of shares and likes on social media, featuring in publications such as *The AJ, Texworld, A10 Magazine, PSBJ Magazine* and *The Big Issue*. Winning an international award, the scheme enabled the pods to become a tool that ensured the issue of homelessness remained current.

The parasitic pods explored the metaphorical concept of raising the homeless community above the negativity of the general public, using the existing services of the host building. Comments received on the scheme led to the development of structures that became stand-alone and self-sufficient with varying forms. By constructing a prototype shelter at the UK's largest home build and renovation show, we were able to test the design on many levels, not only structurally but also socially. Debates held on main stages allowed an engagement with the general public that provided us with real-time reactions and thoughts. This very personal dialogue provided further drivers to aid the development of the scheme. With worldwide support, the project aims to provide all communities the same opportunities to participate equally within society.

We as an industry need to create environments that encourage social interaction, integration, communication and respect. Places that celebrate diversity and difference. There is an opportunity for designers to think outside the box when it comes to inclusive design. Rethinking conventional architecture provides a blank canvas, opening possibilities for innovation and inclusivity within the built environment. We need to continually challenge perceptions of what is considered 'normal' or conventional in architecture.

GROWING TALENTS THROUGH PLACE-MAKING

MDX Living Pavilion, Middlesex University

The MDX Living Pavilion project (shortlisted for sustainable construction in London Construction Award 2019) introduced the fusion of digital and physical learning-by-doing projects for undergraduate students across disciplines and contributed to the sustainable development of the university campus.

Architectural Technology (AT) BSc Hons course year-2 and final-year students were jointly supported by industry-academia experts through the journey of a live project on campus from conception to completion. The real-life interaction with stakeholders that could only be addressed partially by BIM-enabled digital learning environment in the classroom, and the dynamic bi-directional (physical and virtual) experience enhanced students' cognitive skills development for effective learning.

AT students as the ambassadors of student communities participated in key stakeholder groups (planners, consultants, university executive board, potential project sponsors, end users and estate management team) meetings, and were included in the communication process of planning and making technical, design and management decisions.

Regular visits to the project site and Q&A sessions with the site manager throughout the construction phase enhanced AT students' understanding of their design impacts in real project for the campus's sustainable development and engagement with local communities. Several courses across the faculties were using the pavilion as a learning tool in their courses.

Being actively involved in campus development to create a legacy project, students earned work placement opportunities in some of the twenty industry partners. Also, with insightful guidance by the MDX estate management team, students embraced team collaboration, peer and social learning, and interpersonal communication skills with visible impact in their study and satisfaction.

Close communications between academics and the estate management team enabled knowledge sharing on innovative materials, technologies and processes, while upskilling towards community engagement for achieving sustainable campus transformation.

Since this five-year pavilion project (phase one) was completed in July 2019, an inventor in the neighbourhood (winner of *BBC's Dragons' Den*, 2015) who visited and liked how the pavilion space encourages its visitors to connect with nature and each other, has planned to support our new multi-disciplinary learning and teaching projects, and share his experience on design and innovation management with our students.

Fig. 8.37a–b   MDX Living Pavilion on campus. Architectural Technology students celebrate their success and contribution to the pavilion project on their graduation day. (Photo: Tong Yang)

ATELIER TEN BIOPHILIA PROJECTS

Gardens by the Bay, Singapore

Architect: Wilkinson Eyre Architects, Grant Associates
Client: National Parks Board, Singapore
Environmental Design and Engineering: Atelier Ten
Structural Engineer: Atelier One

Gardens by the Bay, completed in 2012, provides Singaporeans with access to 54 hectares of landscaped gardens. Set in these gardens are two cooled conservatories recreating a cool dry Mediterranean springtime and the cool moist conditions of tropical mountain regions.

Plant world

Plants need light levels of at least 45,000 lux; 100 times typical office light levels. To maintain sufficient daylight while blocking heat gains would make the biomes unhospitable for people, so this posed a considerable design challenge.

We worked iteratively with the architects and structural engineers to analyse how the geometry of the building envelope could best respond to the daylighting criteria. A natural shape, the hyperbolic curve is most efficient, enclosing a large volume within a relatively small surface area. The design is based on a spectrally-selective double-glazed unit that transmits 65 per cent of incident daylight with only 35 per cent of solar heat.

Human visitors

Comfort along pathways is from an integrated displacement ventilation system. Chilled water is embedded into the pathways to directly absorb solar heat incident on the floors. Displacement ventilation allows only the occupied areas of the domes to be conditioned, while creating a natural heat reservoir in the unoccupied portions. The cooling and dehumidification system operates on waste timber collected from the pruning of Singapore's street trees, making this a zero carbon project.

Fig. 8.38a–i Gardens by the Bay, Singapore, Atelier Ten. (Photos: (a)–(c) Emma Marchant; (d) Atelier Ten; (e)–(g) Emma Marchant; (h) Atelier Ten; (i) Emma Marchant)

Gallery of case studies 175

Fig. 8.39   Jewel Changi Airport, Singapore, Atelier Ten. (Photo: Timothy Hursley)

Jewel Changi Airport, Singapore

Architect: Safdie Architects
Client: Capital Land
Environmental Design and Engineering: Atelier Ten

Since the vision of Singapore as a 'City in a Garden' was set in 1967, a number of projects have contributed to its status as one of the world's greenest places: 47 percent of Singapore is covered with trees and gardens. No surprise, then, that as the gateway to Singapore, Jewel Changi Airport, completed in 2019, would feature the natural environment in such a central way.

Natural force

From our work on Gardens by the Bay (in Singapore), we knew that resolving the competing demands between abundant heat and light needed for plants, and superior passenger thermal comfort for people and plants, would be the key challenge.

Using a combination of bespoke ray tracing and illuminance prediction software, we modelled the light coming through each triangular cell of the roof, for each hour of the year. In addition to spectrally selective glazing, a frit pattern was applied in varying densities to modulate the light levels throughout the building. We collaborated with PWP landscape design to develop a planting palette. Species that require higher light levels were placed in areas with less frit, and vice versa.

Human epicentre

People are never happier than when they are comfortably immersed in and awed by nature. Temperature, humidity and air movement had to be carefully controlled to ensure that human occupants could stay comfortable while traversing the airport on their way to or from their flights. Keeping these elements constant over such a large space would require significant amounts of energy – so instead we developed a strategy to only condition the occupied zones. Some of the zones are conditioned like outdoor spaces, with higher air movement simulating breezes and providing additional cooling effects.

The majority of the hard floor surfaces have embedded chilled water pipes, providing cooling only at the lowest level and allowing heat gains to rise through the space. The waterfall, supplied with collected rainwater from the roof, provides a minor cooling effect on the space through direct evaporation. Nature also contributes to making the airport a calm environment.

WWF-UK Living Planet Centre, Woking, UK

Architect: Hopkins Architects
Client: World Wildlife Fund UK
Environmental Design and Engineering: Atelier Ten
Landscape architect: Grant Associates
Structural Engineer: Expedition Engineering

From the outset of this project, it was evident that exceptional standards of environmental performance were a prerequisite for the headquarters of the Worldwide Fund for Nature (WWF), completed in 2013.

Fig. 8.40   WWF-UK Living Planet Centre, Atelier Ten. (Photo: Morley von Sternberg)

Conservation centre

Six years after its completion, this building still serves as an industry exemplar of sustainable design and high quality office space.

The headquarters of the WWF in the UK were designed to tread lightly on the environment, and increase human connection to nature. We worked with the architect to create well daylit spaces for visual comfort, occupant wellbeing and ecological enhancement. In addition to bringing in daylight, the windows provide a visual connection to the trees and planting surrounding the building.

Air is supplied naturally to the building for most of the year. As it is drawn in through earth ducts, the air is tempered; warm exhaust air leaves via roof cowls.

Embodied nature

By designing a building that enhances occupant connection to their environment, the design team realised we had also designed a building in which plants would thrive. Natural light, natural ventilation – plants love these in their environment as well. The air conditioning system in the building is not very strong, used only when the indoor temperature exceeds 28°C. This reduces energy consumption and the plants are kept healthy.

NBBJ DESIGN

American International College, Kuwait

The mission of American International College is to improve and enrich lives by meeting the higher education, training, partnership, and economic development needs of the State of Kuwait and the Gulf

Fig. 8.41a–d   American International College, Kuwait. (NBBJ Design and Britni Stone)

Gallery of case studies   **177**

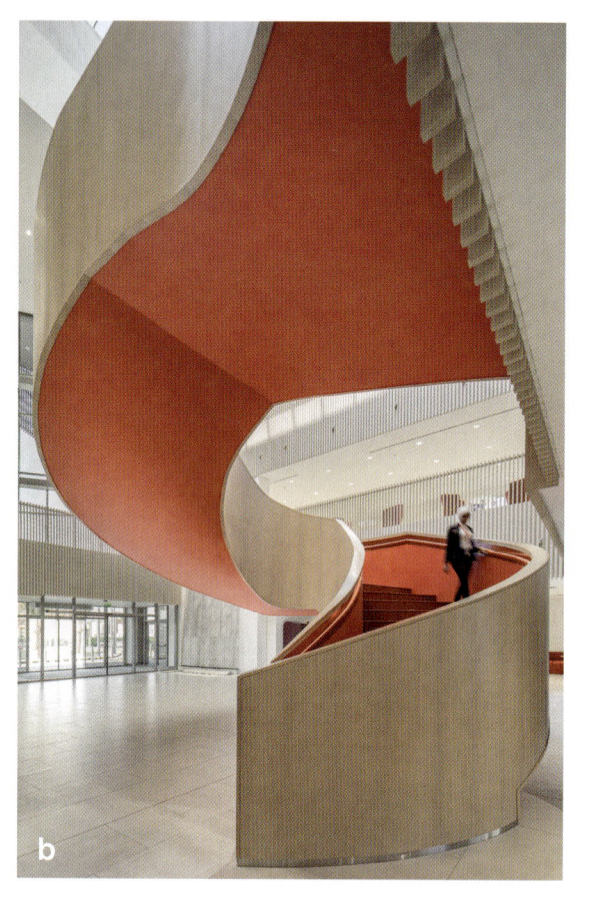

region. The College provides high-quality, innovative, and responsive programmes centered on the intellectual, cultural, and personal growth of all learners. In pursuit of its mission, AIC puts student success first. It will become a student-centered college, academically rigorous and focused on learning outcomes, with strong, integrated support services, including English foundation programmes, advising, and career services.

American International College (AIC) officially opened its doors in Autumn 2019. Located in Al Jahra, about an hour from Kuwait City, it is targeted towards Kuwaiti students who choose to stay in their home country but also desire the progressive, 'gold standard' educational experiences that have earned US schools worldwide respect. AIC offers a curriculum, faculty, staff and student life opportunities that mirror what is available at top-tier schools in the States. As important, the leader of the College recognized from the start that the design of this new institution would be crucial to its success, both to support new models of education as well as to attract high-calibre students and faculty.

I wanted to give students that authenticity of space, to feel as though they had left Kuwait and truly entered an American campus.

Jackie Shaw, Provost of AIC

Shaw chose NBBJ, a premier global firm, as the project's design resource, impressed by their work with leading American universities including Stanford as well as several recent projects in Kuwait. She challenged the NBBJ team to create a user-centered design that would be timeless, magnetic, engaging and intuitive. She also emphasized the need for highly flexible spaces and quality materials so AIC could remain relevant and impressive well into the future.

END NOTES

[1]Vincent Callebaut is a Belgian ecological architect working in Paris. Virtual projects include the Dragonfly and the Lilypad; live projects include Tao Zhu Yin Yuan in Taipei and The Gate.

The following descriptions are partly sourced from Wikipedia (30 June 2019).

- *Dragonfly.* This project involves developing vertical farms in Manhattan, the aim being to rethink the city's food production by encouraging inhabitants to become involved in the life of the gardens, much like city dwellers in the UK having access to garden allotments. The Dragonfly building is 575m tall, and is shaped like a dragonfly's wings. It is composed of two towers connected by a bio-climatic glasshouse. It is positioned between two crystalline wings made out of glass and steel. The honeycomb structure allows sunlight to pass through the building. This is seen as a feeder farm and reconnects the consumers with producers.
- *Lilypad.* This is a model designed as a long-term solution to various possible rising water level scenarios as indicated by the IPCC. It is a self-sufficient amphibious city and satisfies the four challenges laid down by the OECD (Organisation for Economic Co-operation and Development) in March 2008, namely climate, biodiversity, water and health. The floating structure can shelter 50,000 individuals. It comprises three marinas and three mountains, meant for entertainment purposes, surrounding a centrally located lagoon that performs the task of collecting and purifying water. The design was inspired from the ribbed leaf of the *Amazonica Victoria Regia* waterlily. The double skin of this structure is made of polyester fibres covered by a layer of titanium dioxide. The titanium dioxide reacts with UV rays and absorbs atmospheric pollution. By only using renewable energies, this design has zero carbon emission and produces more energy than it consumes. Energy sources could include:

1. Biomass
2. Osmotic power
3. Phytopurification
4. Solar thermal
5. Solar photovoltaic
6. Tidal power
7. Wind energy

This concept has been considered for a possible project in the Philippines.

- *The Gate.* This is under construction in Cairo, and is a multi-use complex of $450,000m_2$ with housing, work spaces and leisure facilities. The roof top is a garden where occupants can swim or run.

[2]Post-occupancy evaluation in action: Techau *et al.* (2016) give three case studies from Australia. A more detailed example is described for the new Greater London Campus developed by AECOM. *See* Gillen *et al.* (2018).

Appendix

The Flourish Questionnaire and Wellbeing Scales

Hanc (2019) compiled Tables 1–4. The user's assessment of environmental factors can be studied using semantic differential scales as described by Watson *et al.* (1988).

Table 1 The Flourish Questionnaire.

1	2	3	4	5	6	7
Very slightly or not at all	A little	Moderately	Quite a bit	Extremely		

_____	Interested*	_____	Irritable**	_____	Distressed**	_____	Alert*
_____	Excited*	_____	Ashamed**	_____	Upset**	_____	Inspired*
_____	Strong*	_____	Nervous**	_____	Guilty**	_____	Determined*
_____	Scared**	_____	Attentive*	_____	Hostile**	_____	Jittery**
_____	Enthusiastic*	_____	Active*	_____	Proud*	_____	Afraid**

*Positive descriptors **Negative descriptors
Scoring: Positive and Negative scores are added separately (Hanc, 2019).

Perceptual factors can be assessed using the Satisfaction with Life Scale (Diener *et al.*, 1985) and the Flourishing Scale (Diener, 2010).

Table 2 The Satisfaction with Life Scale (SWLS).

SWLS instructions: Below are five statements with which you may agree or disagree. Using the 1–7 scale below, indicate your agreement with each item by placing the appropriate number on the line preceding that item. Please be open and honest in your responding (Hanc, 2019).

1	2	3	4	5	6	7
Strongly disagree	Disagree	Slightly disagree	Neither agree nor disagree	Slightly agree	Agree	Strongly agree

_____ In most ways my life is close to my ideal.
_____ The conditions of my life are excellent.
_____ I am satisfied with my life.
_____ So far I have gotten the important things I want in life.
_____ If I could live my life over, I would change almost nothing.

Scoring: Add the responses for all five items. Possible range of scores: 5 (low satisfaction) to 35 (high satisfaction).

Table 3 The Flourishing Scale.

Instructions: Below are eight statements with which you may agree or disagree. Using the 1–7 scale below, indicate your agreement with each item by indicating that response for each statement.

1	2	3	4	5	6	7
Strongly disagree	Disagree	Slightly disagree	Neither agree nor disagree	Slightly agree	Agree	Strongly agree

_____ I lead a purposeful and meaningful life.
_____ My social relationships are supportive and rewarding.
_____ I am engaged and interested in my daily activities.
_____ I actively contribute to the happiness and well-being of others.
_____ I am competent and capable in the activities that are important to me.
_____ I am a good person and live a good life.
_____ I am optimistic about my future.
_____ People respect me.

Scoring: Add the responses, varying from 1 to 7, for all eight items. The possible range of scores is from 8 (lowest possible) to 56 (highest possible). A high score represents a person with many psychological resources and strengths (Hanc, 2019).

Table 4 The Warwick-Edinburgh Mental Wellbeing Scale (WEMWBS) (Tennant *et al.*, 2007).

Users' experience of each over the last two weeks.

Statements	None of the time	Rarely	Some of the time	Often	All of the time
I've been feeling optimistic about the future					
I've been feeling useful					
I've been feeling relaxed					
I've been feeling interested in other people					
I've had energy to spare					
I've been dealing with problems well					
I've been thinking clearly					
I've been feeling good about myself					
I've been feeling close to other people					
I've been feeling confident					
I've been able to make up my own mind about things					
I've been feeling loved					
I've been interested in new things					
I've been feeling cheerful					

Note: The shortened version of the scale has been described by Fat *et al.*, 2017.

Cost of Renewables

Table 5 Cost of electricity from renewable resources.

Listed below are the figures for 2017 in $/kWh (IRENA, 2018). (Data from Raconteur Responsible Business, 19 September 2018.)

0.07	Biomass
0.07	Geothermal
0.05	Hydro
0.10	Solar PV
0.22	Solar concentrated
0.14	Offshore wind
0.06	Onshore wind

Table 6 Renewables' generation capacity worldwide in GW (Energy Information Administration, 2017).

Year	GW
2020	2579
2025	2887
2030	3192
2035	3432
2040	3734
2045	4040
2050	4347

Table 7 Predicted change in energy mix (BP, 2018).

Year	Hydro %	Renewables %
2018	15	10
2040	12	21

Table 8 General conversion factors for energy.

To: From:	TJ Multiply by:	Gcal	Mtoe	MBtu	GWh
TJ	1	238.8	2.388×10^{-5}	947.8	0.2778
Gcal	$4.1868 \times x{-3}$	1	10^{-7}	3.968	1.163×10^{-3}
Mtoe	4.1868×10^{4}	10^{7}	1	3.968×10^{7}	11630
MBtu	1.0551×10^{-3}	0.252	2.52×10^{-8}	1	2.931×10^{-4}
GWh	3.6	860	8.6×10^{-5}	3412	1

1 kWh = 278 GJ.

References

Abdul-Wahab S.A. (ed.), *Sick Building Syndrome in Public Buildings and Workplaces*. Berlin: Springer-Verlag.

Alberti, L.B., 1955. *Ten Books on Architecture*. Alec Tiranti.

Aldersey-Williams, H., 2003. *Zoomorphic: New Animal Architecture*. Laurence King.

Alexander, C., 1977. *A Pattern Language*. Oxford University Press.

Alexander, C., 1979. *The Timeless Way of Building*. Oxford University Press.

Allen, M., and Allen, J., 2015. 'Health inequalities and the role of the physical and social environment', in Hugh Barton *et al*. (eds) *The Routledge Handbook of Planning for Health and Well-Being*. Routledge.

Alnaes, E. *et al.*, 1950. *Norwegian Architecture Throughout the Ages*. Oslo: Aschehang and Co.

Alomar, G., 1967. 'An example of Spanish vernacular architecture: Castropol', in *Arquitectura*, February, 1–35.

Alomar, G., 1978. 'Western Mediterranean European vernacular architecture', in *METU Journal of the Faculty of Architecture*, 4(2), 149–159.

Alvarsson, J.J., Wiens, S., Nilsson, M.E., 2010. 'Stress recovery during exposure to nature sound and environmental noise', in *International Journal of Environmental Research and Public Health*, 7(3), 1036–1046.

Anderson, J., and French, M., 2010. *Sustainability as Promoting Well-being: Psychological Dimensions of Thermal Comfort*. Personal Communication, Institute of Wellbeing, University of Cambridge.

Anderson, J., and Shiers, D., 2002. *The Green Guide to Specification*. Oxford: Blackwell Science.

ANFA, 2013. Selected papers from the Academy of Neuroscience for Architecture Conference September 2012 in San Diego. *Intelligent Buildings International*, 5(S1).

Antonovsky, A., 1979. *Health, Stress and Coping*. San Francisco: Jossey-Bass.

Arantes, B., 2015. 'Neuroscience: The next great competitive advantage', in *Work and Place*, October, 10–13.

Arbib, M.A., 2012. 'Brains, machines and buildings: Towards a neuromorphic architecture', in *Intelligent Buildings International*, 4(3), 147–168. https://doi.org/10.1080/17508975.2012.702863

Armstrong, R., and Spiller, N., 2010. 'Living quarters: Synthetic biology', in *Nature*, 467, 916–918.

Asquith, L., and Vellinga, M., 2006. *Vernacular Architecture in the Twenty-First Century*. Taylor and Francis.

Attenborough, D., 2005. *Life in the Undergrowth*. BBC Books.

Bakó-Biró, Zs., Clements-Croome, D.J., Kochhar, N., Awbi, H.B., Williams, M.J., 2012. 'Ventilation rates in schools and pupils' performance', in *Building and Environment*, 48, February, 215–223.

Balfe, S., 1998. 'Creative writing for health', in *Stress* 33 (October).

Barker, M., 2003. 'Waste to energy: Fired up for growth', in *Waste Management World*, Review Issue, July/August, 29–46.

Barley, M.W., 1971. *The House and Home: A Review of 900 Years of House Planning in Britain*. New York: Graphic Society Ltd.

Barnett, L., 2007. 'Sarah Chang, violinist', in *The Guardian*, 20 November.

Baron, R.A., 1990. 'Environmentally induced positive effect: Its impacts on self-efficacy, task performance, negotiation and conflict', in *Journal of Applied Social Sociology*, 20(5), 368–384.

Barrett, P., 2018. 'Lessons from schools for productive office environments: The SIN model', in Clements-Croome, D.J. (ed.), *Creating the Productive Workplace: Places to Work Creatively*. 3rd edition, Routledge.

Barrett, C., Bascombe, A., Bostock, M., Collis, H., Farnham, G., Guthrie, A., 2002. 'Creating the Eden environment', in *The Arup Journal*, 1, 3–12.

Barrett, P., and Barrett, L., 2010. 'The potential of positive places: Senses, brain and spaces' in *Intelligent Buildings International*, 2, 218–228.

Barrett, P., and Zhang, Y., 2012. 'Teachers' views on the designs of their primary schools', in *Intelligent Buildings International*, 4(2), 89–110.

Barrett, P., Zhang, Y., Moffat J., Kobbacy, K., 2013. 'A holistic, multi-level analysis identifying the impact of classroom design on pupils' learning', in *Building and Environment*, 59, 678–689.

Barrett, P., Barrett, L., Zhang, Y., 2016. 'Teachers' views of their primary school classrooms', *Intelligent Buildings International*, 8(3): 176–191.

BCO, 2003. *Fuel Cells for Offices? A BCO Guide to the New Technology*. Roberts and Partners; British Council for Offices.

BCO, 2012. *Making Art Work in the Workplace*. International Art Consultants; British Council for Offices.

BCO, 2014. *Making the Business Case for Wellbeing*. Wellbeing at Work Study by British Council for Offices; Morgan Lovell and Hatch.

BCO, 2016. *What Workers Want*. British Council for Offices.

BCO, 2018. *Wellness Matters: Health and Wellbeing in Offices and What to Do About It*. British Council for Offices.

Beatley T., 2011. *Biophilic Cities*. Island Press.

Beatley T., 2016. *Handbook of Biophilic City Planning and Design*. Island Press.

Becker, F., 1990. *The Total Workplace*. John Wiley and Sons.

Beil, K. and Hanes, D., 2013. 'The influence of urban natural and built environments on physiological and psychological measures of stress: A pilot study', in *International Journal of Environmental Research and Public Health*, 10(4), 1250–1267.

Bennett, A., 1910. *How to Live on 24 Hours Per Day*. Hodder & Stoughton.

Bennett, N., 2014. 'My proposition? Infrastructure planning needs more foxes, fewer hedgehogs', in *New Civil Engineer*, 2 April.

Bensaid, S., Centi, G., Garrone, E., Perathone, S., Saracco, G., 2012. 'Towards artificial leaves for solar hydrogen fuels from carbon dioxide', in *ChemSusChem: Energy Conversion and Storage*, 5(3), 500–521.

Benyus, J.M., 2002. *Biomimicry*. Harper Perennial.

Berger, J., 1972. *Ways of Seeing*. Penguin.

Berlin, I., 1953. *The Hedgehog and the Fox*. Weidenfeld & Nicolson.

Bernheimer, L., 2017. *The Shaping of Us: How Everyday Spaces Structure Our Lives, Behaviour and Wellbeing*. Hachette.

Bersin J., 2015. 'Becoming irresistible: A new model for employee engagement', in *Deloitte Review*, 16. Graphic: Deloitte University Press.

Bertini, V. and Damluji, S.S., 2018. *Hassan Fathy: Earth and Utopia*. Laurence King Publishing.

Bluyssen, P.M., 2014. *The Healthy Indoor Environment: How to Assess Occupants' Wellbeing in Buildings*. Routledge.

Boerstra, A.C., Beuker, T., Loomans, M.G.L.C., Hensen, J.L.M., 2013. 'Impact of available and perceived control on comfort and health in European offices', in *Architectural Science Review*, 56(1), 30–41.

Boerstra, A.C., Loomans, M.G.L.C., Hensen J.L.M., 2014. 'Personal control over indoor climate and productivity', in *Proceedings of the Indoor Air Conference, Hong Kong*. Santa Cruz, CA, USA:

International Society for Indoor Air Quality and Climate.

Boger, J., Jackson, P., Mulvenna, M., Sixsmith, J., Sixsmith, A., Mihailidis, A., Kontos, P., Polgar, J.M., Grigorovich, A., Martin, S., 2017. 'Principles for fostering the transdisciplinary development of assistive technologies', in *Disability and Rehabilitation: Assistive Technology*, 12(5):480–490.

Bouvier, Y. and Cousin, C., 2015. Ronchamp: *Chapel of Light*. Canope: Château d'Autrey.

Bowman, C., 2015. 'Whatever the politicians decide in Paris, industry's resolve must not falter', in *Building Design*, 3 December.

Bowyer, J., 1977. *Vernacular Building Conservation*. London: The Architectural Press Ltd.

Boyle, G., 1996. *Renewable Energy: Power for a Sustainable Future*. New York: Oxford University Press.

Bradley, F.H., 1914. *Essays on Truth and Reality*. Oxford: Clarendon Press.

Brand, S., 1995. *How Buildings Learn*. London: Penguin Books.

BRE, 2015. Home Quality Mark Technical Manual SD 232.0.0. Beta England.

BREEAM, 2018. UK New Construction: Non-Domestic Buildings (United Kingdom) Technical Manual SD5078 2.0, BRE Global Ltd.

Brekke, H., 2016. 'How does the built environment affect behaviour and cognition?', in Anne Fritz (ed.) *Conscious Cities: An Anthology*, No.1. London: The Cube and the Museum of Architecture.

Brewer, D., Brown, R., Stanfield, G., 2001. *Rainwater and Greywater in Buildings*, Technical Note TN7/2001, Building Services Research and Information Association.

Brewer, P.G., 2000. 'Contemplating action: storing carbon dioxide in the ocean', in Roger Revelle Commemorative Lecture, *Oceanography*, 13, 84–92.

Brewer, P.G., Friederich, G., Peltzer, E.T., Orr, F.M., 1999. 'Direct experiments on the ocean disposal of fossil fuel CO_2', in *Science*, 284, 943–945.

Broll, B., 2010. *Microcosmos*. Firefly Books.

Brown, C., Efstratiou, C., Leontiadis, I., Quercia, D., Mascolo, C., Scott, J., Key, P., 2014. 'The architecture of innovation: Tracking face-to-face interactions with ubicomp technologies', in *Proceedings of the ACM International Joint Conference on Pervasive and Ubiquitous Computing* (Ubicomp 2014). Seattle, WA, USA.

Brown, V.A., 2015. 'Utopian thinking and the collective mind: Beyond transdisciplinarity', *Futures* 65, 209–216.

Brown, V.A. and Harris, J.A., 2014. *The Human Capacity for Transformational Change: Harnessing the Collective Mind*. Routledge.

Brown, V.A., Harris, J.A., Russell, J.Y., 2010. *Tackling Wicked Problems: Through the Transdisciplinary Imagination*. Earthscan.

Browning, W.D., 2012. *The Economics of Biophilia*. Terrapin Bright Green.

Browning, W.D., Ryan, C.O., Clancy, J.O., 2014. *14 Patterns of Biophilic Design*. New York: Terrapin Bright Green, LLC.

Bruce, J.P., Lee, H., Hailes, E.F. (eds), 1996. *Climate Change 1995: Economic and Social Dimensions of Climate Change*, 27. New York: Cambridge University Press.

Brundtland, O., 1987. *Our Common Future: The World Commission on Environment and Development*. Oxford: Oxford University Press.

Brunskill, R.W., 1971. *Illustrated Handbook of Vernacular Architecture*. New York: Universe Books.

BSRIA, 2017. *At a Glance – 3D Printing*. August, TG14/2017.

Building Research Establishment, 1994. *Thermal Insulation: Avoiding Risks*. Report C1/SfB(A3j)(M2). London: HMSO.

Building Research Establishment, 2015. Home Quality Mark Technical Manual SD232: 0.0 (Beta England). London: HMSO.

Building Services Journal, 2003. 'Down the tube' (editorial), September, 37–38.

Bullock, A. and Trombley, S., (eds). 1999. *The New Fontana Dictionary of Modern Thought.* HarperCollins.

Burton, E., 2015. 'Mental wellbeing and place', in Barton, H. *et al.* (eds), *The Routledge Handbook of Planning for Health and Well-Being*, 150–161. Routledge.

Burton, E.J., Bird, W., Maryon-Davis, A., Murphy, M., Stewart-Brown, S., Weare, K., Wilson, P., 2011. *Thinking Ahead: Why We Need to Improve Children's Mental Health and Wellbeing.* Faculty of Public Health, London, UK.

Cabanac, M., 2006. 'Pleasure and joy, and their role in human life', in Clements-Croome, D.J. (ed.) *Creating the Productive Workplace*, 40–50. London: E & FN Spon.

CABE, 2005. *The Impact of Office Design on Business Performance.* Design Council.

Cain, S., 2012. Quiet. London: Penguin.

Callebaut, V., 2011. 'Lilypad', in *Artco Magazine*, 224, 63–64. Taipei, Taiwan.

Cañizares, A. and Bahamón, A., 2013. *Igloo: Contemporary Vernacular Architecture.* Shiffer Publishing, Ltd.

Cao, M. and Wei, J., 2005. 'Stock market returns: A note on temperature anomaly', in *Journal of Banking and Finance*, 29, 1559–1573.

Carfrae, T., 2018. 'Plug-in-to-the-future: Changing approaches to design' (event). Arup, London, 9 November 2018–1 March 2019.

Carson, S., 2010. 'Your creative brain', in *Harvard Medical Publications.* Jossey-Bass.

Chappells, H., 2010. 'Comfort, wellbeing and the socio-technical dynamics of everyday life', in *Intelligent Buildings International Journal*, 2(4), 286–298.

Chen, C.J., Yao, J., Zhu, W., Chao, J.-H., Shang, A., Lee, Y.-G., Yin, S., 2019. 'Ultrahigh light extraction efficiency light emitting diodes by harnessing asymmetric obtuse angle microstructured surfaces', in *Optik*, 182, 400–407.

Chen, Z., Li, H., Wong, C.T.C., 2003. 'Environmental priority evaluation of construction planning', in Anumba, C.J. (ed.), *Proceedings of Innovative Developments in Architecture, Engineering and Construction*, 315–324. Loughborough: Millpress.

Cheshire, D., 2016. *Building Revolutions: Applying the Circular Economy to the Built Environment.* RIBA Publishing.

Chew, M.Y.L., Conejos, S., Law, J.S.L., 2017. 'Green maintainability design criteria for nanostructured titanium dioxide (TiO2) façade coatings', in *Journal of Building Pathology and Adaptation*, 35(2), 139–158.

Childe, G.V., 1951. *Man Makes Himself.* New York: New American Library, 1936.

Chrenko, F.A., (ed.) 1974. *Bedford's Basic Principles of Ventilation and Heating.* 3rd edition, H.K. Lewis, London.

CIBSE, 2000. *Understanding Building Integrated Photovoltaics*, TM25. London: CIBSE.

CIBSE, 2002. *HVAC Strategies for Well-insulated Airtight Buildings*, TM29. London: CIBSE.

CIBSE, 2017. 'Fuel cells for buildings', Data sheet, CHP and Districs Heating Group, 4 May.

Ciftcioglu, Ö., 2003. 'Enhanced decision-making in the construction industry by intelligent technologies', in Anumba, C.J. (ed.), *Proceedings of Innovative Developments in Architecture, Engineering and Construction*, 81–101.

Classen, C., 2013. 'Green pleasures', in Ong, B.L. (ed.) *Beyond Environmental Comfort.* Routledge.

Clements-Croome, D.J., 1985. 'Covered northern township', in *International Journal of Ambient Energy*, 6(4), 171–186.

Clements-Croome, D.J., 1996. 'Freshness, ventilation and temperature in offices', in *Building Services Engineering Research and Technology*, 17(1), 21–27.

Clements-Croome, D.J., 1997. 'Specifying indoor climate', in *Naturally Ventilated Buildings.* E & FN Spon.

Clements-Croome, D. J., 1997. 'What do we mean by

intelligent buildings?' in *Automation in Construction*, 6, 395–400.

Clements-Croome, D.J., 2000a. 'Computers and health in the workplace', in *Proceedings of Healthy Buildings*, University of Technology, Helsinki, 1, 119–124.

Clements-Croome, D.J., Jones, K.G., John G., *et al*, 2003, 'Through Life Environmental Business Modelling for Sustainable Architecture', CIBSE Proceedings of Conference on Building Sustainability, Value and Profit, Edinburgh, September 24–26. Awarded Best Poster Paper.

Clements-Croome, D.J., 2004. 'Healthy buildings', in *Electromagnetic Environments and Health in Buildings*. Routledge.

Clements-Croome, D.J., 2004a. *Intelligent Buildings: Design, Management & Operation*. London: Thomas Telford.

Clements-Croome, D.J., 2004b. *Electromagnetic Environments and Health in Buildings*. London: E & FN Spon.

Clements-Croome, D.J., 2006. *Creating the Productive Workplace*. 2nd edition, Routledge.

Clements-Croome, D.J., 2008. 'Work performance, productivity and Indoor air', in *Scandinavian Journal of Work Environment and Health*, Supplement (4), 69–78.

Clements-Croome, D.J., 2011. 'Sustainable intelligent buildings for people: A review', in *Intelligent Buildings International*, 3(2), 67–86.

Clements-Croome D.J., 2011. 'The interaction between the physical environment and people' in Abdul-Wahab, S.A. (ed.), *Sick Building Syndrome in Public Buildings and Workplaces*. Berlin: Springer-Verlag.

Clements-Croome, D.J. (ed.), 2013. *Intelligent Buildings: An Introduction*. Routledge.

Clements-Croome, D.J., 2013. *Intelligent Buildings: Design, Management and Operation*. London: ICE Publishing.

Clements-Croome, D.J., 2014. 'Sustainable intelligent buildings for better health, comfort and wellbeing', EU Report for Denzero Project.

Clements-Croome, D.J., 2016. 'Intelligent liveable buildings: Health and wellbeing perspectives'. Lecture at Bath University, 4 March. www.derekcroome.com

Clements-Croome, D.J., 2017. 'Innovations in wearables and sensors'. CIBSE Intelligent Buildings Group Innovation Seminar, 19 October, Arup.

Clements-Croome, D.J., 2018. *Creating the Productive Workplace: Places to Work Creatively*. 3rd edition, Routledge.

Clements-Croome, D.J., 2018. Editorial, *Intelligent Buildings International Journal* 10(2), 59–60, 6 April.

Clements-Croome, D.J., Li, B., 2000. 'Productivity and environment', presented at Healthy Buildings 2000 Conference, Finland.

Clements-Croome, D.J., Jones, K.G., John, G., *et al.*, 2003. 'Through life environmental business modelling for sustainable architecture' in *CIBSE Proceedings of Conference on Building Sustainability, Value and Profit*, Edinburgh, 24–26 September.

Clements-Croome, D.J., Marson, M., Yang, T. and Airaksinen, M., 2017. 'Planning and design scenarios for liveable cities', in Abraham, M.A. (ed.) *Encyclopedia of Sustainable Technologies*. Elsevier.

Clements-Croome, D.J., Yang, T., 2018. *Roadmap for Intelligent and Responsive Buildings*. CIB General Secretariat.

Cole, R.J., 2000. 'Cost and value in building green' (editorial), in *Building Research and Information*, 28(5–6), 304–309.

Cole, R.J., Sterner, E., 2000. 'Reconciling theory and practice of life cycle costing', in *Building Research and Information*, 28(5–6), 368–375.

Collins, P., 1965. *Changing Ideals in Modern Architecture*. London: Faber and Faber.

Colls, J., 2002. *Air Pollution*. E & FN Spon.

Consales, C., Merla, C., Marino, C., Benassi, B., 2012. 'Electromagnetic fields, oxidative stress, and neurodegeneration', in *International Journal of Cell Biology* ID 683897.

Cooper, C. and Browning. B., 2015. *The Global Impact of Biophilic Design in the Workplace.* Human Spaces Report.

COP24 Katowice 2018. '24th Conference of the Parties to the United Nations Framework Convention on Climate Change'. Katowice, Poland, 2–14 December.

CoreNet Global, 2014. *International Sustainability Systems Comparison: Key International Sustainability Systems: Energy and Water Conservation Requirements.* Ove Arup and Partners Ltd.

Csikszentmihalyi, M., 2014. *Flow and the Foundations of Positive Psychology: The Collected Works of Mihaly Csikszentmihalyi.* Dordrecht: Springer.

Cui, W., Cao, G., HoPark, J., Ouyang, Q., Zhu, Y., 2013. 'Influence of indoor air temperature on human thermal comfort, motivation and performance', in *Building and Environment* 68, 114–122.

D'Alessandro, A., Pisello, A.L., Fabiani, C., Ubertini, F., Cabeza, L.F., Cotana, F., Materazzi, A.L., 2018. 'Innovative structural concretes with phase change materials for sustainable constructions: Mechanical and thermal characterization', in *Proceedings of Italian Concrete Days 2016.*

Darwin, C., 1859. *On the Origin of Species.* John Murray.

Darwin, C., 1871. *The Descent of Man, and Selection in Relation to Sex.* John Murray.

Davies, D., 2003. 'Exploding some myths', in *Waste Management World*, May/June, 63–68.

Davis, M.C., Leach, D.J., Clegg, C.W., 2011. 'The physical environment of the office: Contemporary and emerging issues' in Hodgkinson, G.P. and Ford, J.K. (eds) *International Review of Industrial and Organisational Psychology*, 26, 193–235. Chichester: Wiley.

de Dear, R., 2004. 'Thermal comfort in practice', in *Indoor Air* 14 (S7), 32–39.

de Dear, R., 2011. 'Revisiting an old hypothesis of human perception: Alliesthesia', in *Building Research and Information*, 39(2), 108–117.

de Dear, R., Akimoto, T., Arens, E.A., Brager, G., Candido, C., Cheong, K.W.D., Zhu, Y., 2013. 'Progress in thermal comfort research over the last twenty years', in *Indoor Air* 23(6), 442–461.

de Looze M.P., Kuijt-Evers L.F., van Dieën J., 2003. 'Sitting comfort and discomfort and the relationships with objective measures', in *Ergonomics* 46(10), 985–997.

de Regules, S., 2016. 'Complex interactions', in *Physics World* 29(4), 27–30.

Deloitte Monitor, 2017. 'Mental health and wellbeing in employment'. Supporting study for the Independent Review. Deloitte.

Dember, W.N., Warm, J.S., Parasuraman, R., 1995. 'Olfactory stimulation and sustained attention' in Gilbert, A.N. (ed.), *Compendium of Olfactory Research.* Kendall/Hunt.

Desmet, P.M.A., 2015. 'Design for mood: Twenty activity-based opportunities to design for mood regulation', in *International Journal of Design* 9(2), 1–19.

Desmyter, J., Garvin, S., Lefèbvre, P.H., Stirano, F., Vaturi, A., 2010. 'A review of safety, security accessibility and positive stimulation indicators', in Perfection Workshop at VTT Helsinki 4 February, final report 30 August (*Performance Indicators for Health Comfort and Safety of the Indoor Environment*).

DETR, 2000a. *Climate Change: Draft UK Programme.* Department of the Environment Transport and Regions. London: The Stationery Office.

DETR, 2000b. *Climate Change, The UK Programme*, Department of the Environment Transport and Regions. London: The Stationery Office.

Diener, E., Biswas-Diener, R., 2008. *Happiness: Unlocking the Mysteries of Psychological Wealth.* Malden, MA: Free Press.

Diener, E., Emmons, R.A., Larsen, R.J., Griffin, S., 1985. 'The satisfaction with life scale', in *Journal of Personality Assessment* 49(1), 71–75.

Diener, E., Wirtz, D., Tov, W., Kim-Prieto, C., Choi, D., Oishi, S., Biswas-Diener, R., 2010. 'New wellbeing measures: Short scales to assess flourishing and positive and negative feelings', in *Social Indicators Research* 97(2), 143–156.

Dolan, P., 2014. *Happiness by Design*. Allen Lane.

Dolan, P., Foy, C., Smith, S., 2016. 'The SALIENT checklist: Gathering up the ways in which built environments affect what we do and how we feel', in *Buildings* 6(1), 9.

Dollens, D., 2010. *The Pangolin Guide to Bio-Digital Movement in Architecture*. Sites Books.

Donev, J., Afework, B., Hanania, J., Stenhouse, K., Yyelland, B., 2018. 'Types of photovoltaic cells', in *Energy Education*.

Drew, P., 1976. *Frei Otto: Form and Structure*. Westview Press.

DTI, 2003. *UK Energy in Brief*. London: Department of Trade and Industry/National Statistics.

du Plessis, C., 2001. *Agenda 21 for Sustainable Construction in Developing Countries*. Pretoria: CSIR Building and Construction Technology.

Du Sautoy, M., 2010. *The Number Mysteries*. HarperCollins.

Dunster, W., 2003. 'BedZED: Beddington Zero-fossil Energy Development' in Thomas, R. (ed.), *Sustainable Urban Design*. E & FN Spon.

Eberhard, J., 2009. *Brain Landscape: The Coexistence of Neuroscience and Architecture*. New York: Oxford University Press.

Ebrahimi, A., Najafpour, G., Yousefi Kebria, D.Y., 2018. 'Performance of microbial desalination cell for salt removal and energy generation using different catholyte solutions', in *Desalination* 432, 1–9.

Edwards, B. (ed.), 2001. 'Green architecture', in *Architectural Design* 71(4).

Edwards, B., 2002. *Rough Guide to Sustainability*. London: RIBA Publications.

EEA, 2000. *Environmental Signals in 2000*. Copenhagen: European Environment Agency; Luxembourg: Office for Official Publications of the European Communities.

Ekelund, U., Steene-Johannessen, J., Brown, W.J., Wang Fagerland, M.W., Owen, N., Powell, K.E., Bauman, A., Lee, I.M., 2016. 'Does physical activity attenuate, or even eliminate, the detrimental association of sitting time with mortality? A harmonised meta-analysis of data from more than 1 million men and women', in *The Lancet*, 388 (10051), 1302–1310.

Ellen MacArthur Foundation, 2012. 'A circular economy tackles the root problems of overconsumption', in *The Guardian*, 31 January.

Elliott, G. and Corey D., 2018. *Build It: The Rebel Playbook for World-Class Employee Engagement*. Wiley: Chichester.

Erwine, B., 2017. *Creating Sensory Spaces: The Architecture of the Invisible*. Routledge.

Eurostat for European Commission Waste management in the EU, 2018. Infographic with facts and figures, 6 April TO00751/eu-waste-management-infographic-with-facts-and-figures.

Evans, R., Haste, N., Jones, A., Haryott, R., 1998. *The Long Term Costs of Owning and Using Buildings*. Royal Academy of Engineering.

Evans, R., Stoddart, G., 1990. 'Producing health, consuming health care', in *Social Science Medicine* 31(12), 1347–1363.

Fanger, P.O., 1970. *Thermal Comfort: Analysis and Applications in Environmental Engineering*. Copenhagen: Danish Technical Press.

Fanger, P.O., 2002. 'Human requirements in future air-conditioned environments', in *Advances in Building Technology* 1, 29–38.

Fat, L., Scholes, S., Boniface, S., Mindell, J., Stewart-Brown, S., 2017. 'Evaluating and establishing national norms for mental wellbeing using the short Warwick-Edinburgh Mental Wellbeing Scale (SWEMWBS): Findings from the Health Survey for England', in *Quality of Life Research* 26(5), 1129–1144.

Fawcett, T., Hurst, A., Boardman, B., 2002. *Carbon UK*. Oxford: Industrial Sustainable Development Group, Environmental Change Institute, University of Oxford.

Fay, R., Treloar, G., Iyer-Raniga, U., 2000. 'Life- cycle energy of a building: life study', in *Building Research and Information*, 28(1), 31–41.

Fergusson, J., *History of Architecture in All Countries*. London: John Murray, 1884.

Figari, L.F., 1997. *Horizontes de Reconciliacion*. Lima: Asociación Vida y Espiritualidad.

Filarete, A., 1965. *Treatise on Architecture*. New Haven: Yale University Press.

Filindra, M., 1975. 'Development and contemporary changes in vernacular housing of Patmos Island', in *Architecture in Greece* 9, 166.

Fisk, W.J., 1999. 'Estimates of potential nationwide productivity and health benefits from better indoor environments: An update', in Spengler, J.D., Samet, J.M. and McCarthy, J.F. (eds), *Indoor Air Quality Handbook*. New York: McGraw-Hill.

Fitch, J.M. and Branch D.P., 1961. 'Primitive Architecture and Climate', in *Scientific American* 205(6), 134–144.

Fitch, J.M., 1961. *Architecture and the Esthetics of Plenty*. New York: Columbia University Press.

Fitch, J.M., 1976. *American Building: The Environmental Forces That Shape It*. New York: Schocken Books.

Foroohar, R., 2018. 'Vivienne Ming: "The professional class is about to be blindsided by AI"', in *Financial Times*, 27 July.

Fords, D., 1963. *Habitat, Economy and Society*. New York: EP Dutton Co. Inc.

Fromm, E., 1964. *The Heart of Man*. Harper & Row.

Fujiwara, D., Vine, J., 2015. *The Wellbeing Value of Tackling Homelessness*. HACT.

Galasiu, A.D., Newsham, G.R., Suvagau, C., Sander, D.M., 2007. 'Energy saving lighting control systems for open-plan offices: A field study', in *LEUKOS* 4(1), 7–29.

Galliers, S., 2003. *Fuel Cell Technology*. Building Services Research and Information Association, BG 9/2003.

Gann, D.M., Salter, A.T., Whyte, J.K., 2003. 'Design quality indicator as a tool for thinking', in *Building Research and Information* 31(5), 318–333.

Gans, D. (ed.), 1989. *Bridging the Gap: Rethinking the Relationship of Architect and Engineer*. Proceedings of the Building Arts Forum/New York Symposium held at the Guggenheim Museum.

Garfinkel, S., 2019. Interview in *Times Higher Education Supplement* 15 August.

Gates, B., 2019. '10 Breakthrough Technologies 2019', in *MIT Technology Review* March/April.

Gebhart, D., 1963. 'The traditional wood houses of Turkey', in *American Institute of Architects Journal*, March, 36ff.

Gehl, J., 2010. *Cities for People*. Washington, DC: Island Press.

George, B., 2012. 'Mindfulness helps you become a better leader', in *Harvard Business Review Blog Network* 26 October.

Gerbert, P., Castagnino, S., Rothballer, C., Witthöft, S., 2017. Report: 'Shaping the future of construction; inspiring innovators redefine the industry'. The World Economic Forum with the Boston Consulting Group, REF 020117.

Germen, A., 1974. 'Yöre Mimarisi', in *Mimarlık* 11(127), 5–9.

Gething, B., 2011. Green Overlay to the *RIBA Outline Plan of Work*. RIBA.

Ghaffarianhoseini, A., Berardi U., AlWaer H., Chang, S., Halawa, E., Ghaffarianhoseini, Ali., and Clements-Croome, D.J., 2015. 'What is an intelligent building? Analysis of recent interpretations from an international perspective', in *Architectural Science Review* 58(3).

Ghaffarianhoseini, A., Berardi, U., AlWaer, H., Chang, S., Halawa, E., Ghaffarianhoseini, A., and Clements-Croome, D.J., 2016. 'What is an intelligent building? Analysis of recent interpretations from an international perspective', in *Architectural Science Review*, 59(5), 238–257.

Ghaffarianhoseini, A., AlWaer, H., Ghaffarianhoseini, A., Clements-Croome, D.J., Berardi, U.,

Raahemifar, K. and Tookey, J., 2017. 'Intelligent or smart cities: A critical exposition and a way forward', in *Intelligent Buildings International Journal* 10(2), 122–129.

Gilder, J.J. and Clements-Croome, D.J., 2010. 'Bio-inspired intelligent design for the future of buildings'. Paper 517 at the CIB World Congress 12–14 May, Salford, UK.

Gillen, N., 2019. Interview in *Modern Building Services* 4 May.

Gillen, N., 2019. *Future Office: Next-generation Workplace Design*. RIBA Publishing.

Gillen, N., Jeffery, H., Hermans, C., Verhees, R., Louth, M., Barrett, D., Bott, R., 2018. People, performance and place: How using perceptive and cognitive data can create inspiring and collaborative workspaces that enable growth and innovation', in *Corporate Real Estate Journal* 8(2), 118–134.

Gillis, K. and Gatersleben, B., 2015. 'A review of psychological literature on the health and wellbeing benefits of biophilic design', in *Buildings* 5(3), 948–963.

Giradet, H., 1999. *Creating Sustainable Cities*. Bristol: Green Books.

Givoni, B. Man., 1969. *Climate, Architecture*. New York: Elsevier.

Giuliani, I., 2000. 'Sustainability – towards mysticism or rational humanism?' MSc dissertation, School of Planning Studies, University of Reading.

Glassie, H., 1975. *Folk Housing in Middle Virginia*. Knoxville, TN: University of Tennessee Press.

Gleick, J., 1997. *Chaos*. Vintage.

Gorb, S.N. and Gorb, E.V., 2016. 'Insect-inspired architecture: Insects and other arthropods as a source for creative design in architecture' in Knippers, J., Nickel, K., Speck, T. (eds), *Biomimetic Research for Architecture and Building Construction*. Springer.

Gou, Z., Lau, S.S.Y., Ye, H., 2014. 'Visual alliesthesia: The gap between comfortable and stimulating illuminance settings', in *Building and Environment*, 82, 42–49.

Gould, J.E. and Gould, C.G., 2007. *Animal Architects: Building and the Evolution of Intelligence*. Oxford.

Göynük: A., 1974. *Town in a Timber Region*. Ankara: METU Department of Restoration, 30–33.

Graeber, D., 2015. *The Utopia of Rules: On Technology, Stupidity and the Secret Joys of Bureaucracy*. New York and London: Melville House.

Gray, A., 2017. World Economic Forum, 18 December.

Grigoriou, E., 2019. *Wellbeing in Interiors*. RIBA.

Gruber P., 2011. *Biomimetics in Architecture: Architecture of Life and Buildings*. Springer.

Guevarra, L., 2011. 'Empire State Building's green transformation earns LEED Gold', in GreenBiz.com, 14 September.

Guy, S. and Moore, S., 2005. *The Paradoxes of Sustainable Architecture in Sustainable Architecture: Critical Explorations of Green Building Practice In Europe and North America*. New York: E & FN Spon Press.

Habraken, N.J., 1998. *The Structure of the Ordinary*. Cambridge, MA: MIT Press.

Hamza, N., 2019. 'Contested legacies: Vernacular architecture between sustainability and the exotic', in Sayigh A. (ed.) *Sustainable Vernacular Architecture: How the Past Can Enrich the Future*.

Hanc, M.L., 2019. 'Productivity and wellbeing in the 21st century workplace: Implications of choice'. PhD Thesis, UCL Institute for Environmental Design and Engineering, Bartlett School of Environment, Energy and Resources. London.

Hancocks, D., 1971. *Animals and Architecture*. Evelyn.

Hansell, M.H., 1984. *Animal Architecture and Building Behaviour*. Longman.

Hansell, M.H., 2007. *Built by Animals*. Oxford.

Harrop, S., 2019. 'Hydrogen trains are coming – can they get rid of diesel for good?' The Conversation, University of Reading, 1 February.

Harvard Medical School, 2018. 'What is blue light? The effect blue light has on your sleep', in *Harvard Health Letter*, 13. Harvard Health Publishing.

Heerwagen, J.H., 1998. Productivity and well-being: what are the links?, presented at the American Institute of Architects Conference on Highly Effective Facilities, Cincinnati, OH, 12–14 March.

Heerwagen, J.H., 2000. 'Green buildings, organizational success and occupant productivity', in *Building Research and Information*, 28(5–6), 353–367.

Heerwagen, J., 2009. 'Biophilia, health and well-being', in Campbell, L., Wiesen, A., *Restorative Commons: Creating Health and Well-Being Through Urban Landscapes*. Gen. Tech. Rep. NRS-P-39. Newtown Square, PA: U.S. Department of Agriculture.

Heerwagen, J.H. et al., 1999. 'Towards a general theory of the human factors of sustainability', presented at the ATA-USGBC Conference on Mainstreaming Green, Chattanooga, TN, 15–17 October.

Heidegger, M., 1977. *The Question Concerning Technology, and Other Essays*. Garland Publishing.

Henshaw, V., 2014. *Urban Smellscapes*. Routledge.

Hermans, V., 2016. 'Office work innovation: What about wellbeing?', in *Modern Economy* 7, 815–821.

Hersey, G.L., 1999. *The Monumental Impulse*. MIT Press.

Herzberg, F., 1966. *Work and the Nature of Man*. New York: World Publishing Company.

Heschong, L., 1979. *Thermal Delight in Architecture*. Cambridge, MA: MIT Press.

Hocking, V.T., Brown, V.A., Harris, J.A., 2016. 'Tackling wicked problems through collective design', in *Intelligent Buildings International* 8(1), 24–36.

Hoffmann, D., 1986. *Frank Lloyd Wright: Architecture and Nature*. Dover Publications.

Holl, S., 2015. 'The Pantheon: A lesson in designing with light'. Video by Studio 360, 2 April.

Hook, L., 2019. 'Could a superplant save the planet?', in *Financial Times*, 31 January.

Hoornweg, D., Hosseini, M., Kennedy, C., 2018. 'Sustainability cost curves for urban infrastructure planning', in *Proceedings of ICE: Civil Engineering*, 171(6), 11–21.

Horn, R., Dahy, H., Gantner, J., Speck, O., Leistner, P., 2018. 'Bio-inspired sustainability assessment for building product development – Concept and case study', in *Sustainability* (MDPI), 10(1), 130.

Hosey, L., 2012. *The Shape of Green*. Island Press.

Humphreys, M., Nicol, N., Roaf, S., 2016. *Adaptive Thermal Comfort*. Oxford: Routledge.

Huppert, F.A., Baylis, N., Keverne, B., 2005. *The Science of Wellbeing*. Oxford University Press.

Huppert, F.A. and So, T., 2013. 'Flourishing across Europe: Application of a new conceptual framework for defining wellbeing', in *Social Indicators Research*, 110(3), 815–821, 837–861.

IBI Group Nightingale, 2012. Sense Sensitive Design. www.ibigroup.com

IEA, 2002. *International Energy Agency Factsheet: Renewables in Global Energy Supply*. November.

Ingalhalikar, M., Smith, A., Parker, D., Satterthwaite, T.D., Elliott, M.A., Ruparel, K., Hakonarson, H., Gur, R.E., Gur, R.C., Verma, R., 2014. 'Sex differences in the structural connectome of the human brain', in *Proceedings of the National Academy of Sciences of the United States of America*, 111(2), 823–828.

IPCC, 1994. *Climate Change 1994: Radiative Forcing of the Climate Change and an Evaluation of the IPCC Emission Scenarios*. Houghton J.T., Meira Filho, L.G., Bruce, J., Ito, K. and Harding, R., 2019. 'Master of Science: Materials – building blocks of the future', in Financial Times Weekend Magazine 10–11 August, 22–27.

IPCC, 1996. 'Climate change 1995: The science of

climate change', in: Houghton, J.T., Meira Filho, L.G., Callander, B.A., Harris, N., Kattenberg, A. and Maskell, K. (eds), Climate Change 1995: *The Science of Climate Change* 572. Cambridge: Cambridge University Press.

IPCC, 2001. *Climate Change – Third Assessment Report.* Cambridge: Cambridge University Press.

Isenberg, B., 2009. *Conversations with Frank Gehry.* New York: Knopf.

Jahncke H., Hongisto, V., Virjonen, P., 2013. 'Cognitive performance during irrelevant speech: Effects of speech intelligibility and office-task characteristics', in *Applied Acoustics* 74(3), 307–316.

Jahnke, I., 2011. 'How to foster creativity in technology enhanced learning', in White, B., King, I., Tsang, Ph. (eds), *Social Media Tools and Platforms in Learning Environments: Present and Future*, 95–116. Springer.

Jibreal, J.M., Azab, E.A., Elsayed, A.S.I., 2018. 'Disturbance in haematological parameters induced by exposure to electromagnetic fields', in *American Journal of Hematology* 6(6), 242–251.

Jodidio, P., 2007. *Santiago Calatrava.* Taschen.

Johannson, T.B., Kelly, H., Reddy, A.K.N., Williams, R.H. (eds), 1993. *Renewable Energy: Sources for Fuels and Electricity.* Washington, DC: Island Press.

John, G., Loy, H., Clements-Croome, D.J., Fairey, V., Neale, K., 2002. 'Enhancing the design of building services for whole life performance' in *CIBSE National Conference Part 2*, 24 October. London: Royal College of Physicians.

John, G.A., Clements-Croome, D.J., Jeronimidis, G., 2005. 'Sustainable building solutions: A review of lessons from the natural world', in *Building and Environment* 40, 319–328.

Jones, B., 2015. *Building with Straw Bales: A Practical Manual for Self-Builders and Architects.* Green Books.

Juniper, B., Bellamy, P., White, N., 2011. 'Testing the performance of a new approach to measuring employee well-being', in *Leadership and Organization Development Journal* 25(4), 344–357.

Juniper, B., White, N., Bellamy, P., 2009. 'Assessing employee wellbeing – is there another way?', in *International Journal of Workplace Health Management* 2(3), 220–230.

Kagge, E., 2018. *Silence in the Age of Noise.* Penguin: Viking.

Kahn, L. (ed.), 1973. *Shelter.* Bolinas, CA: Shelter Pub. Inc.

Kahn, L. (ed.), 1978. *Shelter II.* Bolinas, CA: Shelter Pub. Inc.

Kahneman, D., 2011. *Thinking, Fast and Slow.* Farrar, Straus and Giroux.

Kairamo, M., 1978. 'Features of Vernacular Architecture in Finland', in *METU Journal of the Faculty of Architecture* 4(4), 179–195.

Kaku, M., 2011. *Physics of the Future: How Science Will Shape Human Destiny and Our Daily Lives by the Year 2100.* Allen Lane.

Kaku, M., 2014. *The Future of the Mind: The Scientific Quest to Understand, Enhance, and Empower the Mind – Street Smart.* Doubleday Books.

Kano, N., Seraku, N., Takahashi, F. and Tsuji, S., 1984. 'Attractive quality and must-be quality', in *Journal of the Japanese Society for Quality Control* 41, 39–48.

Kapsali, V., 2016. *Biomimetics for Designers.* Thames and Hudson.

Kellert, S.R., 2016. 'Biophilia and biomimicry: evolutionary adaptation of human versus nonhuman nature', in *Intelligent Buildings International* 8(2), 51–56.

Kellert, S.R., Heerwagen, J.H., Mador, M.L., 2008. *Biophilic Design: The Theory, Science and Practice of Bringing Buildings to Life.* Hoboken, NJ: Wiley.

Kim, J., de Dear, R., 2012. 'Nonlinear relationships between individual IEQ factors and overall workspace satisfaction', in *Building and Environment* 49(1), 33–40.

Kincaid, D., 2002. *Adapting Buildings for Changing Uses.* London: E & FN Spon.

King, G., 1976. 'Some observations on the architecture of southwest Saudi Arabia', in *Architectural Association Quarterly* 8(1), 20–29.

Kirkwood, R., 1998. 'Solar dawn: Challenging the horizon', CIBSE Presidential Address, May, London.

Knasko, S.C., 1993. 'Performance mood and health during exposure to intermittent odours', in *Archives of Environmental Health* 48(5), 305–308.

Knight, C. and Haslam, S.A., 2010. 'The relative merits of lean, enriched, and empowered offices: an experimental examination of the impact of workspace management strategies on wellbeing and productivity', in *Journal of Experimental Psychology*, 16(2), 158–172.

Knippers, J., Nickel, K.G., Speck, T., 2016. *Biomimetic Research for Architecture and Building Construction: Biological Design and Integrative Structure.* Reprint, Springer.

Knowles, R., 1969. *Owens Valley Study: A Natural Ecological Framework for Settlement.* Los Angeles, CA: University of Southern California.

Knowles, R., 1974. *Energy and Form: An Ecological Approach to Urban Growth.* Cambridge, MA: MIT Press.

Kohler, N., 2002. 'Sustainability and indoor quality' in Proceedings of the 9th International Conference on Indoor Air Quality and Climate, Monterey, CA, 30 June–5 July, Vol. 4, 1–9.

Kohler, N. and Lütkendorf, T., 2002. 'Integrated life-cycle analysis', in *Building Research and Information* 30(5), 338–348.

Korcak, P., 1978. 'The goals and means of preserving vernacular architecture', in *METU Journal of the Faculty of Architecture* 4(2), 20–29, 139–149.

Kuncic, Z., 2019. 'In search of smarter machines', in *Financial Times Magazine* August 3–4.

Kurzweil, R., 2006. *The Singularity is Near: When Humans Transcend Biology.* Gerald Duckworth & Co., Ltd.

Kurzweil, R., 2012. *How to Create a Mind: The Secret of Human Thought Revealed.* Gerald Duckworth & Co., Ltd.

Laar, M. and Grimme, F.W., 2002. 'German developments in daylight guidance systems', in *Building Research and Information*, 30(4), 282–301.

Lacy, M.L., 1996. *The Power of Colour to Heal the Environment.* London: Rainbow Bridge.

Laloux, F., 2014. *Reinventing Organizations: A Guide to Creating Organizations Inspired by the Next Stage in Human Consciousness.* First edition: Nelson Parker.

Lan, L., Wargocki, P., Wyon, D.P., Lian, Z., 2011. 'Effects of thermal discomfort in an office on perceived air quality, SBS symptoms, physiological responses and human performance', in *Indoor Air*, 21(5), 376–390.

Langdon, F.J., 1973. 'Human sciences and the environment in buildings', in *Build International*, 6 (January–February), 106.

Laugier, M.A.P., 1755. *Essai sur l'Architecture.* Paris: Duchesne Librarie. London: Osborne and Shipton.

Lazarus, M., Greber, L., Hall, J., Bartels, C., Bernow, S., Hansen, E., Raskin, P., Von Hippel, D., 1993. *Towards a Fossil Free Energy Future: The Next Energy Transition.* Boston, MA: Stockholm Environment Institute.

Leaman, A. and Bordass, B., 1999. 'Productivity in buildings: the "killer" variables', in *Building Research and Information* 27, 4–19.

Lee, D., 2010. *Nature's Palette.* University of Chicago Press.

Lee, H., Callander, B.A., Haites, E., Harris, N., and Maskell K. (eds). Cambridge: Cambridge University Press.

Lehrer, J., 2011. 'Building a thinking room', in *The Wall Street Journal* 30 April.

Leiper, Q., Fagan, N., Entrostrom, S., Fenn, G., 2003.

'A strategy for sustainability', in *Proceedings of the Institution of Civil Engineers* 156(ES1), 59–66 (paper 13063).

Leslie, T., 2003. 'Form as a diagram of forces: the equiangular spiral in the work of Pier Luigi Nervi', in *Journal of Architectural Education*, 57(2), 45–54.

Levete, A., 2008. 'To live in a great space that inspires you', in *Financial Times*, 16 February.

Levin, H., 2002. 'Sustainable building', presented at Seminar Terve Vera (Healthy and Productive Buildings), University of Technology, Helsinki, 17 October.

Levine, J.A., 2015. 'Sick of sitting', in *Diabetologia*, 58(8), 1751–1758.

Lewcock, R., 1976. 'Towns and Buildings in Arabia: North Yemen', in *Association Quarterly* 8(1), 3–19.

Lipman, A., 1966. 'The architectural belief system and social behaviour', in *The British Journal of Sociology* 20(2), 154, 190–204.

Liu, C., Colón, B.C., Ziesack, M., Silver, P.A., Nocera, D.G., 2016. 'Water splitting biosynthetic system with CO_2 reduction efficiencies exceeding photosynthesis', in *Science* 352(6290), 1210–1213.

Lo Dico, J., 2019. 'Vertical gardens breathe life into the city', in *Financial Times* 10–11 August.

Loehr. J. and Schwartz, T., 2010. *The Power of Full Engagement*. Simon and Schuster.

Lomeihing, D., 2017. 'Sight Unseen': exhibition curated by Alia El-Bermani, 24 February–25 March. Abend Gallery, Congress Park, Denver, CO.

Lovelock, J., 2019. *Novacene*. Allen Lane.

Lu, X., Clements-Croome, D.J., Viljanen, M., 2010. 'Integration of chaos theory and mathematical models in building simulation', in *Automation in Construction*, 19, 447–457.

Lu, X., Clements-Croome, D.J., Viljanen, M., 2012. 'Fractal geometry and architecture design: Case study review', in *Chaotic Modeling and Simulation (CMSIM) Journal* 2, 311–322, presented at 5th Chaotic Modeling and Simulation International Conference, Athens, 12–15 June.

Ludvigson, H.W., Rottman, T.R., 1989. 'Effects of odours of lavender and cloves on cognition, memory, affect and mood', in *Chemical Senses*, 14(4), 525–536.

Lyman, M., 2019. *The Remarkable Life of the Skin*. Bantam Press.

Maass, J., 1969. 'Where Architectural Historians Fear to Tread', in *Journal of the Society of Architectural Historians* 28(1), 3–8.

Macaro, A. and Baggini, J., 2014. 'Do we need to focus?' in *Financial Times*, 24 January.

Mace, V., 2014. 'Sensing the urban interior', INArch International Conference, 10–11 September, Universitas Indonesia In Depok, Jakarta, Indonesia.

MacNaughton, P., Satish, U., Guillermo, J., Laurent, C., Flanigan, S., Vallarino, J., Coull, B., … Allen, J., 2017. 'The impact of working in a green certified building on cognitive function and health', in *Building and Environment*, 114, 178–186.

MacNaughton P., Cao, X., Buonocore, J., Cedeno-Laurent, J.G., Spengler, J.D., Bernstein, A., Allen, J.G., 2019. 'Response to "A critical look at energy savings, emissions reductions, and health co-benefits of the green building movement"', in *Journal of Exposure Science and Environmental Epidemiology*. 29(4), 594–596.

Magadley, W. and Birdi, K., 2009, Innovation labs: An examination into the use of physical spaces to enhance organizational creativity', in *Creativity and Innovation Management* 18(4).

Maldonado, T., 1960. 'New developments in industry and the training of designers', in Dannatt, T. (ed.), *Architect's Yearbook* 9. London: Elek Books.

Maldonado, T., 1972. *Design, Nature, and Revolution: Toward a Critical Ecology*. Translated by M. Domandi. New York: Harper and Row.

Malinowski, B., 1968. *The Dynamics of the Cultural Change*. London: Yale University Press.

Malnar, J.M., Vodvarka, F., 2004. *Sensory Design*. Minneapolis, MN: University of Minnesota Press.

Mandelbrot, B., 1982. *The Fractal Geometry of Nature*. W.H. Freeman and Point Press Company.

Mangone, G., Kurvers, S.R., Luscuere, P.G., 2014. 'Constructing thermal comfort: Investigating the effect of vegetation on indoor thermal comfort through a four-season thermal comfort quasi-experiment'. Building and Environment, 81, 410–426

Markham, S.F., 1944. Climate and the Energy of Nations. New York: Oxford University Press)

Marmot, A., 2016. 'Space on demand: Co-workspace and space matchmaker apps', BCO Report: www.bco.org.uk

Marmot, A. and Ucci, M., 2015. 'Sitting less, moving more: the indoor built environment as a tool for change', in *Physical Activity, Sedentary Behaviour and the Indoor Environment, Building Research and Information*, 43(5), 561–565

Marston, W., 1979. *The Emotions of Normal People*. Minneapolis, MN: Persona Press Inc.

Maslow, A.H., 1943. 'A theory of human motivation', in *Psychology Review* 50(4), 370–396

Mazzoleni, I., 2013. *Architecture Follows Nature*. Taylor and Francis CRC Press.

Mazzucato, M., 2018. *The Value of Everything: Making and Taking in the Global Economy*. First edition, Allen Lane.

McAllister, P., 2003. 'Putting management into practice: Property management and the environment', part of *Property Management in Practice Module*, University of Reading, Department of Real Estate and Planning.

McDonough, W. and Braungart, M., 2002. *Cradle to Cradle: Remaking the Way we Make Things*. New York, North Point.

McGraw Hill Construction, 2013. 'New and retrofit green schools: The cost benefits and influence of a green school on its occupants', Smart Market Report.

McGraw Hill Construction, 2014. 'The drive toward healthier buildings: The market drivers and impact of building design and construction on occupant health, wellbeing and productivity', Smart Market Report.

McLean, K., 2013. Sensory maps of cities (www.sensorymaps.com).

Menuhin, Y., 1972. *Theme and Variations*. Heinemann.

Mercer, E., 1976, *English Vernacular Houses: A Study of Traditional Farmhouses and Cottages*. London: HMSO.

Michell, G., 1995. *Architecture of the Islamic World: Its History and Social Meaning*. Thames and Hudson.

Miller, A.B., Sears, M.E., Lloyd Morgan, L., Davis, D.L., Hardell, L., Oremus, M., Soskolne, C., 2019. 'Risks to health and well-being from radio-frequency radiation emitted by cell phones and other wireless devices', in *Frontiers in Public Health* 13 August.

Milner, C. and Cote, K.A., 2009. 'Benefits of napping in healthy adults: Impact of nap length, time of day, age, and experience with napping', in *Journal of Sleep Research* 18(2), 272–281.

Miodownik, M., 2018. 'No more potholes: Cities that can repair themselves', in *Financial Times*, 28 March.

Mitra, R. and Pattanayak, S., 2018. 'Mobile phone and tower radiation: A challenge to all living entities', in *Exploring Animal Medical Research* 8(1), 5–10.

Moram M., 2011. Proceedings of ICE, *Energy* 164, 17–24.

Morgan, L.H., 1965. *Houses and House-Life of the American Aborigines*. Chicago, IL: University of Chicago Press.

Morris, G.P., Beck, S.A., Hanlon, P., Robertson, R., 2006. 'Getting strategic about the environment and health', in *Public Health Journal*, 120(10), 889–903.

Mott Green and Wall, Davis Langdon & Everest, 2003. *Building Services Journal*, September, 16–18.

Nature, 2010. 'Animal behaviour: Avian optical illusions', Nature Publishing Group, 467(16), 255.

Nayak, T., Zhang, T., Mao, Z., Xu, X., Zhang, L., Pack, D.J., Dong, B., Huang, Y., 2018. 'Prediction of human performance using electroencephalography under different indoor room temperatures', in *Brain Science* 8(4), 23 April.

Nedved, M., 2011. 'Ventilation and the air ion effect in the indoor environments: Impact on human health and wellbeing' in Abdul-Wahab S.A. (ed.), *Sick Building Syndrome in Public Buildings and Workplaces*. Springer-Verlag, Berlin.

Nelson, E.C. and Holzer, D., 2017. *The Healthy Office Revolution: A True Story of Burnout, a Wakeup Call and Better Working Through Science*. Learn Adapt Build Publishing.

Nelson, R., 2018. 'Micro-management of learning is the kiss of death for creativity', in *Times Higher Education*, 12 July, 29.

Neville, S., 2018. 'Is Britain loving the NHS to death?' in *Financial Times* 15 June.

Newman, M., 2010. 'Get happy, and get on with it', in *Times Higher Education*, 21 January, 34–36.

Newsham, G., Birt, B., Arsenault, C., Thompson, L., Veitch, J., Mancini, S., Galasiu, A., Gover, B., Macdonald, I., Burns, G., 2012. 'Do green buildings outperform conventional buildings? Indoor environment and energy performance in North American offices', in *National Research Council Canada Research*, Report RR-329.

Nicol, F., Humphreys, M., Roaf, S., 2012. *Adaptive Thermal Comfort: Principles and Practice*. London: Routledge.

Nocera, D.G., 2012. 'The artificial leaf', in *Accounts of Chemical Research* 45(5), 767–776.

Nonell, J.B., 2000. *Antonio Gaudi: Master Builder*. New York: Abbeville Press.

OECD, 2013. OECD *Guidelines on Measuring Subjective Wellbeing*. OECD Publishing.

Oh, S.Y.J., 2005. 'Indoor air quality and productivity in offices in Malaysia', Dissertation (Masters), School of Construction Management and Engineering, University of Reading, UK.

Ojala, M., 2019. 'Eco-anxiety', in *Royal Society of Arts Journal* 4, 11.

Oliver, P. (ed.), 1969. *Shelter and Society*. New York: Praeger.

Oliver, P. (ed.), 1971. *Shelter in Africa*. London: Barrie and Jenkins.

Oliver, P. (ed.), 1975. *Shelter, Sign and Symbol*. London: Barrie and Jenkins.

Oliver, P.D., 2003. *Dwellings: The Vernacular House Worldwide*. London: Phaidon Press (see also *Encyclopaedia of the World Vernacular Architecture, 1997*. Cambridge: Cambridge University Press.)

Ong, B.L., 2013. *Beyond Environmental Comfort*. London: Routledge.

Otto, F. and Rasch, B., 1995. *Finding Form*. Munich: Edition Axel Menges (translation: Michael Robinson).

Owen, J., 2016. 'How to save parks and other urban green spaces', in *Financial Times, Weekend House and Homes*, 7 February.

Oxman, N., 2016. 'What if buildings were grown, not built?', World Economic Forum, July 10.

Özkan, S. and Önür, S., 1975. 'Another thick-wall pattern: Cappadocia', in Oliver, P. (ed.) *Shelter, Sign and Symbol*, 95–106. London: Barrie and Jenkins.

Özkan, S., Turan M., Üstünkök, O., Lowenstein, M., 1974. 'Towards an old architecture by new techniques', in *Architectural Association Quarterly* 6(1), 4–11.

Pacheco-Torgal, F., Diamanti, M.V., Nazari, A., Goran-Granqvist, C., Pruna, A., Amirkhanian, S., 2019. *Nanotechnology in Eco-efficient Construction Materials, Processes and Applications*. 2nd edition, Woodhead Publishing.

Pallasmaa, J., 1996. *The Eyes of the Skin*. London: Polemics: Academy Editions.

Pallasmaa, J., 2016. 'Body, mind and imagination: Neuroscience and the mental essence of architecture', in Fritz, A. (ed.), *Conscious Cities: An*

Anthology – No.1. London: The Cube and the Museum of Architecture.

Papas, C., 1957. *L'Urbanisme et Architecture Populaire dans le Cyclades.* Paris: Edition, Dunod.

Parkin, S., Sommer, F., Uren, S., 2003. 'Sustainable development: Understanding the concept and challenge', Proceedings of the Institution of Civil Engineers, 156 (ES1), 19–26 (paper 13264).

Parmar, S.R.S. and Saini, M.K., 2018. 'Research for technical advancement in developing of shield material to protect from wireless devices', in *International Journal of Emerging Technologies and Innovative Research* 5(12), 644–652.

Pawlyn, M., 2011. *Biomimicry in Architecture.* First edition, RIBA Publishing.

Pearson, D., 2001. *The Breaking Wave: New Organic Architecture.* Stroud: Gaia.

Penn, A. and Turner, J.S., 2018. 'Can we identify general architectural principles that impact the collective behaviour of both human and animal systems?' in *Philosophical Transactions of the Royal Society* B 373: 20180253.

Perin, C., 1970. *With Man in Mind.* Cambridge, MA: MIT Press.

Peters, T., 2016. 'Social sustainability in context: Rediscovering Ingrid Gehl's Bo-Miljo (Living Environment)', in *Architectural Research Quarterly*, 20 April, 371–380. Cambridge University Press.

Philipp, R., 2001. 'Aesthetic quality of the built and natural environment: Why does it matter?', in Pasini, W. and Rusticali, F. (eds), *Green Cities: Blue Cities of Europe*; WHO Collaborating Centre for Tourist Health and Travel Medicine, Rimini, Italy, with the WHO Regional Office for Europe.

Philipp, R. and Thorne, P., 2018. 'The art of wellbeing: A public perspective', in *Athens Journal of Health* 5(2), 107–120.

Pinter-Wollman, N., Penn, A., Theraulaz, G., Fiore, S.M., 2018. 'Interdisciplinary approaches for uncovering the impacts of architecture on collective behaviour', in *Philosophical Transactions of the Royal Society* B 373: 20170232.

Plunz, R. and Özkhan, S., forthcoming. *Houses on the Aegean.* New York: Praeger.

Pongrácz, E., 2003. 'Sustainable waste management: A matter of definition', in *Waste Management World*, Review Issue, July/August, 21–27.

Poole, R., 1991. Extract from Society of Experimental Biology Bulletin, January 2007.

POST, 2016. 'Green Space and Health, POST Note 538'. The UK Parliamentary Office for Science and Technology (POST), October.

PricewaterhouseCoopers LLP, 2008. 'Building the case for wellness', 4 February.

Raglan (Lord), *The Temple and the House.* New York: W.W. Norton and Co. Inc.

Rainham, D., Cantwell, R., Jason, T., 2013. 'Nature appropriation and associations with population health in Canada's largest cities', in *International Journal of Environmental Research and Public Health* 10(4), 1268–1283.

Rapoport, A., 1969. *House Form and Culture.* Englewood Cliffs, NJ: Prentice Hall.

Rapoport, A., 1970. 'Symbolism and environmental design', in *International Journal of Symbology*, April, 1–10.

Rapoport, R.A. 1971. 'Nature, culture and ecological anthropology', in Shapiro, H.L. (ed.), *Man, Culture and Society.* Revised edition, London: Oxford University Press, 237–267.

Rapoport, A., 1977. *Human Aspects of Urban Form.* Oxford: Pergamon Press.

Rawlings, R., 1999. 'Environmental rules of thumb', Technical Note TN12/99, Building Services Research and Information Association.

Reddy, S., Fox, J., Purohit, M.P., 2019. 'Artificial intelligence-enabled healthcare delivery', in Journal of the *Royal Society of Medicine*, 112(1), 22–28.

Rees, M., 2018. *On the Future: Prospects for Humanity.* Princeton.

Riefstahl, R.M. (n.p.). *Turkish Architecture in South-Western Anatolia.* Cambridge: 1931.

Rittel, H.W.J. and Webber, M.M., 1973. 'Dilemmas in a general theory of planning', in *Policy Sciences* 4, 155–169.

Roaf, S., 2001. *Ecohome: A Design Guide*. London: Architectural Press.

Roe, J., Aspinall, P.A., Mavros, P., Coyne, R., 2013. 'Engaging the brain: the impact of natural versus urban scenes using novel EEG methods in an experimental setting', in *Environmental Sciences*, 1(2), 93–104.

Rotton, J., 1983. 'Affective and cognitive consequences of malodorous pollution', in *Basic and Applied Psychology*, 4(2), 171–191.

Roulet, C.A., Johner, N., Foradini, F., Bluyssen, P., Cox, C., Fernandes, E.D., Müller, B., Aizlewood, C., 2006. 'Perceived health and comfort in relation to energy use and building characteristics', in *Building Research and Information*, 34(5), 467–474.

Royal Commission on Environmental Pollution, 2000. 'Energy – The changing climate', 22nd Report, Cm 4749. London: The Stationery Office.

Rudofsky, B., 1964. *Architecture without Architects*. London: Academy Editions.

Russell, B., 1968. 'The vernacular, the industrialised vernacular and other convenient myths', in *METU Journal of the Faculty of Architecture*, 5(1), 101–107.

Salingaros, N.A., 2015. *Biophilia and Healing Environments: Healthy Principles for Designing the Built World*. New York: Terrapin Bright Green, LLC.

Sallomi, A.H., Ahmed, S., Wali, M.H., 2018. 'Specific absorption rate (sar) and thermal effect prediction in human head exposed to cell phone radiations', in *Science International* 30(4), 653–656.

Samad, Z.A., Macmillan, S., 2005. 'The Valuation of Intangibles: Explored by Primary School Design' in Emmitt, S. (ed.) *Proceedings of the CIB W096 Conference on Designing Value: New Directions in Architectural Management*, November. Technical University of Denmark, Lyngby.

Satish, U., Fisk, W.J., Mendell, M.J., Eliseeva, E., Hotchi,T., Sullivan, D.P., Cleckner, L.B., Shekhar, K. Teng, K., 2011. 'Impact of CO2 on human decision making and productivity' in *Proceedings of Indoor Air*, a574 3.

Satish, U., Mendell, M.J., Shekhar, K., Hotchi, T., Sullivan, D., Streufert, S., Fisk, W.J., 2012. 'Is CO2 an indoor pollutant? Direct effects of low-to-moderate CO2 concentrations on human decision-making performance', in *Environmental Health Perspectives* 120(12) 1671–1677.

Sayigh, A. (ed.), 2019. *Sustainable Vernacular Architecture: How the Past Can Enrich the Future*. Springer Nature, Switzerland AG.

Schafer, R.M., 1977. *The Tuning of the World*. New York: Knopf.

Schlittmeier, S.J., Hellbrück, J., Thaden, R., Vorländer, M., 2008. 'The impact of background speech varying in intelligibility: Effects on cognitive performance and perceived disturbance', in *Ergonomics* 51, 719–36.

Schmidt-Nielsen, K., Crawford, E.C., Hammel, H.T., 1981. 'Respiratory water loss in camels', in *Proceedings of the Royal Society of London* Series B, 211(1184), 291–303.

Schumacher, E.F., 1973. *Small is Beautiful*. London: Blond & Briggs.

Schwab, K., 2017. *The Fourth Industrial Revolution*. Penguin: Portfolio.

Schwartz, T. and McCarthy, C., 2007. 'Manage your energy, not your time', in *Harvard Business Review*, October.

Scottish Government, 2006. *Health in Scotland 2006: Annual Report of the Chief Medical Officer*.

Searle, S., Burke, B., Cearley, D., Walker, M., 2017. 'Top 10 Strategic Technology Trends for 2018', in *Gartner,* 3 October, ID: G00327329.

Seligman, M., 2011. *Flourish*. New York: Free Press.

Semple, E.C., 1911. *Influences of Ideographic Environment*. New York: Russel and Russel.

Senge, P.M., 1990. *The Fifth Discipline: The Art and*

Practice of the Learning Organization. Second revised edition, Random House Business.

Seresinhe, C.I., Preis, T., MacKerron, G., Moat, H.S., 2019. 'Happiness is greater in more scenic locations', in *Nature (Scientific Reports)* 9,4498.

Shane, J., 2018. 'Neural networks, explained', in *Physicsworld*, 9 July.

Shepherd, D., Welch, D., Dirks, K., McBride, D., 2013. 'Do quiet areas afford greater health-related quality of life than noisy areas?', in *International Journal of Environmental Research and Public Health* 10(4), 1284–1303.

Shields, B., 2003. 'Learning's sound barrier, by Nina Morgan', in *Newsline*, 26, 10–11.

Silchenko, V., 2018. 'Michio Kaku on bitcoin, perfect capitalism and the recipe for becoming a billionaire', in *The Fintech Times*, 24 April.

Sillén, F., 2003. 'Bo01: an ecological city district in Malmö, Sweden', in Thomas, R. (ed.), *Sustainable Urban Design.* London: E & FN Spon.

Sivaram, V., 2018. *Taming the Sun.* MIT Press.

Smale, K., 2019. 'Change makers', in *New Civil Engineer* March, 26–32.

Snow, S., Boyson, A., King, M., Paas, K.,H.W., L., Noakes, C., Gough, H., Barlow, J., Schraefel, M.C., 2019. 'Exploring the physiological, neurophysiological and cognitive performance effects of elevated carbon dioxide concentrations indoors'. *Building and Environment*, 156. pp.243–252.

Smalley, A., 2019. 'Forest 404: Why we should listen to trees', BBC Radio 4, 4 May.

Sörqvist, P., 2015. 'On interpretation of the effects of noise on cognitive performance: the fallacy of confusing the definition of an effect with the explanation of that effect', in *Frontiers in Psychology* 6, 754.

Spengler, J.D. *et al.*, 2015. 'Associations of cognitive function scores with carbon dioxide, ventilation, and volatile organic compound exposures in office workers: a controlled exposure study of green and conventional office environments', in *Environmental Health Perspectives* 124(6), 805–812

Spengler, M., Brunner, M., Damian, R.I., Lüdtke, O., Martin, R., Roberts, B.W., 2015. 'Student characteristics and behaviors at age 12 predict occupational success 40 years later over and above childhood IQ and parental socio-economic status' in *Developmental Psychology* 51, 1329–1340.

Steele, J., 1988. *Hassan Fathy.* London: Academy Editions.

Steemers, K., 2015. 'Architecture for wellbeing and health, daylight and architecture', in *Spring* 23, 6–27.

Steemers, K., Manchanda, S., 2010. 'Energy efficient design and occupant wellbeing: Case studies in the UK and India', in *Building and Environment*, 45(2), 270–278.

Stein, Y., Hänninen, O., Huttunen, P., Ahonen, M., Ekman, R., 2015. 'Electromagnetic radiation – environmental indicators in our surroundings', in Armon, R.H. and Hänninen (eds), *Environmental Indicators .* Springer.

Stewart, I., 2010. *Cabinet of Mathematical Curiosities.* Profile Books.

Stewart, I., 2011. 'Nature by numbers', in *The Times – Eureka* 20 (May), 34–3.

Stewart-Brown, S., Tennant, A., Tennant, R., Platt, S., Parkinson, J., Weich, W., 2009. 'Internal construct validity of the Warwick-Edinburgh Mental Wellbeing Scale (WEMWBS): A Rasch analysis using data from the Scottish Health Education Population Survey', in *Health and Quality of Life Outcomes* 7, 15.

Stich, J.F., Monideepa, T., Stacey, P., Cooper, C.L., 2019. 'Email load, workload stress and desired email load: a cybernetic approach', in *Information Technology and People* 32(2), 430–452.

Stich, J.F., Monideepa, T., Stacey, P., Cooper, C.L., 2019a. 'Appraisal of email use as a source of workplace stress: A person–environment fit approach', in *Journal of the Association for Information Systems*, 20(2), 132–160.

Strom-Tjesen, P., Zukowska, D., Wargocki, P., Wyon, D.P., 2015. 'The effects of bedroom air quality on sleep and next-day performance', in *Indoor Air* 26(5), 679–686.

SUIT, 2002. 'Sustainable development of urban historical areas through an active integration within towns', EU FP5 Programme, The City of Tomorrow and Cultural Heritage.

Sullivan, L., 2012. *RIBA Guide to Sustainability in Practice*. RIBA.

Syed, M., 2019. *Rebel Ideas: the Power of Diverse Thinking*. John Murray.

Takenoya, H., 2006. 'Air-conditioning Systems of the KI Building, Tokyo', in Clements-Croome (ed.), *Creating the Productive Workplace*. Taylor and Francis.

Tam, C.M., Vivian, W.Y., Tam, S., Zeng, X, 2002. 'Environmental performance evaluation (EPE) for construction', in *Building Research and Information* 30(5), 349–361.

Tan, F., Lee, S.E., Ho, D., Schafer, W., 2002. 'A framework for intelligent building classification for commercial buildings in the tropics', in Ang, G., and Prins, M., Proceedings of CIB W60/W96 Conference on Performance Concept in Building and Architectural Management, May, Hong Kong, CIB Publication.

Tanabe, S. and Nishihara, N., 2018. 'Workplace productivity: Fatigue and satisfaction', in Clements-Croome, D.J. (ed.), *Creating the Productive Workplace* (third edition), 135–147.

Taub, M., Clements-Croome, D.J., Lockhart, V., 2016. 'The impacts of wearables on designing healthy office environments: A review', BCO Report (www.bco.org.uk).

Taylor, R., 2011. 'Vision of beauty', in *Physics World* 24(5), 22–27.

Techau, D., Owen, C., Paton, D., Fay, R., 2016. 'Buildings, brains and behaviour: Towards an affective neuroscience of architecture: The hedonic impact of sustainable work environments on occupant well-being', in *World Health Design* January, 24–37.

Tennant, R., Hiller, L., Fishwick, R., Platt, S., Joseph, S., Weich, S., Parkinson, J., (...), Stewart-Brown, S., 2007. 'The Warwick-Edinburgh Mental Wellbeing Scale (WEMWBS): Development and UK validation', in *Health and Quality of Life Outcomes* 5, 63.

Teo, M.M.M. and Loosemore, M., 2001. 'A theory of waste behaviour in the construction industry', in *Construction Management and Economics* 19(7), 741–751.

Terrapin LLC, 2012. 'The economics of biophilia: Why designing with nature in wind makes financial sense', May White Paper by Terrapin Bright Green LLC.

Tett, G., 2015. *The Silo Effect: The Peril of Expertise and the Promise of Breaking Down Barriers*. New York: Simon and Schuster.

Tett, G., 2017. 'Why the electoral surprises keep on rolling in', in *Financial Times Magazine*, 16 June.

The Buzz Business, 2018. 'Smart Dubai: Blockchain capital of the world', 19 April.

The Commission of the European Communities, 1992. 'Towards sustainability: a European Community Programme of Policy in Action in relation to the environment and sustainable development', COM (92) 23 Final, Brussels: CEC, 27 March.

The Institute of Occupational Safety and Health (IOSH), 2015. *Working Well: Guidance on Promoting Health and Wellbeing at Work*.

The International Energy Agency (IEA), 2010. 'Technology roadmap – solar photovoltaic energy'. 11 May.

The International Energy Agency (IEA), 2015. 'World energy outlook scenario' (report).

The International Renewable Energy Agency (IRENA), 2018. 'Global energy transformation: A roadmap to 2050', International Renewable Agency, Abu Dhabi.

The United Nations, 2018. Sustainable Development Goals.

Thorburn, G., 2002. *Men and Sheds*. London: New Holland.

Tillotson, J., 2008. 'JENTIL: Responsive clothing that

promotes an holistic approach to fashion as a new vehicle to treat psychological conditions' in *The Body – Connections with Fashion*. Proceedings of the tenth annual IFFTI conference. RMIT School of Fashion and Textiles, Melbourne, Victoria.

Tillotson, J., 2012. 'Live scent, evil stench', in *This Pervasive Day: The Potential Perils of Pervasive Computing*, 53–68. London, UK: Imperial College Press.

Trevia, F.G., 2013. *Take Your Time: Combine Nature and Technology to Relieve Work Related Stress in the Office Environment*. TU Delft Faculty of Industrial Design Engineering.

Trotter, L., Vine, J., Leach, M., Fujiwara, D., 2014. 'Measuring the social impact of community investment: A guide to using the wellbeing valuation approach'. HACT, March. London.

Trusty, W.B. and Horst, S., 2003. Integrating LCA tools in *Green Building Rating Systems*. ATHENA Sustainable Materials Institute in Ontario and Pasadena.

Turan, M., 1975. 'Vernacular architecture and environmental influences: An analytical and comparative study', in METU *Journal of the Faculty of Architecture* 1(2), 227–246.

Türkiye'de Kentsel Çevrenin Biçimlenişinde Planc ı ve Mimarın Etkinliği. *Mimarlık* 14(146), 1976/1, 17–19.

Turner, B., Pallaris K., Clements-Croome D.J., 2018. *Creating the Productive Workplace*. Third edition, Routledge.

Tweed, C., Dixon, D., Hinton, E., Bickerstaff, K., 2014. 'Thermal comfort practices in the home and their impact on energy consumption', in *Architectural Engineering and Design Management*, 10(1–2), 1–24.

Ucko, P.J., Tringham, R. and Dimbleby, G.W. (eds), 1972. *Man, Settlement and Urbanism*. London: Duckworth.

UK Green Building Council, 2016. *Health and Wellbeing in Homes*. (www.ukgbc.org)

Ulrich, R.S., 1984. 'View through a window may influence recovery from surgery', in *Science* 224(4647), 420–421.

Ulrich, R.S., 1991. 'Effects of interior design on wellness: Theory and recent scientific research', in *Journal of Health Care Interior Design*, 1(3), 97–109.

Uluc, H., 1946. Güney Anadolu'da Sivil Mimari Örnekleri. *Arkitekt* 46(179–180), 261.

United Nations Environment, 2019. 'The sky's the limit as architects design UN17 eco-village in Copenhagen', 5 February.

USDAW, 2006. 'Union of Shop, Distributive and Allied Workers', in *The Guardian*, 8 July.

Vehviläinen, T., Lindholm, H., Rintamäki, H., Pääkkönen, R., Hirvonen, A., Niemi, O., Vinha, J., 2016. 'High indoor CO2 concentrations in an office environment increases the transcutaneous CO2 level and sleepiness during cognitive work', in *Journal of Occupational and Environmental Hygiene*, 13(1), 19–29.

Veitch, J., 2018. 'Lighting for productive workplaces', in *Creating the Productive Workplace* (third edition), 175–191.

Veitch, J., Newsham, G., Boyce, P., Jones, C., 2008. 'Lighting appraisal, well-being and performance in open-plan offices: A linked mechanisms approach', in *Lighting Research & Technology* 40(2), 133–151.

Veitch, J.A., Newsham, G.R., Mancini, S., Arsenault, C.D., 2010. 'Lighting and office renovation effects on employee and organisational wellbeing', NRC Report IPC-RR-306.

Veitch, J.A., Galasiu, A.D., 2012. 'The physiological and psychological effects of windows, daylight, and view at home', in *Review and Research Agenda* 325. NRC Institute for Research in Construction, Ottawa, Canada.

Vincent, J.F., 2016. 'Biomimetics in architectural design', in *Intelligent Buildings International*, 8(2), 138–149.

Vink, P. and Hallbeck, S., 2012. 'Comfort and discomfort studies demonstrate the need for a new model' (editorial), in *Applied Ergonomics* 43(2), 271–276.

Violet-Le-Duc, E.E., 1971. *The Habitations of Man in All Ages*. Ann Arbor, MI: Gryphon.

Vitruvius, P.M., 1955. *On Architecture*. London: William Heinemann.

von Frisch, K., 1975. *Animal Architecture*. Hutchinson.

von Weizsäcker, E.L., Lovins, A., Lovins H., 1997. *Factor Four*. London: Earthscan Publications.

Vukusic, P., 2004. 'Natural photonics', in *Physics World*, February, 35–39.

Wade, J., 2018. 'Making health digital', in *Physics World*, 31(5), 27–30.

Walker, A., 2016. *Solar Water Heating*. National Renewable Energy Laboratory. Updated by US Department of Energy Federal Energy Management Program (FEMP).

Ward-Thompson, C. *et al.*, 2012. 'More green space is linked to less stress in deprived communities: Evidence from salivary cortisol patterns', in *Landscape Urban Planning* 105, 220–221.

Wargocki, P., Seppanen, O., Andersson, J., Boerstra, A., Clements-Croome, D., Fitzner, K., and Hanssen, S.O., 2006. 'Indoor climate and productivity in offices', Federation of European Heating and Air-conditioning Associations (REHVA) Guidebook 6.

Warr, P., 1998a. 'What is our current understanding of the relationships between wellbeing and work?', in *Journal of Occupational Psychology* 63, 193–210.

Warr, P., 1998b. 'Well-being and the workplace' in Kahneman, D., El Diener, X. and Schwarz, N. (eds). *Foundations of Hedonic Psychology: Scientific Perspectives on Enjoyment and Suffering*. New York: Russell-Sage.

Warr, P., 2002. *Psychology at Work*. Fifth edition, Penguin Books.

Watson, D., Clark, L.A., Tellegen, A., 1988. 'Development and validation of brief measures of positive and negative affect: The PANAS scales', in *Journal of Personality and Social Psychology* 54(6), 1063–1070.

Watson, K., 2018. 'Establishing psychological wellbeing metrics for the built environment', in *Building Services Engineering Research and Technology* 39(2).

Watson, K., Evans, J., Karvonen, A., Whitley, T., 2016. 'Capturing the social value of buildings: The promise of Social Return on Investment', in *Building and Environment*, 103, 289–301.

Watson, K. and Whitley, T., 2017. 'Applying social return on investment (SROI) to the built environment', in *Building Research & Information* 45(8), 875–891.

Weiss, M.L., 1997. 'Division of behavior and cognitive science', PhD thesis, Rochester University, New York.

WELL Building Standard, 2015. ASC/all/DV/S001/Feb15/V1.0 21, info@wellcertified.com. International Well Building Institute, Washington, DC.

Welter, V.M., 2002. Biopolis: Patrick Geddes and the *City Life*. MIT Press.

Wen, K.-C. and Kao, Y.-N., 2005. 'An analytic study of architectural design style by fractal dimension method', in *Proceedings of the 22nd International Symposium on Automation and Robotics in Construction*, ISARC 2005, Italy, 1–6.

West, G.B., Brown, J.H., Enquist, B.J., 1997. 'A generic model for the origin of the allometric scaling laws in biology', in *Science* 276(5309), 122–126.

Whipple, T., 2016. 'Super fuel from artificial leaves "is ready to replace oil"', in *The Times*, 29 July.

Whipple, T., 2017. 'Bionic leaf could help feed the world's hungry', in *The Times*, 4 April.

White, M.P. et al., 2019. 'Spending at least 120 minutes a week in nature is associated with good health and wellbeing', in *Nature, Scientific Reports* 9(7730).

Whittingham, J., Griffiths, E., Richardson, J., 2003. 'Sustainability accounting in the construction industry', in *Proceedings of the Institution of Civil Engineers* 156 (ES1), 13–15 (paper 12354).

WHO, 1989. European Charter on Environment and Health. ICP/RUD 113/Conf.Doc/l Rev.2, 8303r, World Health Organization Regional Office for Europe, Copenhagen.

Widder, E., 2002. *The Bioluminescent Coloring Book*. Harbour Branch Oceanographic Institute.

Widder, E., 2010. 'Bioluminescense in the ocean: Origins of biological, chemical and ecological diversity', in *Science* 329(5979), 704–708.

Wiener, N., 1954. 'The human use of human beings', in *Cybernetics and Society*. First edition, Houghton Mifflin.

Wikipedia, 2018. 'Paris Agreement', https://en.wikipedia.org/wiki/Paris_Agreement

Williams, B., 2000. *An Introduction to Benchmarking Facilities*. Bromley: Building Economics Bureau.

Williams, B., 2006. 'Building performance: the value management approach', in Clements-Croome, D.J. (ed.), *Creating the Productive Workplace*. Oxford: Routledge.

Williams, J., Read, C., Norton, A., Dovers, S., Burgman, M., Proctor, W., Anderson, H., 2001. *Biodiversity: Australia State of the Environment Report 2001*. Theme Report, Canberra: CSIRO Publishing on behalf of the Department of the Environment and Heritage.

Willmott Dixon, 2010. *The Impacts of Construction and the Built Environment*. WD Re-Thinking Ltd. https://www.willmottdixon.co.uk/asset/9462/download

Wilson, E.O., 1984. *Biophilia: Human Bond with Other Species*. Cambridge, MA: Harvard University Press.

Wilson, E.O., 2006. *Nature Revealed*. The John Hopkins University Press.

Wilson, E.O., 2017. *The Origins of Creativity*. First edition, Allen Lane.

Wilson, F., 1984. *A Graphic Survey of Perception and Behaviour for the Design Professions*. New York: Van Nostrand Reinhold.

Woolf, D., 2000. 'Optimal environments: CFD analysis of an igloo', in

Awbi, H.B. (ed.) *Air Distribution in Rooms: Ventilation for Health and Sustainable Environments*, 1087. Elsevier.

Wong, P., 2011. 'Frank Lloyd Wright's Fallingwater House: A design icon?'. Essay, Hiram Bingham British International School of Lima.

World Economic Forum, 2018. 'In Davos, firms meditate on quest for mental well-being', in *The Straits Times*, 25 January.

World Green Building Council (WGBC), 2013. *The Business Case for Green Building*.

World Green Building Council (WGBC), 2014. *Health, Wellbeing and Productivity in Offices: The Next Chapter for Green Building*.

World Green Building Council (WGBC), 2016. *Health, Wellbeing and Productivity in Retail: The Impact of Green Buildings on People and Profit*.

World Health Assembly, 2001. Fifty-fourth World Health Assembly, Geneva, 14–22 May 2001: Resolutions and Decisions'. World Health Organization.

Wright, A., 1995. *The Beginner's Guide to Colour Psychology*. London: Kyle Cathie.

Wurm, J., 2016. *Cities Alive*. Arup.

Wurm, J., 2016. 'Solar Leaf: A Bioreactive Façade', in *Cities Alive Green Building Envelope*. Arup.

WWDR, 2003. *World Water Development Report, Water for People: Water for Life*. Berghan Books.

Wyatt, T., 2003. 'Adapt or die: the major challenges ahead for the building services industry'. CIBSE presidential address, London.

Wyon, D. and Wargocki, P., 2013. 'How indoor environment affects performance', in *ASHRAE Journal*, 55(3), 46–52.

Yakymenko, I., Tsybulin, O., Sidorik, E., Henshel, D., Kyrylenko, O., Kyrylenko, S., 2016. 'Oxidative mechanisms of biological activity of low-intensity radiofrequency radiation', in *Electro-*

magnetic Biology and Medicine 35(2), 186–202.

Yang, T., and Clements-Croome, D.J., 2012. 'Natural ventilation in built environment', in Meyers, R.A. (ed) *Encyclopaedia of Sustainability, Science and Technology*, Springer.

Yeang, K. and Spector, A., 2011. *Green Design: From Theory to Practice.* Black Dog Publishing.

Yessios, C.I., 1987. 'A fractal studio', ACADIA '87 Workshop Proceedings.

Yin, J., Zhu, S., MacNaughton, P., Allen, J.G., Spengler, J.D., 2018. 'Physiological and cognitive performance of exposure to biophilic indoor environment', in *Building and Environment* 132, 255–262.

Zhao, X. and Zhang, X., 2013. 'Solar photovoltaic/thermal technologies and their application in building tetrofitting', in Pacheco Torgal F., Mistretta M., Kaklauskas A., Granqvist C., Cabeza L. (eds), *Nearly Zero Energy Building Refurbishment.* London: Springer.

Index

22, Bishopsgate, London   160
3D printing   92, 94, 120, 131

absenteeism   74–6
Aecom   167–8
AI   89, 91–2, 100–101, 131
air quality & temperature   21–7, 68, 69–71, 103
Aldgate Tower, London   167–8
Alhambra, Granada   32–3
American International College, Kuwait   177–9
Arctic City   29
artificial leaf, research on   44–9
Arup, Ove & Partners   7, 111, 137
Atelier Ten   173–7

bamboo   94
Barcelona   45, 49, 138, 139
Bee Brick   96
Beirut Terraces   144–5
Believe in Better, London   141
Benzecry, Toby   153–5
BIM (Building Information Modelling)   92–3, 129, 131, 133
Bio Intelligent Quotient Building (BIQ), Hamburg   44, 145
biomimetic/biophilic architecture   34–56, 65, 98, 131, 133
Bjarke Ingels Group   160–2
Blockchain   93, 129, 133
breakout spaces   69, 75
BREEAM (Building Research Establishment Environmental assessment Method)   79–80, 94, 111
bricks, smart   94–6
Broadgate Circle, London   143–4
Buckminster Fuller, Richard   29
building materials, new   93–6
   self-repairing/smart   94–5
building rating systems   79–80

Callebaut, Vincent, Architectures   158, 179
CapitaLand tower, Singapore   160–2

Carlo Ratti Associati   160–1
Casablanca, Market   47
Castellón   48
cellulose, as building material   94
Centre Pompidou   18
Cetec   165–7
Chrysler Building, NY   18
Circular Building prototype   140–1
climate change   103, 106–8
CO_2 43, 69–71, 99, 108–9, 111
concentration & engagement   59–60, 69–71, 131
colour, & wellbeing   68–70, 76–7
concrene   102
concrete, self-healing   94–5, 102
Cornellà   48
cost cutting   128
courtyard houses   30–1
creativity, & architecture   63–7
cybertecture   97, 146–7

data speed   89
De Montfort University, UK   26
desert architecture   26–7
Design Museum, London   138–39
digital twin   92, 101
Dragonfly Project, Manhattan   179

EDGE Building, Amsterdam   8, 15, 64, 155–6
Egg Office Building, Mumbai   146–7
Eliasson, Olafur, No Future is Possible Without a Past   80
Empire State Building   18
energy efficiency   114
energy levels   59–60
energy-emotion map (Loehr & Schwartz)   59
environmental factors, & physical wellbeing   68–9
Estevez, Alberto T., research of   45–9

Fallingwater House   12
Fathy, Hassan   27, 30, 33
FCB Studios   158–59
Fibonacci sequences   37–8

Finc Architects   169–72
'flourish' approach   76–9
Fosters Intelligent Buildings   147–50
fractal geometry   19, 39–40
fuel cells   116

garden cities   43
Gardens by the Bay, Singapore   173–6
Gate Project, Cairo   179
Gaudí, Antoni   39
Gehry, Frank   39, 63
gender differences   127
Gherkin, The, London   122
golden number   38
graphene   91, 94, 97–8
Green Development Strategy/Green Plan 2015   123–4
greenery, value of   40–3, 50–5, 118
greenhouse effect   106, 108–9
grey water/rainwater use   116–17

Hadid, Zaha   39, 137
health & well-being, buildings for   16–19, 57ff
   assessing & rating   62–3, 79–80
   factors   59–63
   futures   80–83
   neuroscience studies   62–3
heat & ventilation control   21–7, 44, 68
Hemcrete   94
Hok case studies   156–8
homeless pods   170–2
hot water systems   116
Housing Quality Indicator   111
hydrogen, as fuel   98–9
hygge   58

igloos   8, 22, 31
ikigai   58
Innsbruck housing   47, 48
insect-inspired architecture/building   27, 65
intelligence v. smartness   6–7
Intelligent buildings, qualities & criteria   6–20
Internet of Things   89, 90–1 131, 133
ionization   70
Iranian/Persian architecture   22–3
IRENA (International Renewable Energy Agency)   112–13
Islamic architecture   21, 22–6

Jaguar Land Rover Advanced Engine facility, Wolverhampton   140

James Law Cybertecture   146–7
Jean-Marie Tjibaou Cultural Centre   12–14
Jewel Chang Airport, Singapore   176

Kajima HQ, Japan   76
Kapsarc, Riyadh   137
Kathleen Grimm School, New York   152–3
Kings Place, London   164–5
Kuala Lumpur, International School   157–58

landscape, greening   42–3, 118
Landsecurities   162–4
LCA (life-cycle assessment)   110
Le Corbusier   12, 38, 39, 67, 70
LEED (leadership in Energy & Environmental Design)   79, 111
light, & wellbeing   68, 69–70, 75, 114–15
lightweight structures   28–30
Lilypad Project   179
lime mortar   94
Limebrook Park Garden Suburb, Maldon   169–70
Lloyd Wright, Frank   12, 39
Lloyds Building, London   17–18
Los Angeles Courthouse   150–2
lotus leaf effect   43–4
Lykouria, Yorga   169

Malay houses   21–2
Mansueto Library, University of Chicago   169
Masdar City, Abu Dhabi   147–48
MIT (Massachusetts Institute of Technology)   18, 63–4
MDX Living Pavilion, Middlesex University   172–73
Metal Organic Frameworks (MOF)   97
Microbial Fuel Cell (MFC)   95
mingle space   64
music, impact on brain   69

NABERS (National Australian Building Environmental Rating System)   79, 111
Namibia   120–1
nature, as inspiration, *see* biomimetic/biophilic architecture
NBBJ Design   177–9
neural networks, artificial   90–1
neuroscience studies   62–3
nickel   96
Notre Dame du Haut, Ronchamp   12, 67, 70

parks   43
Pearl River Tower, Guangzhou, China   150

PCM (Phase Change Materials)   95
photovoltaic systems   115
Piano, Renzo, & RPBW   12–13
Pixar HQ   64
PLP Architecture   155–6, 160
POE (Post occupancy evaluation)   8, 125
productivity, & architecture   63–7
Project Milestone, Netherlands   120
Putney High School, classroom study   50–1

Rain Light Studio, London   169
recycling   117, 118
renewable energy   112–14
Riyadh, Diplomatic Quarters   29–30
Robotics   92, 95, 131
Rose Bowl Building, Leeds Beckett University   165–7
Royal Society of Arts, London   66–7

Sagrada Familia, Barcelona   138, 139
Salvinia effect   44
Savills UK   164–5
Second Home   80
Shard, The, London   72, 74, 154
siheyuan   30
silence   70
silo effect   128, 129
SIN holistic model   76
sitting   72
SLG Project, Cheltenham   153–4
slide-ring materials   102
solar power   113–6
SOM   150–2
space & layout   63–4, 71–3
Spence, Charles   11
spirals   37–8
straw bale construction   94
sustainability   43–4, 79, 103–25
   assessing   110–12
   circles of Global Goals   104–5
   future   118–24
Sydney Opera House   16–17

Taipei Tower (Tao Zhu Yin Yuan)   158
technology, new   58–9, 72, 88–96, 131–3

Television Centre, London   142–3
Teng Fong Hospital, Singapore   156–7
tents   28–30
termite dwellings   27
thinking, modes of   126–8
titanium dioxide coatings   96
TLEBM (Through Life Environment Business Model)   111
transdisciplinarity   130–1
trogladitic towns   28

ventilation   21–7, 68, 71, 114
vernacular architecture   21–33
Vertico Boscale, Milan   145–6
Victoria & Albert Museum, London   81–2, 143
Victoria St, London   162–3
Vitruvius   6, 31, 128
volatile organic compounds (VOC)   96–7

Warwick-Edinburgh Mental Wellbeing Scale (WEMWBS)   62
waste recycling   117
water usage   116–17
wearable sensors/technology   72, 76, 90, 91, 92, 93, 125
WELL   79–80
wellbeing, *see* health & well-being
White Collar Factory, London   137
wind towers/catchers (badgirs)   24–5, 26
wood, as building material   94, 96, 102
Worcester, The Hive   158–159
workplaces   17, 20, 57–87
   & creativity   63–7
   layout, *see* space & layout
   healthy environment   57–63, 67–76
   lighting   75

ventilation   71, 75

Wotton, Sir Henry, The Elements of Architecture   6
WWF Living Planet Centre, Woking, UK   177

Yale University, School of Architecture   26
yurt (ger)   29